T0342178

"Mark Kruger has made a significant contribution to understanding the events of the St. Louis area in the late nineteenth century. Not since 1966, with the publication of *The Reign of the Rabble*, have we heard some of the details of those violent and fearful days. Now some fifty years later we receive, in a sense, the details of the details. . . . It is [Kruger's] use of a diversity of sources that gives this work its richness."

—ELIZABETH KOLMER, retired professor of American studies at Saint Louis University

"Mark Kruger has brought alive the labor struggles of the nineteenth century as they culminated in the St. Louis Commune. He skillfully shows how the 1848 revolutions in Europe, the Paris Commune of 1871, the First International, the 1873 depression, and the Great Railroad Strike of 1877 all converged to produce remarkable events in St. Louis. This is an excellent example of a local history set on a world stage."

—CLIFF DURAND, research associate at the Center for Global Justice and author of *Moving beyond Capitalism*

"*The St. Louis Commune of 1877* brings new life to the story of the St. Louis Commune, demonstrating its connections to the German revolution of 1848, the Paris Commune, and the First International. The commune, which has too often been seen as a story of only local interest, can now be fully understood in its national and international context."

—KRISTEN ANDERSON, associate professor of history at Webster University

"The Great Upheaval of 1877 was the first of the great mass strikes that have periodically shaken the United States, and its acme was the St. Louis general strike, in which workers took over and ran one of America's major cities. *The St. Louis Commune of 1877* provides the fascinating backstory of the German immigrants—many veterans of the European revolutions of 1848—who helped define the character and provide the leadership for America's first general strike."

—JEREMY BRECHER, labor historian, filmmaker, and author of *Strike!*

The St. Louis
Commune of
1877

Communism in the Heartland

MARK KRUGER

UNIVERSITY OF NEBRASKA PRESS LINCOLN

Library of Congress Cataloging-in-Publication Data
Names: Kruger, Mark, 1948– author.
Title: The St. Louis Commune of 1877:
communism in the heartland / Mark Kruger.
Other titles: Communism in the heartland
Description: Lincoln: University of Nebraska Press,
[2021] | Includes bibliographical references and index.
Identifiers: LCCN 2020057472
ISBN 9781496228130 (paperback)
ISBN 9781496228925 (epub)
ISBN 9781496228932 (pdf)
Subjects: LCSH: General Strike, Saint Louis, Mo.,
1877. | Working class—Economic conditions—
Missouri—Saint Louis. | Socialism—History—19th
century. | Forty-Eighters (American immigrants)—
Missouri—Saint Louis. | Workingmen's Party of the
United States—History. | International Workingmen's
Association (1864–1876) | BISAC: POLITICAL
SCIENCE / Political Ideologies / Communism,
Post-Communism & Socialism | HISTORY /
United States / State & Local / Midwest (IA, IL,
IN, KS, MI, MN, MO, ND, NE, OH, SD, WI)
Classification: LCC HD5326.S24 K78 2021 |
DDC 331.892/5097786609034—dc23
LC record available at https://lccn.loc.gov/2020057472

Set in Arno by Laura Buis.
Designed by N. Putens.

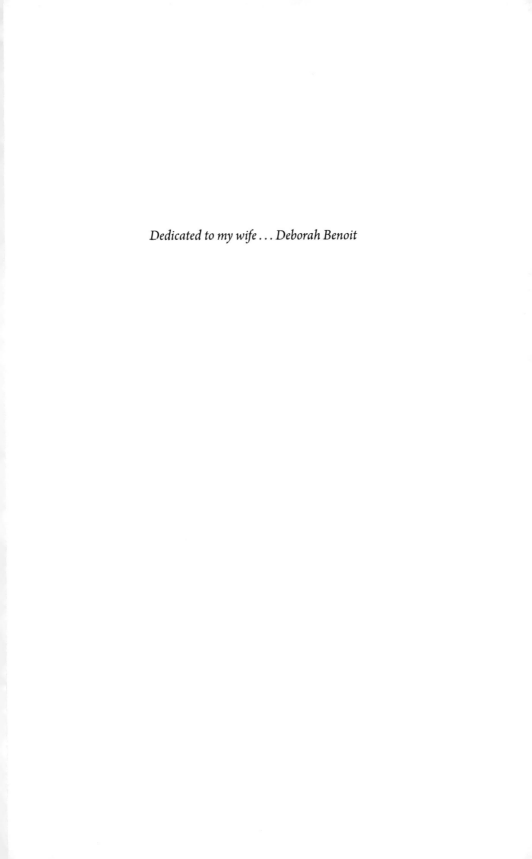

Dedicated to my wife . . . Deborah Benoit

CONTENTS

ILLUSTRATIONS

PREFACE

Many years ago, while reading a book on American labor history, I came across a short paragraph that referenced the takeover of the city of St. Louis by its workers during the 1877 railroad strike, led by the Workingmen's Party of the United States, which was at the time the only Marxist political party in the United States.

I was surprised that hardly anything had been written about the incident aside from mostly brief references, since it constituted the first general strike in American history and the only occasion when workers took control of a major American city and when the city was ruled by a communist party.

I was immediately curious about how the St. Louis General Strike and the St. Louis Commune came to be. What factors led to workers in the United States capturing municipal power from the city's elected leaders and government? Who were the people who led the takeover? Was the action part of a larger revolutionary attempt to gain power? What were the elements that led to such a radical action? What was the government's response?

The answers to those questions were largely to be found in both European and American history. A series of events over the course of approximately thirty years that occurred in the leading capitals of the world, including Berlin, Vienna, London, Paris, and New York, came together and ultimately resulted in what became known as the St. Louis Commune.

It is especially important today to understand the history of American labor and the philosophy of socialism within the labor movement. Young people today are more interested in the concept of socialism than they have been in over fifty years. The issue of the gap in wealth between classes is not new, but interest in it has been accelerated by its recent growth and the virtual disappearance of any social net meant to protect our most vulnerable people. The gains of labor over many years have been reduced by continuous attacks upon working people during the past twenty years, not only on those gains but on unions themselves. The 2020 presidential election brought the idea of democratic socialism to the forefront of political focus and reflected its embrace by millions of Americans.

The establishment of the St. Louis Commune was the result of a number of historical events both in Europe and in the United States. Without the German Revolution of 1848, the Paris Commune, and the First International, it is doubtful that St. Louis workers would have rebelled as they did against the industrial world that had emerged following the American Civil War.

Many books have described and analyzed the German Revolution, the Paris Commune, the First International, and American labor history and the 1877 railroad strike. Jonathan Sperber's *Rhineland Radicals* and Wolfram Siemann's *The German Revolution of 1848–49* provide a good background for the 1848 Revolution in Germany; Stewart Edwards's *The Paris Commune 1871* explains the importance of the Paris Commune; and *The First International in America* by Samuel Bernstein describes the effect of the First International in the United States. The history of the American labor movement, the condition of the working class in the United States, and the railroad strike of 1877 are well covered by Herbert Gutman in *Work, Culture and Society in Industrializing America*, Philip Foner's *History of the Labor Movement in the United States*, and *Annals of the Great Strikes in the United States* by J. A. Dacus. There has been only one book written about the St. Louis Commune, *Reign of the Rabble* by David Burbank, which provides an excellent day-to-day description of the Commune's rule of the city. However, none of the existing literature focuses on the effect of European socialism on the St. Louis Commune, the reason the Commune arose, and its nature and philosophical foundations. It is the purpose of this book to fill that void.

The history of socialism and labor is relevant and important to the political issues we face today. Hopefully this work can shed some light on those ideas and challenges and the part they played in the establishment of the St. Louis Commune.

ACKNOWLEDGMENTS

I was fortunate to have had the advice of a number of people and institutions in preparing this work.

I want to thank Professors Elizabeth Kolmer and Bob Swacker, who served as my mentors for many years and whose advice greatly enriched this work. Thanks also to Deborah Benoit, Steve Rinsler, Miriam Karp, Tony Cuneo, and Professor Deborah Henry, who read the manuscript and offered valuable suggestions. Rebecca Kettler and John Siebel were invaluable in translating documents from Old German to English, and Jacqui Cox was extremely helpful regarding technical matters. Deborah Weinstein's aid was crucial in securing the photographs that appear in the book. Professor Pat Gregory was very helpful with the intricacies of research, as were the staffs of the following institutions: Tamiment Library and Robert F. Wagner Labor Archives at New York University, the Wisconsin Historical Society, University of Wisconsin Library, Newberry Library, Missouri Historical Society, State Historical Society of Missouri, Mercantile Library, New York Public Library, Chicago Public Library, and the St. Louis Public Library. Thanks also to Nancy Oliver at the St. Louis Public Library, Dennis Northcutt at the Missouri Historical Society, and Nicholas Fry at the Mercantile Library. Special thanks to Matt Bokovoy of the University of Nebraska Press, who patiently offered valuable insights and suggestions while leading me through the publication process, and to my project editor, Sara Springsteen, and my copyeditor, Judith Hoover, both of whom were relentless in their efforts to make this a better book.

THE ST. LOUIS COMMUNE OF 1877

Introduction

The Mississippi Valley had been settled and influenced by both the Spanish and the French before the territory was purchased by the United States in 1803. The city of St. Louis was founded near the confluence of the Missouri and Mississippi rivers and grew as a result of the rich fur trade. Furs were purchased from Native Americans or French trappers and sold to eastern markets, much of the product making its way to East Coast and European shops. Many of the original founding families of St. Louis grew wealthy as a result. However, overhunting and changing fashions caused the end of the fur trade, and, as a result, St. Louis capitalists redirected their attention to agriculture, manufacturing, and speculation in real estate. Manufactured goods were sold to pioneers heading west. At the same time, Native American lands were privatized, and rich St. Louisans took control of those previously common areas. One founding family of St. Louis, the Chouteaus, obtained hundreds of thousands of acres of land that had been controlled by the Osage tribe.

Following the Civil War, huge corporations emerged in the United States, intent on maximizing their power and profits. Corruption permeated American society as those corporate entities grew and spread across the country by bribery and exploitation. Corporate interests sought to expand their markets, decrease their overhead, maximize their profits, and gain political power. Expansion into new areas, lower payrolls, and corporate control of state governments followed. The worst example of such corporate behavior and the most obvious to the public was that of the railroads, which experienced tremendous growth in the postwar years, invaded city streets, forced their workers to labor under dangerous conditions, paid their employees as little as possible, and compelled state legislatures and the federal government to award them public lands and to pass legislation favorable to them. The new power of corporations, particularly railroads, caused terrific resentment among railroad workers, the working-class generally, and the public.

During the summer of 1877, railroad workers across the United States struck against all of the major railroads. Hundreds of thousands of workers joined the strike, which spread across the United States from Baltimore to San Francisco. The railroad workers were generally supported by ordinary people in their various communities. In those cities and towns that consisted largely of railroad workers, residents provided strikers with financial and material support, and local merchants provided them with food and other commodities. Large corporations and especially railroad companies were generally unpopular among the working masses, who supported those who challenged them.

The issues giving rise to the strike were primarily wages and working conditions. Railroad work was dangerous, and many workers were killed or maimed each year. In addition, during the summer of 1877 virtually all major railroads instituted wage reductions, some for the third time in months, that made it impossible for railroad workers to live, much less support their families. The railroad lines laid off many workers, often doubling the work load of those who remained. The payment of wages was sometimes months late, and those living paycheck to paycheck were unable to feed their families or heat their homes during the winter months.

Finally, the workers at Martinsburg, West Virginia, spontaneously struck, and railroad workers in other cities immediately followed their lead. Within days hundreds of thousands of railroad workers were on strike across the country. The strike was for the most part peaceful, but extensive violence did erupt in some cities, especially Baltimore, Chicago, and Pittsburgh. A number of strikers were killed, as were many innocent bystanders, including women and children.

There was no national leadership nor coordination of the strike. When railroad workers in one city heard that those in another were striking over common issues, they too stopped working. The spontaneity of the individual strikes evidenced the harsh working conditions and poor wages of the railroad workers in every locale, many of whom were earning only half of what they were paid only a few years earlier. But although the strikes spread like a wave from east to west, there was no common strategy. As a result, they appeared as separate brush fires, which in the end failed to merge or connect with each other.

In time other workers struck both in support of those employed by railroads and on account of their own issues. While workers across the country shared many grievances against their employers, many also confronted issues specific to their own workplaces. Miners, canal workers, those working in manufacturing, and others joined the strike. Freight transportation in the United States was virtually shut down. Most businesses at the time depended on railroad transportation for their livelihood, so when their goods sat unshipped on railroad side tracks, those businesses failed.

In St. Louis railroad workers successfully encouraged those not engaged in railroad work to join their strike, which resulted in the first general strike in American history. Virtually all businesses in the city were closed down. Shortages of coal because of the strike meant many manufacturing businesses could not operate, and the lack of freight transportation caused food to spoil en route to its destination and thus be in short supply. The city in effect was shut down, and municipal authority was nonexistent. Shortly after the beginning of the strike, the Workingmen's Party of the United States (WPUSA), the first Marxist political party in the country, took over leadership of the strike and of the city. Its Executive Committee governed the city, operated city services, moved into City Hall, and patrolled the streets in order to protect private property, including railroad property.

Although the spontaneity and suddenness of the strike surprised many, it had been influenced by actions and philosophies of the past and a continent away. Communism was not at the time unknown in the United States. A number of utopian communist intentional communities had existed in the country for many years. Many of those were religious communities, such as the Shakers, which practiced the communism of early Christian groups. Others were secular, such as the Harmonists, Owenites, Fourierists, and Icarians.

Utopian communists sought to give people some control over their lives by creating communities based on democratic principles and equality and the sharing of resources, and were operated for the benefit of all members.

The American utopian socialists were influenced largely, although not entirely, by Robert Owen and Charles Fourier. Owen was a Welsh factory owner who sought to solve some of the problems of the new industrial society. He operated model textile mills, paid fair wages, shortened the workday, and provided decent housing for his employees. He argued that the producers of goods should themselves own the means of production, private property should be abolished, and communities should be run by cooperative labor. Fourier's philosophy was not unlike that of Owens. He believed everyone in a community would be an owner of the means of production, and profits should be divided, with one-third paid out as dividends, one-fourth paid to those with special talents, and the rest given to the remaining laborers. One fatal problem with Owen's and Fourier's plans was that they depended on capitalists ending labor exploitation voluntarily. The workers were therefore dependent on the goodwill of business owners and did not have a role in their own emancipation. This position was to set the utopians apart from later socialists.[1]

An Owenite community was established in New Harmony, Indiana, on thirty thousand acres of land that Owen bought from a former intentional community. It had about a thousand members but ultimately failed. Albert Brisbane brought Fourier's ideas to the United States in 1834. In Brisbane's community, property was held by a joint stock association in which each member of the community was a partner and stockholder. Fourierism had a large following in the United States, and many such communities were established. Even Horace Greeley, the editor of the *New York Tribune*, was a Fourier supporter. Their failure was largely the result of a lack of sufficient capital.

During the 1840s and 1850s there was also a movement to create producers' and consumers' cooperatives, which can be traced back to the ideas of French socialism and the French Revolution of 1848. However, raising capital also proved to be a problem for the cooperatives. An Ohio cooperative failed to compete with private companies because of insufficient capital, and similar co-ops were attempted in Cincinnati, Boston, Pittsburgh, Wisconsin, Michigan, Illinois, and throughout New England. In New York, coopers, painters, cabinet makers, and tailors organized cooperatives. All eventually failed as a result of insufficient capital and an inability to engage in price wars with private businesses, which had more money with which to compete.[2]

But the communism that arose in the midst of the railroad strike was not the same communism that had previously appeared in the United States. This new communism, like the utopian communism, had its roots in Europe but was the result of new events and a new revolutionary philosophy that had spread and was then spreading throughout Europe. Karl Marx's so-called scientific socialism claimed that class conflict drove society forward and ultimately resulted in a classless or communist society. The achievement of socialism was not dependent on well-meaning capitalists but would be accomplished by the workers themselves as a result of their ultimate confrontation with the bourgeoisie, those who owned the factories and other means of production and distribution.

In 1789 in France and again in 1830, monarchies in Europe, remnants of the feudal age, came under attack. The European bourgeoisie demanded more political and financial power that was based on merit, not birth, within their societies. It sought to destroy the feudal rights of monarchs and aristocrats. There was a temporary coalition between the middle-class bourgeoisie and the working classes against the ruling royal families, which both sought to overthrow. However, insurgents were suppressed by the more powerful forces in control of European societies.

In 1848 revolution again spread across Europe and for similar reasons. The emerging middle class of merchants and manufacturers again sought to challenge the remaining feudal power of monarchs, aristocrats, and the Church. There were demands for a republican form of government, more political power for the new bourgeoisie, and limits on the powers of the Church. In Germany, while the revolution was not entirely successful, it did result in reforms. However, the repression by the government there was tremendous, and many German revolutionaries were forced to leave; a large number of them immigrated to the United States, mostly settling in St. Louis, Milwaukee, and Cincinnati, where there were already large German communities.

Marx, who was forced to flee Germany as a result of his political activities and writings, organized the International Workingmen's Association (IWA), or First

International, in London in order to unite working people from different countries. Its headquarters was eventually moved to New York, with local sections throughout the United States, including St. Louis. Members of those sections were largely followers of Marx and Ferdinand Lassalle. It was from the remnants of the IWA that the Workingmen's Party of the United States was born.

In 1871 workers in Paris revolted against the French government during the Franco-Prussian War. They established their own government in that city, raised an army, fought Prussian and French troops, and passed legislation beneficial to the poor and laboring classes. Many, though not all, of the workers of Paris were socialists and put into practice many socialist demands of the period, including free public education, a republican system of government, a people's army, and workers' control of the workplace. As a result, the French government was forced to flee to Versailles, and the French workers, socialists, and communists who remained led and were in control of what became known as the Paris Commune. The Commune became a rallying cry for both rich and poor during the 1877 strikes in the United States, but for different reasons. The rich pointed to it as an example of the dangers of a conscious working class which sought to overthrow existing governments, while to the poor and laborers it represented an egalitarian society that could be achieved and led by working people.

The WPUSA, a communist party, was made up largely of followers of Marx and Lassalle. In St. Louis it was led by German revolutionaries who had fled Germany after the failure of the Revolution of 1848–49 and who had settled in St. Louis. After the American Civil War, St. Louis flourished as a business, industrial, and agriculture center until the financial Panic of 1873. At the same time, it was a magnet for emigrants from Germany, who sought to live in a republic with a familiar German population and culture. When the railroad strike and general strike of 1877 reached St. Louis, the Workingmen's Party took over leadership of the strike and the city. It moved into City Hall and virtually ruled the city. Almost no business operated in St. Louis without its consent or permission. The city's elite referred to the emergence of WPUSA leadership as the St. Louis Commune, fearfully equating it with the Paris group. It led the first general strike in American history, and St. Louis became the only city in the United States to be governed by communists.

I

Revolution Comes to St. Louis

"The Internationalists have taken control of the strike, same as the communists who took control of Paris in 1870" was the headline in the *Missouri Republican* on July 27, 1877.[1] "The Internationalists" referred to the membership in the First International of the workers who had taken control of St. Louis, while the reference to Paris concerned the seizure of that city and its government by French workers only six years earlier. Both the First International and the Paris Commune were in the minds of St. Louis leaders in the summer of 1877, when St. Louis's working class took control of the city and established the St. Louis Commune.

The International was a working-class organization established in Europe by Marx just a few years earlier and had recently moved its headquarters to the United States. It boasted branches or sections in all major American cities and sought to organize the workers of the world for the purpose of taking power from the bourgeoisie, those who owned the means of production and distribution and who employed wage-labor at the cheapest cost to them in order to maximize their profits. Leaders of the First International were largely followers of Marx and Lassalle, although a number of anarchists also belonged to the organization. The International sought to unite workers' organizations throughout the world with regard to their common interests and to support their actions.

The Paris Commune had seized power from the French government and the bourgeoisie in the midst of great bloodshed in 1871. Following the Franco-Prussian War, the workers of Paris took control of the city and instituted social reforms along the lines of European socialism. The government of France and many of the bourgeois class had fled Paris for Versailles, and the workers took possession of and operated businesses and factories and the municipal government itself. Marx described the Paris Commune as an example of the dictatorship of the proletariat, which he believed to be a necessary step in a society's transformation from capitalism to socialism. Worker control of the institutions of business and government would result in a more equitable society and the end of the exploitation of man by man.

The St. Louis Commune emerged from the railroad strike of 1877, which began in the east United States and rapidly moved westward, as workers along the railroad lines spontaneously stopped working. Following a series of wage reductions, railroad workers struck in Martinsburg, West Virginia, and Baltimore on July 16. In a matter of a few days the strike spread to Philadelphia and Altoona, Pennsylvania; Cleveland and Cincinnati and Columbus, Ohio; Syracuse, New York; Terre Haute, Indiana; Chicago, Illinois; and numerous other cities along the way. On July 18 the strike grew to include Cumberland, Maryland, and Newark, Ohio. Railroad workers struck in Pittsburgh a day later, and by July 22 railroad workers in Hornellsville and Buffalo in New York, and Harrisburg and Reading in Pennsylvania had joined the strike. Philip Van Patten, the national secretary of the Workingmen's Party of the United States, called on all sections of the party to support the strike and to aid railroad workers across the nation, and also called for government ownership of the railroad and telegraph companies and an eight-hour workday. The strike quickly reached the cities of East St. Louis and St. Louis and their environs.

Directly across the Mississippi River from St. Louis, East St. Louis, Illinois, in 1877 was a railroad center for transportation and commerce moving horizontally throughout the United States, and most of the railroads around St. Louis came together there. St. Louis and East St. Louis together were second only to Chicago as a railroad center. The railroad industry was the lifeblood of East St. Louis. Even today many residents of the city ignore warnings at railroad crossings, claiming that because so many tracks intersect with city streets they could never reach their destinations if they stopped every time the gates went down. In 1877 East St. Louis was largely working class, and the villages immediately surrounding it included several company towns and a stockyard that serviced those transporting cattle east. But above all it was a railroad town, and its economy and politics centered around the railroad industry.

The railroad workers of East St. Louis watched with interest as, like an out-of-control conflagration, the strikes moved through West Virginia, Pennsylvania, Ohio, and Indiana, ever closer to their city. As workers in city after city struck, national guards and militias were called out, and violence often erupted. Railroad property was burned, and workers and spectators were often killed. The labor issues involved were virtually the same everywhere, including ignoring workers' safety, instituting wage reductions, and running two trains coupled together without increasing the number of crew.

Following the outbreak of spontaneous strikes in the East, on Saturday, July 21, railroad workers in East St. Louis met and announced their support for those striking workers. The next night a number of East St. Louis railroad workers, representing different lines, elected an executive committee, which issued General Order No. 1, directing workers to stop all freight traffic in East St. Louis at midnight. Passenger and mail trains would be allowed to run so that the traveling public was not inconvenienced more than was necessary and so the federal government had no excuse to intervene. A huge meeting of a thousand workers was held at the oppressively hot railway depot in East St. Louis. More than four hundred St. Louis workers ferried across the Mississippi River to join them while singing the French revolutionary anthem, the "Marseillaise."[2] American workers taking up the anthem of the French Revolution had the effect of connecting American labor with European revolution.

In East St. Louis the railroad workers established their strike headquarters in the railroad depot and from there controlled the entire city. As yet they had met with no opposition, and there was no violence. The city had only twelve policemen, and a large part of the population was employed by the railroads. The mayor, John Bowman, supported the strikers, even appointing many of them as special police to protect railroad property. Bowman did not want to alienate the workers, who constituted a good share of East St. Louis's citizens and voters.

Prior to his emigration from Germany to the United States, Bowman had engaged in radical and revolutionary politics in Europe. In an attempt to overthrow German royalty and replace it with a more democratic republic, he had participated in the 1848 Revolution in the German-speaking states and had belonged to a conspiratorial group in London, which was made up of former European revolutionaries. Although Bowman was primarily a German nationalist and republican, he was also a revolutionary and was not likely to be spooked by political radicalism, socialism, or even cries for revolution.

The strikers' executive committee trusted Bowman and authorized him to meet with the railroad managers and owners in an attempt to reach an agreement with regard to a number of wage reductions previously instituted by the railroad companies and other working conditions. Unfortunately, the owners refused the invitation to discuss a settlement of the strike, which then spread from the railroad yards to the stockyards and a car works. Strikers took control of locomotives and telegraph lines between East St. Louis and St. Louis.[3]

Several members of the WPUSA in St. Louis spoke at the East St. Louis meeting. Peter A. Lofgreen, Albert Currlin, and Henry F. Allen, members of the party's executive committee in St. Louis, spoke to the crowd. Luke Hite, a prominent lawyer in St. Clair County, Illinois, also spoke and declared that a war was being waged between labor and capital.

Also on July 21 a meeting was held in support of the railroad strikers in Carondelet, a community characterized by heavy industry and working-class residents, which had only recently been incorporated into the city of St. Louis. Lofgreen and Currlin also spoke at that meeting. On Sunday, July 22, Philip Van Patten, the national secretary of the Workingmen's Party sent a letter to all sections directing them to support the railroad strike and to demand the eight-hour day and the nationalization of all railroads and telegraph companies.

Even many of the authorities believed that the railroad workers had legitimate grievances against the railroad companies. Although he had no legal jurisdiction in Illinois, Missouri's governor, when asked what could be done about the situation, suggested that the railroads negotiate over the workers' legitimate complaints: "It is absurd to say that the men have no cause whatever of grievance, and the railroad officials should be prepared to negotiate with them in a frank and manly way."[4]

While most members of the WPUSA in St. Louis were German immigrants, Lofgreen was originally from Denmark, spoke German and perfect English, had graduated from the University of Copenhagen, and was a member of the bar in Chicago. He was the financial secretary of the St. Louis English-speaking section of the WPUSA. Albert Currlin, a twenty-four-year-old baker, was a leader of the German-language section of the WPUSA in St. Louis. Henry Allen, a sign painter, was a utopian socialist. Another speaker was Harry Eastman, a member of the party in East St. Louis and chair of the strikers' executive committee. Other members of the St. Louis executive committee included James Cope, Thomas Curtis, William Fischer, and Joseph Glenn. At the time, there were approximately one thousand WPUSA members in St. Louis, in German-, English-, French-, and Bohemian-language sections.

Almost all of the St. Louis strike leaders were members of the working class. Forty percent were skilled workers; over 25 percent were white-collar workers or small businessmen; and 25 percent were unskilled workers.[5] The German influence was greater than that of any other ethnic group: 31 percent of the strike leaders had been born in the German states, 21 percent in Ireland, and 21 percent in the United States.

When those German, French, and other immigrants came to the United States, they brought with them their political philosophies and revolutionary experiences, all of which became part of the St. Louis Commune and its leadership. It is therefore helpful to understand what had previously occurred in Europe in order to comprehend what occurred in America.

Although the strike was precipitated by wage reductions and dangerous working conditions, larger and more radical issues arose among the workers from the very beginning. According to one speaker at the meeting in East St. Louis, "The capitalist was trying to starve the workingman, and was educating his children to look down on them, despise and grind them under foot at every chance."[6] The strike that began over bread-and-butter issues expanded its focus and took on the elements of class warfare.

As had occurred in Europe, most significantly in Germany, the strike occurred at the time that independent artisans were losing their favored place in society and were being forced into the ranks of unskilled industrial wage earners. Skilled artisans had previously enjoyed a certain pride in their work, respect in society, and independence that was absent in the factory system. With the coming of industrial capitalism, they no longer were able to produce their own products, manage their own working conditions, or exist as independent workers who enjoyed the proceeds of their labor. As wage earners they were limited to the drudgery of piece work, obeyed the whistle of the factory system, and were dependent on capitalists who reaped the profits of their toil.

The decision to strike was spontaneous, with no existing railroad-related organization calling for or supporting the stoppage at that time. The Workingmen's Party in St. Louis immediately declared its support for the strike and the restoration of the 1873 wage scale, which was about 50 percent higher than that following the wage reductions.[7]

The Monday morning after the meeting the St. Louis papers were full of stories about the strike in Pittsburgh, where a great deal of violence had occurred, many people had been killed, and railroad property was destroyed, including buildings, locomotives, railroad cars, and freight. Since the state militias were, for a variety of reasons, not especially helpful in suppressing the strikes at any location, St. Louis business and political leaders suggested that two former Civil War generals who resided in the city, one from the Union and one from the Confederacy, be used to suppress any disorder in the city. Two former enemies who had fought a war to the death only a decade earlier were to unite in order to suppress the working class.

At the same time, led by Thomas Scott of the Pennsylvania Railroad and John Garrett of the Baltimore and Ohio, pressure was building in Washington to send in federal troops to break the strike. Proclamations issued by President Rutherford B. Hayes referred to "insurgents" in West Virginia, Maryland, and Pennsylvania, a description necessary to support the intervention of the federal government. The seriousness with which the government assessed the situation was clearly evident when the secretary of war authorized Gen. John Pope at Fort Leavenworth to move troops to St. Louis even though no violent or illegal conduct had occurred there.

When the strike reached St. Louis, there was no national or local leadership. The strike was expanding east to west quickly as workers spontaneously left their jobs to join their comrades. In the absence of any local direction, the St.

Louis WPUSA assumed leadership, and the St. Louis Commune was born. The leadership largely consisted of members of the Marxist Workingmen's Party who were German immigrants and who believed that a confrontation between labor and capital was imminent. The party proceeded to hold mass meetings and public marches of thousands of workers several times a day and sought to guide the direction of the strike and the protesting workers.

Ultimately the WPUSA issued a call for a general strike by all workers in the city, with the result that virtually all commerce in St. Louis was brought to a standstill. Where the railroad strike was originally fueled by wage cuts within the industry, in St. Louis it became a general strike with the participation of all members of the working class, no matter in which industries they were employed, and was led by a group of communists who declared the railroad owners and other capitalists to be the enemies of the working class who needed to be removed.

Whether the strike and the St. Louis Commune were viewed as part of an international communist conspiracy bent on overthrowing the government or as working men who were merely attempting to survive in light of starvation wages and hazardous duty somewhat depended on one's perspective. St. Louis's wealthy class remembered the bloodshed of the Paris Commune and feared that their city's lower classes would attempt to take away their property and power. Members of the working class saw the strike instead as a last-minute and desperate attempt to survive. There was some evidence to support each view.

At a mass meeting at St. Louis's Lucas Market, one worker compared his life to that of a slave and surprisingly concluded that slaves were actually better off than he. At least slaves were fed enough to work, he argued, and their health and lives were of some concern to their owners, who had a good deal of money invested in them. Capitalists, on the other hand, had no interest in the health or survival of their workers, and they had no financial incentive in protecting workers' health or lives. For the capitalist, the incentive was actually the opposite: to pay the workers as little as possible and force them to work long hours and to not spend any money on safety measures. With no capital investment in their workers, capitalists could starve them or work them to death and then easily replace them from the large pool of the unemployed. Because they faced death in any event, workers were desperate to change the system that exploited them. The workers, explained another speaker, "might as well be shot as starved to death."[8]

There were also signs of what appeared to be European socialist thought growing among the workers. Calls for class warfare and revolution could be heard at gatherings of working-class citizens. A resolution passed at one mass meeting described the work stoppage as "oppressed labor exercising the inherited right of revolution against the tyrannical exactions of capital."[9] Demanding that the government take over the railroads, one St. Louis Commune leader, Currlin, declared that the entire working class of the United States was "in a condition of revolution."[10] In a very short time, it seemed the railroad strike had developed from one based on bread-and-butter issues to one that challenged the very nature of industrial capitalism itself.

There is no question that the railroad strike evolved from a protest against wage cuts, low wages, and dangerous working conditions to acquire a more radical tone. However, workers were divided as to their ultimate objective. Wages and working conditions were the issues that gave rise to the railroad strike and that existed in every city in which railroad workers struck. However, at mass rallies called by the Workingmen's Party in St. Louis, many speakers attacked capitalism, monopolies, the rich, and the massive corporate interests that had recently emerged in the United States. Workers carried the black and red flags of anarchism and communism as they marched through the streets of St. Louis. Their rhetoric was certainly of a revolutionary nature. But at the same time they also sought a more equitable division of property, even through a mere increase in wages. In none of the actual settlement discussions themselves had workers demanded the forfeiture of private property as part of their demands to end the strike. The seemingly opposing views were the result of not only the thousands of different personalities that participated in the strike but also the speed with which the strike spread and the lack of political direction from its leadership.

The story of the St. Louis Commune cannot be understood merely by a factual description of the events that occurred in the city during the month of July 1877. It can be argued that those events were not unique to the United States or to St. Louis but were actually a continuation of what had been occurring in Europe for thirty years. From that perspective, the uprising of American workers was another episode in the battle between labor and capital that had exploded in the European revolutions of 1848 and the Paris Commune of 1871 and was brought to the United States by members of the First International. Many of the participants in the strike and the St. Louis Commune had fought on the barricades in the 1848 German Revolution and the 1871 Paris Commune. Some, although not all, were dedicated communists. Many were members of the International Workingmen's Association, the First International, which was organized and controlled by communists and anarchists. The International in the United States, after all, had dissolved itself and formed the WPUSA just a year prior to the railroad strike. It is to Europe, then, that one must look to understand the roots of the St. Louis Commune.

2

Revolution in Europe

While the St. Louis Commune arose during the 1877 railroad strike in the United States, its roots were in the Europe that existed thirty years before. The revolutions that characterized Europe in 1848 and 1849 provided American workers with both the philosophy and the workforce that fueled the 1877 strike and specifically the St. Louis Commune. A strong argument could be made that in the absence of the European, especially German, revolutions, the St. Louis Commune would never have existed.

The roots of the revolutions in Europe in 1848 can be found in the French Revolution of 1789 and the years immediately following. A number of political, economic, and social factors led to revolution in France, supported by the French bourgeoisie's call for greater participation in French politics and government.

The period of the Enlightenment in France was marked by scientific thought, science and philosophy challenging religion, and an optimistic view that rational thinking could solve any of a society's problems. Paris was the center of French Enlightenment thought. Some of the leading Enlightenment thinkers there included the philosophers Montesquieu, Rousseau, and Voltaire. Montesquieu called for the separation of powers in government, so that each branch provided a check on the power of the other branches. Rousseau believed that people were naturally free, that they gave up some of their freedom for the good of society, that all citizens were equal, and that the best form of government was a democracy. Voltaire called for civil freedoms, such as speech and religion in the public sphere, and rational solutions to society's problems. The British philosopher John Locke believed that people were born free and entered into an agreement to form governments in order to protect themselves. The purpose of government, according to Locke, was to protect people's lives, liberty, and property. Enlightenment thought was the philosophical and political basis for the middle-class attempt to gain political power from the European feudal monarchies and aristocracy.

Napoleon attempted to spread the philosophy of the French Revolution across Europe. When he was defeated at Waterloo, the Vienna Congress of 1815 attempted to turn back the clock and return France to pre-Revolution days, returning the monarch to the throne and suppressing any traces of republicanism that remained throughout Europe.[1] However, the ideas of the French Revolution remained in many areas that had been conquered by Napoleon, including parts of the German states, such as the Rhineland.[2]

However, despite the intentions and precautions of the Congress of Vienna, revolutions did spread across Europe in 1830, which marked the beginning of the defeat of the aristocracy by the newly emerging middle-class bourgeoisie.[3] As the middle class grew richer and more successful, it sought to gain commensurate political power. The revolutions of 1830 represented an attempt by the bourgeoisie to establish liberal constitutions that were more democratic and less monarchical and aristocratic. The new power of the growing bourgeoisie resulted in a partial retreat by monarchs, aristocrats, and the Church. After 1830 political power in Europe was shifting to the bourgeoisie. While the working class sought more egalitarian ends and social welfare legislation, it was not yet powerful enough to succeed against the monarchy, the aristocracy and the bourgeoisie. The newly emerging bourgeoisie consisted of bankers, industrialists, and manufacturers, while their challengers were small shopkeepers, artisans, and workers. The legacy of the French Revolution was the model it presented for the next generation of European revolutionaries.[4]

The Bourbon king Louis XVIII, placed on the throne of France in 1814, was followed by Charles X, who was replaced by Louis Philippe in 1830 after an insurrection in Paris. The working class, which fought on the barricades, felt that their revolution had been stolen by the industrialists and large landowners. Revolts also occurred in Germany, causing some German princes to agree to constitutional government, and an insurrection took place in Russia by Polish nationalists. In the 1820s Greece successfully rebelled against the Ottoman Empire, and in Italy Giuseppe Mazzini sought to achieve a democratic republic there by ousting the Austrians.[5] It was during this time that underground socialist, revolutionary organizations appeared, along with those who would devote their entire careers and lives to the making of revolution.

According to the historian Eric Hobsbawm, three revolutionary trends emerged after 1815: (1) a group made up largely of moderate upper-middle-class liberals who sought liberal, republican reforms; (2) a more radical democratic group, primarily consisting of lower-middle-class elements; and (3) socialists, represented for the most part by the working poor.[6] Europe's absolute monarchs perceived each group as a threat to their existence. Those groups had different views of a future society, but all were united by their opposition to the monarchies, the aristocracy, and the Church.

Industrialization grew in Europe during the late 1830s and 1840s. Following the example of Great Britain, western Europe was becoming industrialized, including some of the German states. The medieval guild system remained in place for skilled workers until industrialization eventually destroyed it. Railroads were expanding in the 1840s. The Austrian Empire added thirty thousand miles of track between 1830 and 1847. France expanded its road system and railroad track, encouraging the growth of other industries. In Germany in 1835 Krupp installed its first steam engine, and the first shafts were sunk in the Ruhr coalfields in 1837. Even in the United States railroads added approximately 150,000 miles of new track from 1800 to 1850.[7]

The 1830 revolutions, however, exposed divisions within the opposition to the reactionary 1815 governments. With the growth of the new bourgeoisie came the growth of a new working class, the industrial proletariat, many members of which sought a socialist revolution. The urban poor had few choices that could lead them to better lives. They could not work their way into the bourgeoisie, which required either capital or education, neither of which was available to the poor. As a result, they could either suffer the way things were or revolt against those conditions. Such were their limited choices. The working-class poor thus began to unite, forming organizations for their protection. Lower-class organizations in the German states, for example, included the German League of the Outlaws, which later became the League of the Just, and still later the Communist League. Moderates split from radicals and working-class revolutionaries. Skilled workers, artisans, and small shopkeepers, while sympathizing with the poor, were also property owners and therefore had some identification with the rich and the preservation of private property. They believed they had something to lose in a socialist revolution. While moderate liberalism was more successful in Belgium, France, and Great Britain, it was violently suppressed in Italy and the German states, often with the aid of Austria.

With the expansion of industrialism came the growth of the working-class proletariat. As class consciousness grew, so did a labor movement. Led by socialist thinkers, the picture of a new society based on cooperation and collectivism rather than competition and individualism took hold. Socialist leaders introduced the idea of remaking society in its entirety rather than struggling for a few more pieces of bread. This idea, beginning in France and England, spread to other countries. Although all classes were represented, the earliest communists were primarily journeymen craftsmen, carpenters, tailors, and printers, all of whom saw their lives and careers blocked by the end of the guild system and by the replacement of skilled workers by the unskilled, factories, and machines.[8] Instead of practicing their trades, skilled workers were forced to seek jobs operating machinery in factories. Where they were once independent, they became wholly dependent on the factory system, which was displacing them, and wages fell as a result.

Working-class radicals and middle-class liberals sought to bring their societies out of the remnants of feudalism into new, more progressive and modern states, where power was gained by new classes struggling for a place in a new society.[9] In France the revolutionary tradition included communism, led by Auguste Blanqui, who viewed the working class as a socialist engine and the middle-class as its enemy along with the monarchy and the aristocracy. Following repression in Paris and other cities in France in the mid-1830s, Blanqui organized the Society of Seasons, consisting of separate revolutionary cells, and called for a period of revolution until the ruling classes were eliminated and their wealth redistributed. Revolutionary energy was focused in the cities rather than the more conservative rural areas.

Economic crises and poor harvests in the 1840s led to frustration in Europe. There was a potato blight in 1845, bad harvests in 1845 and 1846, and an economic recession between 1847 and 1849. In some places over two-thirds of the population was forced to beg. The years immediately prior to 1848 were especially harsh in the German states. There were demands for political and economic reform by the lower classes and a movement in favor of radical and socialist policies. Between 1816 and 1850, 5 million Europeans emigrated, half of them moving to the Americas.[10] National revolutionary activity became international when revolutionaries were forced to flee their native countries, many emigrating to Switzerland, England, and the United States, where they met others from their country with similar views.

The radical German newspaper *Rheinische Zeitung* was founded in 1842. Although purporting to be a liberal, republican publication in order to survive Prussia's censors, the paper's political beliefs were actually much more radical. Marx became the editor of the paper soon after its birth. Following antigovernment editorials, it was closed by the authorities in 1843, and Marx left for Paris. During his absence, Friedrich Engels met with those interested in communism in the German states, at that time largely students and liberal intellectuals such as lawyers, journalists, and teachers. In 1846 the Big St. Martin Parish Fair in Cologne was attacked by police and soldiers, who beat people and stabbed them with bayonets. Thousands marched against the government the next day, resulting in the removal of the troops.

In January 1848 Alexis de Tocqueville warned the French Chamber of Deputies that parliamentary reform was necessary or the masses would explode in rebellion. Most of the people's anger was directed at the conservatives, and when such reforms were not forthcoming, the explosion Tocqueville warned against did occur.

In 1848 revolutions broke out throughout Europe, including France, Italy, the German states, the Habsburg Empire, and Switzerland. A march in Paris to the Chamber of Deputies demanding reforms was attacked by French soldiers, and fighting broke out in the streets. Insurgents constructed barricades and captured an arsenal. Soldiers fired into a crowd, killing fifty people. Fearing for his own position, Louis Philippe called for reforms in order to appease the growing discontent. But he also sent troops to clear away the barricades. The national guard, who refused to fight civilians, instead joined the insurgents and captured the Hôtel de Ville, Paris's city hall. The crowd attacked the palace, overwhelmed the palace guards, destroyed property, and took turns sitting on the throne. The king fled to England for safety. A provisional government was appointed to lead France, a Republic was proclaimed, and the radical Louis Blanc was appointed a minister without portfolio.

News of the events in Paris spread quickly throughout the continent, and monarchs all over Europe agreed to the writing of constitutions in efforts to quiet the masses. The revolts were not limited to France. A tobacco riot in Milan resulted in the killing of six and the wounding of fifty civilians. Thirty-six were killed in Palermo in Sicily when peasants took the city after the army withdrew. Peasants rose up in Naples in January 1848, with twenty-five thousand demonstrating in front of the royal palace until the army stood down and King Ferdinand agreed to a constitution. In March of that year Leopold of Tuscany and Charles Albert of Piedmont agreed to constitutions.[11] In Wurttemberg, Nassau, and the Grand Duchy of Baden, rulers conceded to liberal demands. The Grand Duke of Hesse-Darmstadt abdicated, and following the seizure of an armory King Ludwig of Bavaria also gave in to revolutionary demands. King Frederick Augustus II of Saxony agreed to reforms, including freedom of the press, trial by jury, jobs, free secular education, welfare for the poor, and a popular militia and constitutions.[12]

Ethnic tensions and a spirit of nationalism contributed to the revolutionary fervor in Europe, especially affecting the Austrian Empire. In March 1848 Lajos Kossuth, a Hungarian revolutionary, demanded an independent Hungary, free from the Habsburg Empire. When Foreign Minister Klemens von Metternich refused, students in Vienna occupied the university and encouraged workers to join them. Workers attacked factories; four thousand students and some middle-class reformers who were demonstrating were confronted by police and soldiers, and six were killed.[13] Street fighting broke out throughout Vienna, workers poured through the city gates, Metternich fled the city, and Emperor Ferdinand agreed to liberal reforms and a constitution.

Revolts broke out in Budapest, where twenty thousand marched on Buda Castle, which yielded to their demands for free speech, a parliament, religious freedom, a national guard, and trial by jury. Two weeks later thousands of Czechs demanded a constitution, freedom of the press, trial by jury, and a unified kingdom independent of Vienna. Absolute monarchy was under attack throughout the Habsburg Empire.

In Milan and Venice, Austria's two Italian provinces, people demanded greater autonomy, freedom of the press, and the establishment of a national guard. Fifteen thousand marched on the government, took over government buildings, and held the vice governor hostage. Austrian troops were again called out, church bells again rang, and barricades once more appeared. The troops were attacked from all sides, men shooting and women pouring boiling water on them from the windows of buildings. Nationalists, liberals, workers, and armed peasants finally forced the army to withdraw. In the more conservative rural areas, landlords and priests supported the monarchists.

When word of Metternich's fall reached Venice, a crowd gathered in St. Mark's Square, attacked the governor's residence, and raised the Italian flag. Croatian and Hungarian troops fired into the crowd, killing or wounding nine protesters. Venetian troops counterattacked and captured an arsenal; Italian troops joined the insurrection; and cannon that were aimed at the crowd were turned around to face the governor's palace. The Austrian army and government retreated, and a new provisional government was proclaimed in Venice. In the Netherlands, King William II agreed to reforms providing for freedom of the press, assembly, and religion.

Russia was more backward than Europe at this time; whereas 60 percent of the population of France and Austria were literate, as were 80 percent of Prussians, only 5 percent of Russians could read. In an attempt to keep revolutionary ideas out of Russia, news of the European revolutions was banned, foreigners were not allowed to enter the country, and any discussion of reform was prohibited. Tsar Nicholas I mobilized the army and attempted to build a wall between Russia and Europe, at the same time forcefully repressing any dissent. In April universities were closed, 252 Russians were arrested, 51 exiled, and 21 sentenced to death.[14] All of this unrest could not help but affect the German states, leading Rudolph Stadelman to conclude that the German

Revolution of 1848 was caused by the introduction of the new proletarian into a "half feudal, half bourgeois world."[15]

Prussia at the time was ruled by a king and a feudal aristocracy. German princes governed their own domains, where their rule extended over local courts and political life. They served at a level between the sovereign and the masses, with their own infrastructure and bureaucracy.[16] Each German state was seemingly independent, though under the watchful eye of a powerful Prussia.

By 1848 the feudal remnants were under attack by both the bourgeoisie and the proletariat. While the latter two classes were united against the institutions of the monarchy, the aristocracy, and the Church, they faced off against each other in the struggle for the form of a new society. As a result of new machines and industrialization, there was a glut in the labor market in the German states. Master craftsmen could still earn a decent wage, but their journeymen lived on the edge of starvation. The poorest elements of the working poor were the day laborers, who, in many cases, earned less than they needed to survive. While profits were greater for employers, wages for workers dropped as commodity prices increased. The factory system was still growing, and there were about 550,000 factory workers. Textiles employers hired more women than men and at lower wages, creating financial stress on families.

Artisans and master craftsmen were attempting to hold on to their privileges, to control their production, income, and work environments, while journeymen sought to become masters at the time that guilds were dying and industrialism was about to replace them. Under the new factory system, artisans were working machines as skilled workers in a controlled environment. Those skilled and semiskilled workers were to become important elements in the 1848 Revolution. The factory system would introduce long hours, child labor, dangerous working conditions, and reduced wages to the extent that many working-class families were forced to share small apartments and witness family members starve or work as prostitutes. Reform at that time in Prussia consisted of prohibiting the employment of children under nine years of age and limiting those children age nine to sixteen to ten-hour workdays. Those who were most active in revolutionary activities were those who lived at a subsistence level or who felt a threat to their social position.

At this time approximately two-thirds of Germans were employed in agriculture. The number was even greater in Prussia. This glut resulted in a decrease in wages in rural areas. Peasants endured hard lives but were more conservative and more religious than their urban counterparts. Their strong religious views made them vulnerable to the opinions of local priests, who were largely supportive of the monarchy. They lived almost as they had lived in feudal times. As a result, the liberation of peasants demanded confrontation not only with current law but also with feudal obligations, which were passed down from generation to generation. In many cases liberated peasants became day laborers or other forms of wage laborers, hardly improving their lot. They became, in effect, a rural proletariat. Their existence was marginal, and they survived day to day. Weather and the success or failure of a harvest could determine life or death. The potato blight in 1847, for example, resulted in the deaths of sixteen thousand in upper Silesia.

Peasants also complained about the unequal division of the common lands and demanded the use of them by all at a nominal price. The prohibition against hunting and gathering wood on aristocrats' lands sometimes made the difference as to whether a family survived or perished. Their frustration sometimes exploded in breaking the law and violence. In one incident, four hundred peasants burned down the house of a chief forester and carried off wood from the royal forest.[17] Crowds of peasants often interrupted prosecutions for forest offenses and freed prisoners accused of violating the forest laws.

The educated class of lawyers and journalists was dependent on the government or government-sanctioned entities for employment, so the lack of these jobs made them ripe for revolution. In March 1848 five thousand people marched on City Hall in Cologne, led by communists, and demanded the abolition of the standing army, the arming of the people, universal manhood suffrage, the guarantee of a minimum standard of living, and free public secular education.[18] That same month similar demands were made by the people in Berlin and throughout the German states. On March 18 an insurrection broke out, and twenty thousand Prussian troops were sent to Berlin.[19] Paving stones were removed from the streets, and barricades were thrown up throughout the city. Church bells rang out, calling the people to revolution. Workers and parts of the middle class joined the revolt. Soldiers fired at everything moving, and artillery blasted the barricades, resulting in the deaths of nine hundred in one afternoon. The army was eventually withdrawn, and King Frederick William agreed to a constitution and promised that Prussia would become part of a unified Germany.[20]

The places in which revolutions broke out throughout Europe in 1848 included, but were not limited to, France, Italy, the German states, the Habsburg Empire, and Switzerland. Working-class radicals and middle-class liberals sought to advance their societies from the remnants of feudalism to more progressive and modern states, where power would be shared by the new classes struggling for a place in a changing society.[21] French and British socialist ideas spread to the German states, challenging German culture's seeming obedience to authority. On the edge of starvation, peasants were losing trust in government and their traditions. Peasant uprisings in the German provinces were not led by the poorest but rather by small property owners, who resented paying feudal taxes and being prohibited from hunting and gathering on aristocrat-owned property. A new philosophy, that political power and wealth should not be based on birth but that all should have an opportunity to better their situations and that everyone should participate in government, was especially strong in the German Rhineland. Other voices calling for a new society were heard on university campuses, where students sought to spread radical ideas to the masses.

The German Confederation, dominated by Prussia, placed severe limitations on the press, public assembly, and voting. German social and gymnastic societies, such as the Turnverein, often served as fronts for political discourse and activities. In 1849 there were more than fifty such gymnastic societies throughout the German states, many providing military training and hanging red flags from their windows. In reaction to the growing radicalism, Prussian authorities armed forty thousand of their richer citizens in order to suppress the poor. The same strategy would be used in the United States during the railroad strike some thirty years later. One of the revolutionary activists at the time was a young journalist and philosopher whose name would be linked to revolution for the next century.

Karl Marx was active in and a leading theoretician of the European revolutions in 1848. A student of Friedrich Hegel, Marx modified his teacher's dialectical thought into a philosophy supporting communist revolution. He taught that all societies advance as a result of the class conflict caused by a society's changing means of production, and that in 1848 the primary conflict was between the existing monarchies, which represented the feudal stage of social and economic development, and the new bourgeoisie, which represented the emerging capitalist society. Later, Marx explained, the struggle would be between the then ruling bourgeoisie, those who owned the means of production, and the proletariat, those who owned nothing except their own labor power, which they were forced to sell in order to survive. Because the working class in 1848 was new and immature, Marx saw the current battle as between the monarchists and the emerging bourgeoisie. It was therefore necessary to confront the monarchy with a united front of all classes. At a later moment in history, when it was stronger, the proletariat would directly confront the bourgeoisie. Marx set out his philosophy in *The German Ideology*. His manuscript was copied and later published in the United States by another German revolutionary, Joseph Weydemeyer, who later joined German radicals who had emigrated from the German states to St. Louis and served as a colonel in the Union army during the American Civil War.[22] Marx felt that the German states were far behind England and France with regard to social and economic progress. Feudalism, he wrote, had been reduced to insignificance in England and France by a strong bourgeoisie, while German-speaking areas still remained stuck in feudal privilege.[23]

Engels wrote for, and for a time Marx edited, the *Rheinische Zeitung*, the radical, anti-Prussian newspaper in Cologne. Marx also wrote for other publications, including the radical *Vorwarts*, which was published in Paris by Heinrich Boernstein, who would actively participate in the 1848 Revolution in Germany and also later immigrate to St. Louis, where he joined other German radicals and worked as a journalist and editor. Marx joined other Germans in Paris, but he and Boernstein were eventually expelled from that country. In 1848 Marx was asked to prepare a paper setting out the beliefs of the Communist League, which was centered in London, and his work was published as *The Communist Manifesto*. In that document he clearly set forth his philosophy: "The history of all hitherto existing society is the history of class struggle. . . . Freeman and slave, patrician and plebian, lord and serf, guild-master and journeyman, in a word, oppressor and oppressed, stand in constant opposition to one another.... Society as a whole is more and more splitting up into two great camps, into two great classes directly facing each other: *Bourgeoisie* and *Proletariat*."[24]

Intertwined with ideas about a new kind of politics was the issue of the consolidation of the German states. Nationalism was merging with thoughts of liberalism, a republic, and a constitution. The consolidation of the German states into one nation would result in an economically and militarily stronger Germany. The lower classes believed having political power would protect them from harassment by royalists and a faceless bureaucracy. By the spring of 1848 the black, red, and gold flag representing German nationalism and unity was seen at the head of most demonstrations. But the bourgeoisie, who were not experiencing starvation and hunger, were not as interested in a social revolution as in more moderate political reforms giving them some political power, such as freedom of the press, extended suffrage, limitations on the power of the bureaucracy, the end of feudal privileges enjoyed by the aristocracy, and a constitution. For a time the working class joined the bourgeoisie against the monarchy and the aristocracy.

The Rhineland was the center of the democratic movement in the German states.[25] Having once been part of Napoleon's empire, the area had been infiltrated by French ideas of liberty and revolution. It was primarily an agricultural area where farmers who owned some land survived, while the landless workers did not do as well. When the commons were privatized and divided among the rich, the poorer small peasants and day laborers, who grew food on and used the land for pasture, suffered. In addition, by 1848 the wine industry had been hit especially hard there. Producers were earning less due to bad weather and the rising cost of barrels. Many were in debt and forced out of business. The area was also cursed with a potato famine in 1845 and 1846.[26] As a result there was a shortage of bread everywhere. In the more industrial cities of the area, there existed large machine shops, and companies outsourced a good deal of labor at lower wages to independent contractors, who had formerly worked as independent artisans and master craftsmen.

There was not a large number of factory workers in the Rhineland. They were greatly outnumbered by craftsmen under contract to employers. Textiles were the most important manufactured products, and women and children under fourteen provided the workforce for the mechanized spinning mills. Most of that kind of work was outsourced as well. Therefore many workers appeared on the surface to be independent producers, although they depended on the factory owners for their livelihood and competed with each other for available work, thus resulting in lower earnings.[27] Tension between workers and owners was great, and textile workers often attacked the homes of manufacturers over the issue of wages.

Artisans were also threatened, their independence and dignity stolen by the machines that were replacing them. Where they once used their skills and training to turn out finished goods, they now were forced to engage in piecework, losing any pride and dignity that they once had in their skilled workmanship. The introduction of gas lighting meant workers sat at their machines up to fifteen hours a day. In March 1848 Solingen metal workers destroyed factories and foundries, smashing the machines that were taking their jobs.[28]

Capitalism, which was spreading throughout the German states, suffered booms and busts; overproduction resulted in lower wages and unemployment; and rural poverty was staggering. There were not enough jobs in Prussia for the educated middle class, as the state bureaucracy was bloated. In the cities Germans were crowded into tenements and could barely survive on their wages. Half of all German children died before reaching the age of five. Open sewers and other unsanitary conditions led to outbreaks of cholera. Although the law required compulsory education, half of the Rhineland's children did not attend school, promoting a cycle of poverty in the region. From late March to early May 1848 there were clashes between Prussian troops and artisans and day laborers in Aachen, Dusseldorf, Eupen, Mainz, and Trier.[29]

Religion was important to people in the Rhineland. There was no separation of Church and state. There were large numbers of Catholics and pious Calvinist Protestants, each operating their own schools. The Catholic Church was loyal to the monarchy since it had always enjoyed privileges due to its feudal status. Most Protestants supported the Prussian monarchy. Teachers were subordinate to the clergy, especially in Catholic schools; this fostered a feeling of anticlericalism among teachers, who generally demanded a secular education where they would not be required to teach courses on religion or answer to the Church bureaucracy. Because people in the Rhineland were so affected by Napoleon's influence that his written Code of laws was still in effect years after his defeat, the French Enlightenment's rationalism and liberty that he spread throughout the Rhineland made the area's poor peasants and growing proletariat ripe for revolution.

The 1848 revolutions affected all the major governments in Europe. Workers rioted and demonstrated in France and in the German states. Louis Philippe's throne was burned in Paris, and German workers served petitions on the government and marched in the streets. In February 1848 German liberals demanded press freedom, trial by jury, and a parliament. There was discussion of a constitutional monarchy and the uniting of the several German states. In Vienna, the Habsburg Empire gave up Metternich following demands by the people, thereby attempting to save the monarchy from the threat of republicanism. Still, crowds there destroyed the custom house and attacked machines and employers. Those attending a meeting in Frankfurt demanded a parliament, although not all present were in favor of a republic. Uprisings occurred in Vienna, Venice, Milan, Prague, Berlin, and the towns of every German principality. European monarchs were able to keep their position only by agreeing to constitutions that included male suffrage, press freedom, trial by jury, and a limitation on feudal privileges.[30]

Protests and rallies in Berlin began on March 6 and continued thereafter. On March 13 and 14, 1848, a nonviolent crowd in Berlin was confronted by the cavalry. A few days later, shots were fired and the square was ordered to be cleared. Barricades were erected in the streets, and in response the large crowd, which was primarily made up of workers, was met with sabers and rifle shots, and over three hundred were killed.[31]

In order to end the violence, the king met with representatives of the crowd and promised a free press, a legislature, and a constitution in Prussia. But when the aroused crowd demanded the replacement of the military with a civilian guard, more shots were fired, more barricades were constructed, and the angry crowd accused the king of using the army against the people at the exact moment that he pretended to accede to their demands. Fighting continued throughout the night, with social classes joining together in the battle. Aristocrats fled the city. Unsure of the loyalty of his troops, the next day the king ordered the army to withdraw, and a citizen guard was organized and armed.

On September 17 some eight thousand people gathered in Worringen under a huge red flag to listen to speeches by Engels and others.[32] A mass meeting in Bernkastel on October 8 drew over fifteen thousand people. The bourgeoisie and the workers were divided, neither sure of the next steps to take, except to build barricades and seize arms.

In the southern German provinces, peasants rebelled against feudal conditions and burned records of taxes, deeds, and feudal obligations. They demanded that aristocrats pay their fair share of taxes, remove forest wardens, and open hunting and fishing lands to everyone. Their concerns were more local in nature and more concerned with local issues and leaders that affected their daily lives. Similar scenes occurred in Baden, Vienna, and Berlin, with socialist demonstrations in Cologne, all occurring spontaneously, without any leadership. Socialists demanded social reforms, jobs for all, free secular education, the arming of the population, universal suffrage, and freedom of the press and assembly, while the bourgeois liberals demanded state unity and constitutional reforms.

Austria, Prussia, and Russia were the conservative opposition to Enlightenment liberalism in Europe. Austria's hold on Italy had been challenged for years, but especially dangerous for the Austrian Empire were the new calls for nationalism. The 1848 revolutions caused chaos within the empire, as rebellions by Czechs, Poles, Hungarians, Italians, Croatians, and Slovenians endangered the future of the Habsburgs.

Russia too contained a number of nationalities within its borders. It was especially concerned about uprisings by its peasants and by Polish nationalists seeking independence from the empire. Russia had done its best to keep out Western thought after the Enlightenment, but it was not entirely successful. Russian army officers were exposed to Western ideas during the Napoleonic Wars that had led to a liberal insurrection in December 1825, which was successfully crushed by the authorities.[33]

In Germany some workers united with intellectuals and students who were attracted to socialist ideas and the French Revolution. The German working class was not large enough or sufficiently conscious of its own class interests to act independently, so the primary conflict was between the German feudal interests, the monarchy and aristocrats, and the opposition, which consisted of most of the bourgeoisie, republicans, democrats, liberals, constitutionalists, workers, and radicals. There was no united front against the German state, however; for instance, one revolutionary, Arnold Ruge, voiced his concern about the working class cooperating with those he perceived as its ultimate enemies, the bureaucrats, professors, lawyers, and clergy.[34]

One of the only actual working-class activists who was successful in organizing a powerful workers' organization in the German areas of 1848 was Stephen Born, a colleague of Marx in the Communist League, who led a printers' strike in Berlin and sought to unite all workers and establish producers' cooperatives. His idea was for the state to provide low-interest loans to local workers' concerns or cooperatives to enable them to buy raw materials and any necessary machinery; the state would then place orders for the goods produced. He also advocated a progressive income tax, public libraries, free secular public education, and free adult education, all of which was intended to enable the working class to better itself and participate in governing. Another proposal called for the creation of a republic, the arming of workers, the taking over of feudal estates by the state, limitations on inheritance, the regulation of banks, and equalization of wages. In August 1848 a conference seeking to represent all German workers elected Born its first president. Resolutions called for erecting workers' dwellings, establishing a loan bureau, instituting a ten-hour workday, the approval of factory foremen by workers, lowering the voting age, the division of large estates, and free public education.

In April 1848 liberals had made gains against the monarchy and the aristocrats. The Prussian authorities agreed to the creation of a National Assembly and universal male suffrage, democratic elections, and a written constitution under a monarchy. The elections were to be indirect and limited to property holders. Those elected by the people would then elect the delegates. The makeup of the Frankfurt National Assembly was not revolutionary; it contained 436 state employees, 100 businessmen and landowners, 100 lawyers, and 50 clergymen.[35] Still, some leftists were elected to the Frankfurt National

Assembly. Those participating included clerical Catholics, democratic groups, and those in favor of a constitutional monarchy. Divisions occurred when the Cologne Workers' Association protested the indirect elections, and the Church endorsed and ran candidates supported by their parishes. Protestant constitutional monarchists and Catholics combined against the left, while hunger, unemployment, and rising prices fueled uprisings, and artisans and workers joined with middle-class republicans against the aristocracy. However, the middle class, fearing the workers and peasants more than the feudal aristocracy, in the end made their peace with the latter.[36]

In May fighting at election time broke out in Trier between Prussian troops and citizens. Barricades were again constructed, and this time a red flag flew above St. Gangolf's Church. Two weeks later that scene repeated itself in Mainz. Marx returned to Cologne to edit the *Neue Rheinische Zeitung* and warned that the revolution was in danger of being suppressed. Gottfried Kinkel, a German professor, journalist, and revolutionary, alerted citizens to beware of the five fingers of despotism: the clergy, the nobility, the rich, the army, and authoritative officials. Those demanding a democracy, and communists who wished to act under the banner of democracy, opened Democratic Clubs throughout the country, so the revolution was spreading at the same time that it was being suppressed. Those Democratic Clubs were able to unite democrats, republicans, and communists, although the largest single group within the clubs was the liberal bourgeoisie who desired a republic, especially with them at its head.

Although not the largest of the antimonarchy groups, workers did boast substantial numbers and a popular message. With Marx as its president, the Cologne Workers' Association had a membership of eight thousand in 1848. The Prussian government attacked the organization in July 1848 and arrested Marx for inciting the overthrow of the Prussian monarchy. In honor of the French Revolution, the motto of the association and the name of its newspaper was "Liberty, Fraternity, Labor." Encouraged by Marx and Engels, members of the Communist League formed the Workers' Educational Association in Mainz in 1848. By 1849 that organization was engaged in military training. On May 6, 1849, the Cologne Workers' Association called on the population to withhold tax payments and to arm themselves in preparation for revolution. The primary purpose of such organizations, however, was not immediate revolution but rather to politicize and educate workers and the lower classes. At a February 1849 meeting of the Mainz Democratic Club, over two thousand celebrated the anniversary of the French Republic under red, gold, and black flags representing a German republic, the flags of France and the United States, and a much larger red flag of revolution. The main opponents of the progressive forces were the constitutional monarchs and Catholics. In Trier and Mainz, however, over 25 percent of adult males belonged to Democratic Clubs.

The German region was divided into thirty-nine separate states, each with its local prince. Some of the princes had agreed to constitutions for their people, but Prussia, by far the largest and most powerful, was entirely against such sharing of power. Led by King Frederick William IV, whose father had promised the people a constitution but who was against any kind of constitution himself, Prussia was still ruled by nobles and large landowners.

Concerned over the growth of a revolutionary proletariat, a frightened middle class and petit bourgeois artisan shopkeepers confronted working-class revolutionary activity. As a result of the emerging factory system, a few of the petit bourgeois improved their station in society and became factory owners themselves, while most became factory workers and part of the growing proletariat. It was that fear of the loss of property or social status that caused many of that class to hesitate in the face of revolutionary change. As a result of state-directed repression and hesitation by certain groups and allies, in many localities revolutionary reforms were reversed, and thus universal suffrage was lost, rural land was returned to the feudal interests, and other reforms were abandoned.

The German Revolution continued into 1849. Frederick William IV declared that he would never accept a constitution, and so the left attempted to organize pressure for a republic. It sought to publicize and communicate throughout Germany the desire for an armed citizenry and constitution. Democratic Clubs grew to number five hundred thousand members in a thousand branches. Many of the German states, outside of Prussia, were still in a state of rebellion, primarily over the issue of a constitution, and red flags became part of the demonstrations. Barricades appeared in the streets, armories were stormed for weapons, street battles erupted throughout German provinces, and mass meetings of workers numbered in the thousands. The question of the loyalty of the army arose in Erlangen, where students and soldiers together carried a red flag through the streets.[37] Many of the soldiers refused to shoot civilians from their own areas. Confronted with barricades in Elberfeld, troops refused to engage and left the city. In the same city the local militia denounced the Prussian government as traitors, and one thousand soldiers joined citizens ready to revolt. The Committee of Public Safety replaced the government there. Engels was placed in charge of the defense of the city but later was asked to leave because the bourgeoisie was afraid that he would declare a red republic.[38] Some militias refused to be called out against the people, and only three of eight hundred militiamen called for duty appeared in Krefeld.[39] In May 1849 over a hundred barricades were built in Dresden, buildings were burned, and 250 persons were killed in street confrontations.[40] Twenty thousand at a meeting in Reutlingen approved rebellion and allegiance to a constitution and called for a local constituent assembly, the abolition of feudal burdens, an income tax, the arming of the people, and the abolition of a standing army. Journeymen and government troops engaged in bloody battles in Nuremberg. Participating in those insurrections were the Russian anarchist Mikhail Bakunin and the communists Marx and Engels.

The 1848 revolutions in Europe had their roots in the French Revolution of 1789. Monarchists and revolutionaries both looked to France either in fear or for inspiration. The fall of Metternich in Vienna threw gasoline on smoldering revolutionary fires. However, only in France did the monarchy actually fall. In other places a more powerful bourgeoisie, seeking to attain benefits for itself from the monarchy, feared the ascendency of the working class and sought to control it. Added to the fire were the battles between the left and right wings of the bourgeoisie and the new nationalism of different ethnic groups within Europe.[41]

According to Jonathan Sperber, three major elements contributed to the German Revolution: (1) the desire and attempt to create a German national state, (2) the clash between the bourgeoisie and monarchy for political power, and (3) a social crisis as a result of industrial modernization displacing artisans and the state refusing to modernize socially and politically.[42] But that interpretation ignores the contribution of the radical workers, intellectuals, and students who were part of the revolutionary movement for social reform, socialism, and communism. It was they who manned the barricades and demanded a structural change in German political life. Students, workers, peasants, and the liberal bourgeoisie united for a time in the fight against reaction and demanded civil and social reforms in German society.

The 1848 Revolution in German-speaking areas was also the beginning of the German women's movement. Women were active in the revolution as nurses, obtained supplies for fighters, and themselves fought on the barricades.[43] For most Germans, however, the primary issue at stake was the attempt to build a strong, unified German state to replace the federalism of the German Confederation, to end the remaining effects of feudalism, to give birth to a German republic, and to agree on a constitution that provided more political power to the new bourgeoisie and to the German proletariat.[44]

The German Revolution of 1848 had a direct effect on subsequent events in the United States. Many German immigrants to the United States after 1848 had been active republicans, working-class activists, socialists, or communists in German-speaking Europe. They were familiar with socialist philosophy and had fought on the barricades. In the United States they continued the fight for the freedoms they had supported in Europe. They brought with them a radical ideology concerned with a restructuring of society and revolutionary experience. Activists for democratic rights and enemies of slavery, German revolutionaries served in the Union army during the Civil War; were largely responsible for causing Missouri to remain in the Union; served their new homeland as governors, senators, mayors, legislators, and cabinet members in local, state, and federal governments; and played a major role in the American labor movement, the railroad strike of 1877, and the St. Louis Commune.

3

After the Civil War

The St. Louis Commune emerged during a period in which the United States was undergoing tremendous change and was marked by terrific instability. The Civil War had only recently ended; the South was experiencing Reconstruction; American industrial capitalism was expanding at a rapid rate, as was the federal government; the gap between rich and poor had never been as wide; and the country was in the midst of a major depression. All of those factors contributed to the unrest that ultimately led to the strike of 1877 and the St. Louis Commune.

While the Civil War destroyed Southern slave society, businesses and corporations in the North prospered during and after the war. The railroad industry thrived, carrying troops and supplies to battle sites. The closing of the Mississippi River as a means of transportation during the war negatively impacted commerce but resulted in more business for railroad companies. Congress encouraged and financially supported industrial growth and railroad expansion by grants of public land.

When the transcontinental railroad was completed in 1869, it ensured investment in and the development of the West.[1] Between 1865 and 1873 industrial production grew by more than 75 percent. The young Republican Party supported such internal improvements, but the postwar industrial expansion largely ended in 1873 with the onset of the depression. The railroads were not immune to the business downturn, and by 1876 over half of existing railroad companies were in receivership. Capital investment, especially the massive amounts necessary to finance the building of railroads, favors political stability. The Indian wars being fought in the West following the Civil War resulted in severe instability on the frontier, where the railroads were expanding. The laying of railroad track and the construction of stations attracted settlements on what was previously Indian land, and so violence and instability followed the expansion of railroad mileage, especially in the Crow, Northern Cheyenne, and Lakota areas of the northern territories and the Apache lands of the Southwest. Frontier instability added to the financial problems of railroad companies and the selling of bonds, contributing to the pressure on the Northern Pacific bonds and the failure of Jay Cooke. "Simply put," Peter Cozzens explained, "Lakota resistance spooked investors into shedding Northern Pacific bonds."[2] Nevertheless, Gen. William Sherman's top priority was to protect railroad construction crews.[3]

Depending on one's place in American society, the period after the Civil War was a time either of plenty or of suffering. Never before in American history had there been so great a chasm between the haves and the have-nots. The zeitgeist that permeated the United States at the time included unfettered greed. Fortunes were made at that time by those who profited from the war, especially in industry and manufacturing. The economy had grown as a result of the war, factories were humming, and there was no shortage of money for investment and speculation. Industrial development was especially strong in the North, while the South's mostly agricultural and feudal economy bore the brunt of the fighting and was stagnant. For its entire history the South had relied on cotton and slavery for its wealth, both of which were destroyed as a result of the war.

Nationally the United States entered a period involving the reconstruction of the Southern states that had seceded from the Union. The postwar amendments to the U.S. Constitution, the Thirteenth, Fourteenth, and Fifteenth Amendments, ended slavery, conferred citizenship on those who were born in the United States along with equal protection under the laws of the nation, and provided Black males the right to vote. During the period of Reconstruction, attempts were also made to educate and prepare former slaves for lives of freedom and civic engagement.

Unfortunately the death of Abraham Lincoln ended any plans to support newly freed slaves. His successor, Andrew Johnson, though pro-Union, was a Democrat from Tennessee who was sympathetic to the South and its way of life. Johnson did not support the goals of Reconstruction and allowed Southern whites to reclaim their land, which had in many cases been worked by their former slaves in their absence, resulting in newly freed slaves becoming attached to the land as sharecroppers. Black Codes were instituted in Southern states in order to control their Black populations, the Ku Klux Klan emerged to intimidate African Americans, and the South took on a character remarkably similar to the way it functioned prior to the Civil War.[4]

Because of its central geographic location, St. Louis was also a very politically divided city. The explorer, Union officer, and later Republican presidential candidate John C. Frémont had placed it under martial law in 1861, and its residents were governed by a curfew and required passes in order to move around the city. As Grant's army moved south along the Mississippi River, freed slaves made their way to St. Louis looking for work and a less hostile environment. Between 1860 and 1890 the Black population of St. Louis increased by 600 percent, resulting in economic resentment against Blacks, especially by American-born and Irish workers.[5]

Although St. Louis had remained loyal to the Union and provided a number of Union generals and troops to the Northern cause, racism was rampant in the city. Blacks were required to ride on the outside of streetcars, which was not only dangerous but also very uncomfortable in cold or rainy weather. The St. Louisan Carl Schurz, a former German revolutionary, described the Caribbean as being infested by indolent Blacks and referred to Dominicans as lazy and shiftless.[6] Even the Republican German-language newspaper *Anzeiger des Westens* opposed racial integration.[7]

In the West new lands were ripe for settlement and development, encouraged by the Homestead Act of 1862 and the Pacific Railway Acts of 1862 and 1863, which created new markets for American manufacturers.[8] Manifest Destiny, the idea that the United States should rule the entire North American continent, was popular, driving people west to fill what they perceived as unpopulated land, that is, land not populated by whites. Under the Homestead Act, anyone living on 160 acres of unclaimed land for five years became its owner. The historian Frederick Jackson Turner described the settlement of the frontier as a safety valve that released pressure on the cities.[9] With the closing of the frontier, he predicted that American business would turn to foreign imperialism in order to continue its growth.

Smaller corporations combined into trusts after the war, and wealth began to be concentrated into fewer and fewer hands. By the late 1800s, 10 percent of the population held over 70 percent of America's wealth. Profits increased as the introduction of machines allowed unskilled workers to perform the work previously done by more highly paid skilled workers. In the twenty years following the war, the economy surged, and the new "titans of industry" attributed their success to their own superiority, purportedly proven by the social philosophy of Herbert Spencer's Social Darwinism. In the competitive world, it was those of superior intellect and character who survived and prospered; those who did not were obviously inferior and bound to fail.

During the years following the Civil War, it was not enough to be rich and enjoy the fruits of one's fortune. People needed to see one's riches and therefore recognize how smart, successful, and superior the rich were. It was an age of ostentation. William Vanderbilt, son of Cornelius and head of the New York Central Railroad, constructed a mansion at Fifth Avenue and Fifty-Second Street in New York that was modeled on a French Renaissance chateau. The walls were covered with Italian tapestries and paintings of scenes from mythology. A large stained-glass window represented a meeting of King Henry VIII of England with France's Francis I in an effort to tie Europe's hereditary royalty to America's new monied aristocracy. Vanderbilt held a party there with dancers dressed as horses, a friend dressed as Queen Elizabeth, and his wife as a Venetian princess with a diamond-studded dress. Fountains and ferns caused the room to take on the characteristics of a tropical forest. Twelve hundred guests were invited to the ball. William's son Cornelius Vanderbilt II built an even fancier summer house in Newport, Rhode Island, whose sixty-five thousand square feet contained seventy rooms. Much of the wood was brought from Europe, and the paneling came from a house that was built for Marie Antoinette. Another son, George Washington Vanderbilt

II, built Biltmore, a mansion in Asheville, North Carolina, that was even more magnificent than his father's and brother's mansions. Biltmore's 175,000 square feet contained 250 rooms and its 125,000 acres of land included farms, a church, and a village.[10]

The lives of working people were not as glamorous as those of the rich. Long hours of labor in factories, industrial accidents, and child labor were challenged by early organizations of workers. The Knights of Labor, for instance, formed in 1869, sought improvements in the workplace. However, an increase in immigration had the effect of ethnically dividing the working class, which was then making early attempts to unite on a national basis. Those fleeing European repression by immigrating to the United States were often willing to work for lesser wages and were used as strikebreakers by factory owners, incurring anger, resentment, and discrimination against Irish and Italian immigrants. The movement of job seekers from rural areas into the cities increased the competition for jobs and filled tenements with the poor.

Industrial development at the time was so massive and extensive that it even had the effect of changing the focus and nature of American culture. The World's Fair of 1876 in Philadelphia was named the International Exhibition of Arts, Manufactures and Products of the Soil and Mine and stressed the industrial successes of post–Civil War America. The Horatio Alger myth that a poor boy could become rich simply as a result of hard work and perseverance was born, and the simple life described by Romantic writers such as Emerson and Thoreau gave way to a new vein of realism and naturalism in American literature, which was reflected in the writings of Mark Twain, William Dean Howells, Frank Norris, Stephen Crane, and Theodore Dreiser. The realists attempted to show the dark underside of American society.

The greatest expansion of American industry occurred in the building of the railroads. They were the first American large corporations and the first to be publicly traded. Railroads were extremely expensive to build and required contributions from state and federal governments; private investment was not able to raise the amount of money needed for their development. There was a need for large capital investments, and profits were only slowly returned. However, investors' returns on railroad and telegraph stock were considerably higher than on other investments. In 1860 there were over thirty thousand miles of laid track, most of it in the North. Supported by state and federal taxpayers, railroads spread throughout the West, bringing new settlers to the area and creating new markets for business. Since a single railway line had a monopoly in an area, it could charge farmers whatever it desired for shipping their crops. Railroads set high prices on the transportation and warehousing of farm goods and showed favoritism in pricing for large shippers, resulting in the organization of farmers into the Granger movement in 1867 and the passage of the Interstate Commerce Act in 1887. By 1875 the Grange had 750,000 members and 19,000 chapters. Farmers combined to purchase goods and supplies at a lower price and to present a united front to the railroads. However, after 1870 corn prices declined by one-third, wheat by one-half, and cotton by two-thirds, and large corporations bought land and machinery and competed with small farmers. Later the Northern Alliance of Farmers, the Southern Alliance of Farmers, and the People's Party would call for the government ownership of railroads.

Some of the wealthiest capitalists of the period were involved not only with the expansion of railroads but also with related industries and businesses. Cornelius Vanderbilt was involved in the operation of railroads and shipping and grew the New York Central into the largest railway line in the United States. Leland Stanford, the governor of California, along with Collis Huntington and Mark Hopkins, organized the Central Pacific Railway Company. John D. Rockefeller was invested in oil; his operations dwarfed his competitors' so that he was able to negotiate favorable transportation rates with the railroads, thereby placing his competitors at a price disadvantage. Rockefeller consolidated the oil business and created Standard Oil and later the Standard Oil Trust, thereby destroying all his competition in the oil producing and refining business. Mining was a very expensive business that required a substantial amount of labor and expensive equipment. Mining companies were also consolidated into a few, and large corporations also took over the mining business. Both Carnegie Steel and Standard Oil owned coal mines, as did the Philadelphia and Reading Railroad, which primarily transported coal from its own mines.

Jay Gould invested in banking and financial firms as well as railroads. At one time he and James Fisk Jr. attempted to convince President Ulysses Grant to suspend gold sales, which would allow Gould to corner the gold market and drive up the price of gold. The move negatively affected the market, and Grant then released gold onto the market, but not before Gould and Fisk sold and took their profits. Both Gould and Fisk were also directors of the Erie Railroad. Andrew Carnegie operated steel mills, but in the past he had worked for the Pennsylvania Railroad as the personal assistant to Superintendent Thomas Scott and later was superintendent of its Pittsburgh Division. Carnegie's Union Iron Works produced steel rails for the railroad industry, and he was a partner of a manufacturer of sleeping cars, whose largest customer was the Pennsylvania Railroad Company. Carnegie Steel ultimately became the largest steel producer in the world. Carnegie invested in machinery and automation that enabled him to employ unskilled workers at the lowest wages in the industry, giving him an edge on his competitors with regard to pricing. He also fought efforts to shorten the workday from twelve hours to eight. His harsh labor actions led to the 1892 Homestead Strike, which was crushed by three hundred detectives from the antilabor Pinkerton agency and eight thousand federal troops.

Although they primarily focused on one industry, many of the capitalists of the period expanded horizontally as well as vertically. For example, Carnegie was primarily involved in steel but also invested in mining and the transportation of his commodities. Rockefeller, who was primarily focused on oil, also operated his own railroads. Any cost-cutting measure meant larger profits, so what all of these industry leaders had in common was the payment of low wages, the existence of poor working conditions, the demand for long hours of work, and the fear of union organization by their workers.

For the workers this meant a life in shantytowns or urban slums, warehousing in tenement buildings, and the modification of single-family homes into ones able to house multiple families. Working-class life was depicted by Jacob Riis in his classic study of urban slums in New York, *How the Other Half Lives*. Riis estimated that there were thirty-seven thousand tenement houses in New York housing over 1 million people. The overcrowded conditions he described were abhorrent: "In Essex Street two small rooms in a six-story tenement were made to hold a 'family' of father and mother, twelve children and six boarders." He attributed the poor conditions to the greed of the rich: "The greed of capital that wrought the evil must itself undo it, as far as it can now be undone." Failure to resolve the problem of working-class slums would, according to Riis, result in a massive social explosion and class conflict between rich and poor: "The sea of a mighty population, held in galling fetters, heaves uneasily in the tenements. . . . If it rise once more, no human power may avail to check it. The gap between the classes in which it surges, unseen, unsuspected by the thoughtless, is widening day by day."[11]

Others also warned of the dangers of unbridled capitalism. Harvard professor Francis Parkman believed that democracy was perverted by capitalism because of the strong value it placed on self-interest, especially in the United States, where individualism was viewed as a virtue. Henry George, a journalist and reformer, suggested that businessmen, manufacturers, and merchants would benefit from railroad expansion but that the working class would suffer from the introduction of foreign goods and the higher rents caused by the increase of land values due to the railroads. Towns that were not on the railroad line would die out. The growth of huge corporations was dangerous to the American polity. The railroads, he warned, control both capital and men, legislators and governors, and senators and judges.[12]

Originally corporations were intended to serve the public good by, for example, providing capital for the construction of bridges and other public works. That changed with the development of factories and the growth of railroads, when their sole purpose became the maximization of profits for their shareholders, notwithstanding any direct or indirect harm they might cause in that effort. A major problem with the tremendous expansion of business after the Civil War was that it was largely unregulated. Corporations grew into massive organizations that were too large for the government to control. In September 1873, four years after Jay Gould attempted to control the gold market, his financial house was overextended as a result of its financing of the Northern Pacific Railroad and was unable to service its bonds, resulting in the Panic of 1873, which would eventually have a major effect on the railroad strike in 1877. By 1878 over a thousand businesses closed each month as a result of the depression, which continued into 1879. According to Alan Trachtenberg, the railroad strike in 1877 represented the first example of the smashing of machines and national class violence in the United States and destroyed the myth of the American pastoral.[13]

The railroad business was the most productive and profitable financial endeavor after the Civil War. With the settlement of the West, it was necessary to bring consumer goods to settlers and to take their farm products to the East. A whole new and huge market was available to railroad magnates after the war, and railroads dominated the American economy and politics. In order to expand, railroads needed land and laborers. They required the rights to the lands on which their rails were laid and on which their trains operated, and they needed workers to lay the track. The Pacific Railway Act of 1862 authorized the construction of a railroad line from the Missouri River to California. The Central Pacific would build east and the Union Pacific would build west and ultimately the two would connect, creating a transcontinental railroad system. The federal government would provide loans and land grants of ten square miles for each mile constructed in alternating sections along the route. Later an amendment to the Act doubled those land grants. The value of the land would increase greatly after the railroad was completed, thereby effectively reimbursing the railroad corporations for their construction costs. The Pacific Railway Act provided the railroads with the land and money they needed, and freed slaves and Irish and Chinese workers provided the labor. As a financial incentive to the railroads to expand, Congress gave the railroad companies more than 1.5 million acres of land, which they sold off to pay for the costs of their expansion, so that the building costs were paid largely by taxpayers.[14]

The period following the Civil War was also marked by political as well as economic corruption. It was characterized by greed and the uncontrolled growth of industry and large corporations, the new power of big business, political power, and the unregulated settlement of the West.[15] Henry Clay Warmoth, a Republican governor of Louisiana, remarked that he didn't pretend to be honest, only that he was as honest as any current politician and that corruption was the fashion of the time. The corruption involved all levels of government, municipal, state, and federal, and the railroad companies. Examples of such corruption often reached the highest levels of the federal government.

Ohio's governor, Rutherford B. Hayes, won the Republican nomination for the office of president against his opponent, James G. Blaine, who was Speaker of the House of Representatives. Blaine was clearly positioned to affect legislation, and he had been accused of receiving $64,000 from the Union Pacific Railroad in the form of a loan that he never repaid and was not expected to repay. He had also secured a land grant for a railroad in Arkansas in which he owned stock. In the 1876 general presidential election, Hayes lost the popular vote to Samuel Tilden, but as a result of his promise to end Reconstruction and remove federal troops from the South, enough Southern states gave their electoral votes to Hayes to enable him to win the presidency by one electoral vote.

Blatant conflicts of interest between politicians and railroad magnates existed. The Kansas legislature awarded hundreds of thousands of public acreage to the railroad companies. The state's governor, Samuel Crawford, had ties to the Union Pacific Railroad. Senator Lyman Trumbull of Illinois received an annual retainer from the Illinois Central. The Central Pacific awarded Senator William M. Stewart fifty thousand acres of land for services rendered to the company.[16] Any business conducted in New York City had to pass through the hands of Boss Tweed, who received a percentage of any profits. Mark Twain described the period as the Gilded Age and summed up the relationship between government and business this way: "When you come to look at it you cannot deny that we would have to go without the services of some of our ablest men, sir, if the country were opposed to—to—bribery."[17]

When Grant ran for president in 1868, he was largely supported by Northern businessmen, including Jay Cooke, who made substantial contributions to his campaign. The Republican Party became the party of big business. H. W. Brands observes that the Republicans freed capitalism as well as the slaves.[18] All branches of government supported business, including the Supreme Court, which held that local governments could not regulate interstate commerce and that corporations had the same rights as human beings under the Fourteenth Amendment.

The Grant administration became known for its corruption. Nepotism was rampant; Grant's family and his in-laws were awarded lucrative government jobs. Grant gave control of the New York Custom House, the largest source of patronage in the federal government, to the political machine boss Roscoe Conkling. Congress passed a retroactive pay raise for itself and doubled Grant's salary. Grant's commissioner of Indian affairs, Ely Parker, was accused of fraud. Corruption was common among Indian agents, and there was no competitive bidding on Indian contracts. Orville Grant, the president's brother, held a surveying job at which he never appeared, although he did cash his paychecks. Orville also held the contracts for four Indian trading post concessions. Having no desire to service the Indian contracts himself, he took on partners who performed the work and divided the profits with them. The Indian trading post contracts were so lucrative that Ron Chernow, Grant's biographer, describes them as "virtual presses to print money."[19] The wife of Grant's secretary of war, William W. Belknap, who was charged with awarding Indian concessions, obtained a trading post for John Evans, who transferred a percentage of the profits back to her. After her death, Belknap continued to accept the payments.

When Grant's attorney general, Amos Akerman, denied Union Pacific's request for a land subsidy, he was offered a bribe, which he turned down. Under pressure from the railroads, Grant dismissed him.[20] The Crédit Mobilier scandal occurred during the building of the transcontinental railroad. The Union Pacific Railroad set up Crédit Mobilier as a dummy corporation with the same executives as Union Pacific. Its directors received large salaries paid for by government payments over and above the actual costs of building the railway. Crédit Mobilier stock was handed out to politicians and legislators by the railroad. Important officeholders were caught up in the scandal, including House Speaker Blaine, Vice President Schuyler Colfax, and James Garfield, who was the head of the Appropriations Committee in the House of Representatives.[21]

Lincoln had used a tax on whiskey to help finance the Civil War. Unfortunately, many of the revenue agents in the Treasury Department were corrupt, and there was a great deal of bribery and tax evasion. John D. Sanborn was hired to locate tax evaders and was awarded half of what he was able to collect from them. Apparently the award was not sufficient because Sanborn earned extra by threatening to falsely accuse people of tax evasion. Grant appointed his friend Gen. John McDonald as supervisor for internal revenue matters in Missouri and Arkansas. Distillers often falsified records regarding the production of whiskey and bribed revenue agents, who certified the false statements. More whiskey was produced than taxed, and those involved in the deceit divided the saved tax money among themselves. The so-called Whiskey Ring was centered in St. Louis but was also active in Chicago, Milwaukee, and Louisville.

What had emerged from the Civil War was an alliance between people involved in business and government that included bribery and corruption and resulted in economic instability. Although the economy appeared on the surface to be healthy, it was founded on speculation, corruption, and the overextension of railroads. Chernow attributes the postwar corruption in America to the wartime growth of the federal government, the expansion of industry, and the new partnership between government and business.[22] With the failure of Cooke's firm in 1873, the stock market collapsed, gold prices fell, banks failed, and depression set in. As a result of the booms and busts that characterized the emerging financial and industrial capitalism, the gap between rich and poor became even greater. Unsafe working conditions, low pay, child labor, and long hours would eventually result in the growth of national unions, labor unrest, strikes, and violence.

After the Civil War, St. Louis was a microcosm of the nation. It experienced the same benefits and struggled with the same problems that grew out of the expansion of business and railroads. The city was growing at a phenomenal rate, business was booming, and its residents took pride in its development and perceived future success. It was marked by economic and industrial growth, wealth and prosperity, and greed and corruption.[23]

Situated on the Mississippi River and considered to be the westernmost eastern city, St. Louis was the principal trade route between East and West until railroads linked Chicago with New York. Based on the fact that the city was rapidly developing into a business and industry center and that it was located in the middle of the country, a local booster named L. U. Reavis began a movement to make it the nation's capital. In October 1869 delegates from twenty-one states and territories met at the Mercantile Library in St. Louis to discuss the move, which was even favored by the Chicago editor Joseph Medill, Walt Whitman, and Gen. William Tecumseh Sherman. Reavis's book, *The Future Great City of the World*, was translated into German and was credited with encouraging German immigration to the city.

St. Louis was largely a city of immigrants in the mid-nineteenth century. In 1860, 77 percent of its adult population was foreign-born.[24] Most were from the German states and Ireland. Of its 1860s population of 160,000, approximately 60,000 were born in German states and 40,000 in Ireland. During the potato famine in 1845, almost 1 million Irish immigrated to the United States, many arriving in St. Louis. In the 1850s the St. Louis Irish Emigrant Society paid the passage of large numbers of Irish, many of whom went to work on the new railroads. The Irish in St. Louis primarily lived in the Kerry Patch neighborhood; they mostly worked in unskilled jobs, such as ditch digging and hod carrying. Germans had settled in St. Louis in significant numbers during the 1830s, and another wave arrived following the revolution there in 1848. The later German arrivals were more educated and skilled than were the Irish and the earlier German immigrants. Of those St. Louis residents who were born in the United States, most were descendants of French and Spanish creoles, some free African Americans, and easterners who traveled west in search of new opportunities. There were also Bohemians, who had fled the Austro-Hungarian Empire, and French from the Alsace Lorraine region, which was conquered by Germany in 1871 in the Franco-Prussian War. Immigrants usually settled in neighborhoods and wards according to their ethnicity.[25]

The Know Nothings had emerged from the Whig Party and were rabidly xenophobic. There was the usual fear among the general population that new immigrants were different and therefore untrustworthy and that they would take American jobs; therefore, not all were welcomed with open arms, even by those who denied having any bias against ethnic groups. Edward Bates, who was to serve as attorney general under Lincoln, accused them of coming to the United States in order to bring disorder and violence, and the older French families of St. Louis described new arrivals as wild radicals. There were frequent clashes between Irish and German immigrants and Know Nothings and among immigrant groups themselves. In August 1854, after a riot had erupted over voting by immigrants, other citizens led a volunteer group that attempted to return order to the city. The more conservative elements believed that immigrants brought with them ideas of Red Republicanism, socialism, and free living. The leading citizens of St. Louis were from conservative Southern Protestant and French Catholic families.

Before the Civil War, St. Louis was a conglomeration of French and Spanish cultures with a large free Black population, an antislavery city located in a slave state. Never containing a great many slaves, by 1860 St. Louis's slave numbers had been reduced to approximately 1 percent of its population. Most worked as servants in the homes of the rich. Many free Blacks and white women achieved some success both before and after the war. Unlike British common law, whereby women gave up all rights to property and any legal status upon marriage, Spanish law was much more progressive, so that women continued to own the property they had brought to a marriage and received half of a deceased husband's estate. As a result, many St. Louis women, including free women of color, were able to own significant assets in their own right from the early days of the settlement of St. Louis. One free Black woman, called only Esther, had been the mistress of a St. Louis merchant and owned an entire city block, two houses with lots, and two farms in her own name.[26] Free Blacks in St. Louis were said to control several million dollars' worth of real and personal property; they were described as a colored aristocracy.

The Germans who arrived in St. Louis after 1848 were more educated and more radical than the earlier German immigrants. There was division between the two groups, between Catholics and Lutherans, liberals and radicals, and those who were against religion of any kind. Many of the later arrivals had been professionals in Germany. They were sometimes, not without reason, criticized by the older German immigrants for being haughty. Not yet fluent in English, many new immigrants became journalists and published German-language newspapers. The *Anzeiger des Westens* became one of the most read German-language papers in the West.

With the influx of German immigrants and changes in national political parties, politics in the city and in Missouri became more complicated. In the late 1840s Missouri was politically divided between Democrats and Republicans and later Liberal Republicans. In a contest for the U.S. Senate, the small farmers in the state supported Thomas Hart Benton, a lawyer and newspaper editor and Liberal Republican, who had the distinction of having shot Andrew Jackson in a duel. Large landowners favored Henry Geyer, who supported slavery and represented the slave owner in the *Dred Scott* case. For a time Missouri was represented by only one senator because the governor was hesitant to appoint anyone in the overly heated political environment. St. Louis was a center of free labor and antislavery sentiment, and its new German immigrants hated the very idea of slavery. Many German immigrants who arrived in the area had chosen to settle across the river from St. Louis in southern Illinois because they refused to live in a state that allowed slavery. Many chose to farm the Missouri River Valley, although a good number who had never farmed before failed at it and ultimately moved to St. Louis.

Similar to what occurred nationally, the city's rich enjoyed showcasing their wealth. As railroads expanded, communities grew along the railway lines, and towns were born and grew as suburbs of St. Louis. Country estates became fashionable, and mansions were erected containing libraries, European wood and furniture, paintings and sculpture, ballrooms, and in some cases indoor plumbing. The rich entertained by throwing large parties and balls. Even funerals were designed to show wealth. Fancy horses pulled hearses to deliver the wealthy dead to new cemetery cities such as Bellefontaine and Calvary, which contained huge marble mausoleums decorated with marble sculptures of weeping muses and angels.

The St. Louis Agricultural and Mechanical Association was started in 1856, led by Norman Coleman, who would become the nation's first secretary of agriculture. It sponsored an annual fair that resembled a mixture of a carnival and a World's Fair and showcased manufactured goods and agricultural products in an effort to boost St. Louis businesses and trade. People who attended the extravaganzas viewed the latest developments in steam engines and home and kitchen goods such as stoves and washing machines.

Some St. Louis businesses prospered economically during the Civil War, although most suffered financial loss. Those businesses that were able to attract government contracts during the war did well. St. Louis was a major ship manufacturing center and served as the western supply base for a million Union troops. Hundreds of millions of dollars flowed into the city from the U.S. government alone: "From September 1, 1861 to December 31, 1865 the

Commissary of the Department of the West spent $230,700,000 in the city for supplies and transportation."[27]

After the Civil War, St. Louis boasted both small businesses and large factories and manufacturers. Carondelet, which was incorporated into the city of St. Louis in 1876, was a major center for shipbuilding and ironworks. The Belcher Sugar Refining Company took in over 63 million pounds of raw sugar in 1874 and produced 53 million pounds of refined sugar. It was the largest sugar refinery in the United States until its sugar cane plantations in Cuba were seized by the Spanish government, which at the time ruled the island. The Excelsior Stove Works was the country's largest stove manufacturer, producing over twenty thousand stoves a year. St. Louis led the nation in flour milling by the 1870s. The Yaeger Milling Company milled 1,200 barrels of flour each day and 6,000 bushels of winter wheat in twenty-four hours. Joseph Gerneau consumed 500 barrels of flour each day in his cracker-making factory, selling his product as far away as the West Indies. Dozier, Wayl and Company produced 1,500 barrels of crackers a day. St. Louis was second only to Boston in the production of shoes in the United States.[28]

Large iron ore deposits existed near Carondelet. The ore was brought to Carondelet by the Iron Mountain Railroad and then shipped to Pittsburgh. In 1868 businesses in Carondelet began the iron industry there, building large furnaces, factories, and railroad connections. The Vulcan Iron Works emerged as the largest business in Carondelet. Its monthly payroll was $50,000, and it employed 850 men. Carondelet was referred to as "Birmingham on the Mississippi."[29]

Due to its large German immigrant community, St. Louis had boasted local breweries since the 1820s and numbered over thirty at the end of the Civil War. By 1876 it was the largest beer-producing city in the nation and had the largest number of breweries. Because beer spoils quickly, markets for it were necessarily local until Adolphus Busch made use of refrigerated railroad cars and pasteurization and marketed Budweiser on a national basis, producing forty thousand bottles of beer a day. The Lemp Brewery stored its beer in underground caves that could hold fifty thousand barrels. Other breweries in the city included the Anthony and Kuhn Brewery, the Griesedieck Brewery, the Marquard Foster Brewery, and the Fritz and Wainwright Brewery. The

American Wine Company owned three stories of underground caverns and used up to 3 million pounds of grapes a year in its winemaking.

By the middle of the nineteenth century, St. Louis businesses were doing very well. The luxurious Planter's House Hotel, where Planter's Punch was invented, was a meeting place for the discussion of business and politics and was the largest hotel in the West. The Southern Hotel was completed in 1865 at a cost of $700,000. The population of St. Louis had doubled in ten years, and the city's businesses flourished.[30] Twenty-nine railroads served St. Louis. There were 108 boot and shoe shops and 45 brick and tile manufacturers. The Union Press Brick Works manufactured ninety thousand bricks every day, while the Laclede Fire-Brick Company produced fourteen thousand bricks every ten hours. The St. Louis riverfront was crowded with hundreds of boats arriving and departing with goods.[31]

Meat processing was another major business in St. Louis. Henry Ames and Whittaker and Sons each slaughtered and processed a thousand hogs a day. In 1874 the Union Stockyards opened and held twenty-five thousand hogs and two thousand head of cattle. A year earlier the National Stockyards opened across the Mississippi River from St. Louis and was served by twelve different railroads. St. Louis also emerged as a major tobacco center, processing chewing tobacco, cigars, snuff, and pipe tobacco. Liggett and Myers operated an immense facility in St. Louis.[32] The city was second only to Richmond, Virginia, in tobacco products. A major chemical company was founded by the Mallinckrodt brothers, and the Singer Machine Company manufactured sewing machines. The St. Louis Type Foundry supplied type and other printing merchandise throughout the West. Since its founding, St. Louis had had a virtual monopoly on the West's fur trade, and many fortunes had been made in that business since the early days of the city's settlement. The American Fur Trade Company was dominated by the Chouteau family, descendants of one of the founders of St. Louis. James Astor had interests in St. Louis fur companies. By the end of the nineteenth century, the city ranked second in meatpacking plants, third in milling, third in pressed cotton, and second in the West in capital investment in manufacturing.[33]

Banks were important in financing the development of the city. Page and Bacon was the largest banking firm in the West, boasting a branch in San

Francisco. General Sherman had managed the West Coast branch of the bank before the Civil War. It financed the last section of the Ohio and Mississippi Railroad, which connected St. Louis with the East. In June 1855 the Ohio and Mississippi defaulted on a note in an amount over $1 million payable to Page and Bacon, resulting in the insolvency of the firm. Robert Campbell, who made his fortune in fur, was president of the Bank of the State of Missouri and owned the fancy Southern Hotel. The Bank of the United States was established in St. Louis in 1829. John O'Fallon, nephew of the explorer and Missouri territorial governor William Clark, became president of the national bank in St. Louis, while Thomas Biddle, whose brother Nicholas was president of the Second National Bank of the United States, and wealthy St. Louisans Pierre Chouteau Jr., and Peter Lindell were directors of the bank.

Beginning in the 1850s St. Louis real estate values skyrocketed. A tremendous building boom occurred, so that the *Missouri Republican* reported that 2,500 new buildings were erected in one year, 1859.[34] Fourth Street became a fashionable shopping district, which the newspaper compared to New York's Broadway. Real estate and personal property in the city totaled $8.6 million in 1840, grew to $29.7 million in 1850, and then more than tripled to $102.4 million in 1860. Property that sold for $50 to $150 an acre in 1843 sold for $1,200 to $2,000 an acre by 1854. A lot downtown that was purchased for $800 in 1845 was worth $142,000 in 1855, only ten years later.[35]

St. Louis was a major river transportation hub both before and after the Civil War. Over 1 million tons of freight landed at the levee each year. In 1852 there were 3,307 steamboat landings in St. Louis, compared to 2,778 in New Orleans.[36] St. Louis boasted twice the capital investment and product value of Chicago in 1860. While Chicago was connected to the East Coast, St. Louis was better located to serve southern and western markets. However, its economy depended on southern river traffic. During the Civil War, the South blockaded the lower Mississippi, thereby cutting off St. Louis from southern and foreign markets by way of New Orleans. Following the war, the South's economy was devastated, but as the South recovered, trade resumed, and with the development of the Iron Mountain Railroad and the Atlantic and Pacific Railroad, new markets were opened in the Southwest. Cotton-compressing companies opened for business in the city, and the St.

Louis Compress Company became the largest of its kind in the world. It compressed five-hundred-pound bales of cotton into a bundle nine inches thick, thereby allowing fifty such bundles to be loaded onto one railroad car. As a result, St. Louis became the third largest cotton market in the nation. Most of the cotton was shipped to New England textile mills.[37]

Because of the high rates charged by ferry companies for the transport of railway cars across the Mississippi River and the problems associated with the freezing of the river in the winter, a new bridge was built in 1864. Daniel R. Garrison was president of the new bridge corporation and also served as a board member of the Pacific Railroad. The corporation's board was made up primarily of railroad and bank leaders and included Thomas Scott of the Pennsylvania Railroad. The bridge was designed by James Eads, who had manufactured ironclad gunboats for the Union during the Civil War and now operated a river salvage business in Carondelet. Carnegie, a shareholder in the bridge company, sold it the steel necessary to construct the bridge. Two hundred thousand people attended ceremonies for the opening of the bridge, which was hailed as a bond of union between East and West. As a result of the Panic of 1873, the company was unable to meet its debt-service fees and went into receivership, and J. P. Morgan took over the company.

There was a serious movement for the development of railroads in St. Louis both before and after the Civil War. Railroads had a large impact on population growth, bringing new people with new ideas to the area. Railroads also enabled and encouraged the opening of new areas for settlement, bringing farmers, mechanics, and other skilled workers and banks to finance development, and they ended the isolation of many small communities. The Morrill and the Pacific Railroad Acts of 1862 and the Homestead Act of 1863 encouraged settlement of the West and the expansion of railroads. The western army, strengthened by the removal of troops from the South at the end of Reconstruction and their redeployment to the western frontier, assured the building of a western empire for American settlement and business.

Due to the great cost of materials and labor in the construction of railroads and the delay in profit-taking, it was difficult to raise private money to build railroads in the West. Most railroad construction required a combination of private capital and government subsidies or investment. A good deal of capital investment came from eastern sources and from England. Missouri owned stock in the Pilot Knob Railroad, which connected the iron ore region of Missouri, the largest such deposit in the country, to Carondelet. By 1860 Missouri had guaranteed bonds of $7 million for the Pacific Railroad; $4.35 million for the Northern Missouri Railroad, which sought to connect Missouri agriculture to Iowa and Minnesota; $3 million for the Hannibal and St. Joseph; $3.5 million for the St. Louis and Iron Mountain; and almost $4 million for the southwest branch of the Pacific.[38] The state-authorized bonds for railroad construction at that time totaled approximately $25 million. In May 1857 half of the bonded debt of the city was for railroad construction. In the ten-year period prior to the Civil War, Missouri spent more money on railroad building than did any other state.[39]

The construction of the Iron Mountain Railroad was spearheaded by John O'Fallon and James Lucas, two of St. Louis's richest citizens. Mayor Luther Kennett, a vice president of the Pacific Railroad, became the president of the Iron Mountain. Eastern financial interests also were invested in the new railroads in Missouri. Jay Gould took control of the Northern Missouri Railroad, leased out the Missouri Pacific Railroad, and controlled the Missouri, Kansas and Texas, and the St. Louis, Iron Mountain, Southern, and Texas and Pacific railroads. By 1873 Gould had acquired a large portion of Union Pacific stock and controlled the Kansas Pacific, the Denver Pacific, and the Central Pacific railroads. In 1879 he bought a controlling interest in the Missouri Pacific and became its president. A. J. McKay purchased the failing St. Louis and Iron Mountain Railroad from a Missouri state commission and immediately resold it to Thomas Allen for a very significant profit. Allen and his New York partner, Henry Marquard, then consolidated the Iron Mountain with two other railroads and sold their holdings to Gould, where they became part of Gould's southwest railroad system. As a result, several of the bridge and railroad assets were owned or controlled by eastern investors.

In 1849 Missouri business leaders obtained a charter for the Pacific Railroad to connect St. Louis with the Pacific Ocean, but a major fire in the city and a cholera epidemic that year put those plans on hold until groundbreaking finally occurred in July 1851. In 1865 a train connected St. Louis with Kansas City and took only fourteen hours to travel the distance of 250 miles. A number of lines connected Missouri with Texas, including the Texas and Pacific, the International and Great Northern, and the Cairo and Fulton. By 1874 lines connected St. Louis with Houston and Dallas. In 1870 the Missouri, Kansas, Texas railroad acquired land grants to build a rail line all the way to Mexico. The *Missouri Republican* boasted that Mexico would soon become part of the St. Louis commercial empire.[40]

St. Louis was in competition with Chicago as the western railroad capital of the United States. Much of the eastern investment money flowed to Chicago, leaving St. Louis behind in the rivalry. Missouri's geography and terrain were such that it made railroad building more expensive, and there were no major cities to its west. The opening of a number of canals gave Chicago access to the Mississippi River, and a connection to the Erie Canal allowed eastern goods targeted for Chicago and upper Mississippi destinations to entirely bypass St. Louis. The construction of the Chicago and Alton Railroad and the Terre Haute and Alton Railroad allowed goods bound for Chicago to arrive without first passing through St. Louis, even though Alton was only twenty miles from the city. In 1856 a bridge was built across the Mississippi River at Quincy, Illinois, providing access to the Mississippi from the East, thereby allowing goods to be sent to Chicago directly on the Chicago and Rock Island line.

As a result of losing a good amount of the northern and eastern trade, St. Louis began looking to the Southwest for opportunities. Located in the middle of the country, and itself a growing business center, St. Louis hoped to become the center of a great railroad empire, linking trade in every direction. Freight traffic by railroad was more practical and cheaper than by river, and railroads were therefore replacing barges and riverboats for the carrying of freight. The time and distance involved in shipping affected prices and profits. Rivers were long and winding, while railroad tracks went in a straighter line, so that, for example, St. Louis was 612 miles from Pittsburgh by train and twice as far by boat. It took sixteen hours to travel from St. Louis to Cincinnati by rail but three days by boat.

The growth of western capitalism, however, depended on the final removal of Native Americans from western lands. Once that problem was resolved, the entire West would be open for business. Missouri's Thomas Hart Benton envisioned a march west by American business until it reached the Pacific. At the time St. Louis was the military headquarters of the Western Department of the U.S. Army and the staging area for the Indian Wars.[41]

Memphis and Chicago too were seeking investment in and development of railroads in their cities. St. Louis held a railroad convention in 1849 where Benton called for a railroad that would connect St. Louis with the West Coast along a route recommended by his son-in-law, John C. Frémont. The Pacific Railroad received the most interest in the city and was the first railroad construction in Missouri supported by state and federal grants. The Hannibal and St. Joseph Railroad ran parallel to but north of the Pacific Railroad. That line actually received more private investment because the land grants it received were more valuable than those awarded the Pacific. The St. Louis and Iron Mountain Railroad was intended to aid in the development of Missouri's mining region. Railroad construction resulted in Missouri becoming one of the fastest growing states in the nation with regard to population and agricultural output between 1850 and 1870. By 1870 Missouri was the fifth most populated state; the increase was mostly in rural areas, making Missouri an agricultural leader. Between 1850 and 1870 the number of farms in Missouri grew threefold, from approximately 54,000 to 150,000. Its wheat crop in 1870 was five times what it was in 1850.[42]

Many of St. Louis's major business firms profited from railroad construction. In 1860 the city was comparable to Pittsburgh in manufacturing and iron work factories. In 1853 the Pacific Railroad purchased 600 tons and the western division of the Ohio and Mississippi Railroad 250 tons of spikes from St. Louis companies. The Palm and Robertson Foundry and Machine Shop produced locomotives for the Pacific Railroad, each of which required 24,500 pounds of cast iron, 9,200 pounds of plate and sheet iron, 12,000 pounds of rolled iron bar, and 2,500 pounds of hammered iron. Lucas and other St. Louis elites organized the Union Locomotive and Machine Shop for the purpose of manufacturing locomotives and other items needed by the railroads. O'Fallon, Lucas, and Charles Chouteau formed the Missouri Lumber and Car Manufacturing Company to build passenger, freight, cattle, coal, and other railroad cars. Since the stock in some of these companies sold for $500 a share, investment was limited to the wealthy residents of St. Louis.[43]

As with any new industry, many of the railroad companies failed, and others were consolidated into major lines. Many people lost money due to corporate bankruptcies, while others were able to profit from those losses. The St. Louis and Iron Mountain Railroad, the Southwest Pacific, the Cairo and Fulton, and the Platte County were foreclosed on and went into receivership. The Iron Mountain Railroad was bought by Thomas Allen. Part of the reason for railroad failures was the cost of converting track to another gauge so that railroad lines could connect with each other. Operation of the Pacific Railroad was suspended for that reason. The Pacific defaulted on interest, principal, and taxes in the amount of $11 million owed to the state of Missouri, and the state sold the railroad's assets at a loss of $10 million. Private capitalists made huge profits buying state-owned railroads at immensely discounted prices. The Atlantic and Pacific Railroad, which was part of the Pacific Railroad's southwest portion, had been taken over by the state and sold to Frémont, who defaulted, and the line was then sold again, and ultimately was bought by Allen. Missouri sold its interest in the North Missouri Railroad, which had cost the state $2 million, to Henry Blow for $200,000. Blow was a congressman and ambassador during his career, and his family had owned and set free the slave Dred Scott. Twain humorously but accurately described the shenanigans that characterized railroad investment and the race for quick profits during what he called the Gilded Age:

> "We'll buy the lands," explained he, "on long time, backed by the notes of good men; and then mortgage them for money enough to get the road well on. Then get the towns on the line to issue their bonds for stock, and sell their bonds for enough to complete the road, and partly stock it, especially if we mortgage each section as we complete it. We can then sell the rest of the stock on the prospect of the business of the road through an improved country, and also sell the lands at a big advance, on the strength of the road."[44]

If Twain's description of the get-rich-quick mentality of the era is at all accurate, it is not surprising that so many dreams of wealth went unfulfilled.

As was true on a national scale, corruption was rampant in St. Louis. One of the greatest examples during this period was national in scope and involved the Whiskey Ring. At the start of Grant's administration following the Civil War, revenue officials were replaced as part of the important patronage system of the time. In October 1869 John McDonald was named supervisor of internal revenue for the Missouri district, which included Missouri, Arkansas, and Indian territory. McDonald, a friend of Grant, together with William McKee, a co-owner of the *Missouri Democrat*, Orville E. Babcock, Grant's secretary, and C. W. Ford, the district collector of revenue for St. Louis, were all at the heart of the scandal. Only part of the whiskey produced was reported for tax purposes. The rest was sold with no tax paid on it and the extra profit pocketed. Half of the liquor tax saved was to go to the distillers and half to members of the Whiskey Ring. Between November 1871 and November 1872 four distillers paid approximately $300,000 to the five members of the Ring. Some of the money went into a Republican slush fund, but most of it went to the individual participants. Distillers had no choice but to participate in the scheme. While most voluntarily took part, others were threatened with false accusations of violations if they refused to go along. Babcock warned members of the Ring of planned federal investigations and intercepted a letter from St. Louis lawyer Jesse Woodward to John W. Douglas, the internal revenue commissioner in Washington DC, that warned of the scam and provided evidence in the form of documents and witnesses.

Benjamin H. Bristow, secretary of the treasury under Grant, became suspicious of the small amount of revenue received from whiskey sales and began an investigation. He determined that only one-third of the whiskey being distilled in St. Louis was being taxed, though it was difficult to obtain proof because the entire system was corrupt. Finally, Bristow submitted the results of his investigation to Grant, who ordered the seizure of distilleries in St. Louis, Milwaukee, and Chicago. Sixteen distilleries were seized in St. Louis alone. An analysis of the business of one of them for one month showed that taxes had been paid on only one-third of the gallons of whiskey shipped. Ultimately prosecutions were brought. Babcock was acquitted of the charges against him when Grant offered to testify on his behalf. He did, however, resign as Grant's secretary. McKee was convicted and sentenced to two years in prison and fined $10,000; however, he served only a small portion of his sentence. McDonald was convicted and sentenced to three years in prison, but served only one year.[45]

Joseph Pulitzer attempted to shine a light on St. Louis corruption. An immigrant from Hungary, Pulitzer was passionate and idealistic about what he considered to be the American values of freedom and liberty. He was affiliated with the Republican Party. At the recommendation of Carl Schurz, a German revolutionary who became Lincoln's secretary of interior, Pulitzer edited the *Westliche Post*, a German-language newspaper, which supported the Republicans. However, Schurz also led a new movement of Liberal Republicans in St. Louis who were disgusted by the scandals occurring during the Grant administration, and the *Westliche Post*, under Pulitzer's leadership, supported the reformists. In support of the new movement, Pulitzer made countless speeches in German across Missouri and throughout his career attempted to fight corruption through the press.[46]

Poverty was not an issue with which the rich in St. Louis were overly concerned. The belief was that if one was rich, it was because one was superior in intelligence, morals, and perseverance; poor people deserved to be poor because they were lacking in those virtues and characteristics. While the wealthy businessmen were re-creating French chateaus and Versailles-like entertainment, many others in St. Louis were living in or on the verge of poverty. Most of the Irish immigrants were unskilled and competed with free Blacks for low-paying jobs. Many were unemployed, women and children worked at starvation wages, and holding a job did not guarantee a decent life.

The post–Civil War period in the United States and in St. Louis was characterized by economic growth, the emergence of large corporations, and the concentration of wealth into fewer and fewer hands. The rich survived the unstable markets that marked the period and even prospered by buying failed businesses at extremely low prices. The concentration of wealth occurred at both the national and local levels. Railroads emerged as the most profitable and powerful of American businesses. Their wealth and power enabled them to affect national policy and to control city and state governments, which not only failed to regulate them but even financially supported them with gifts of money and land. Greed was the major characteristic of American business, and wealth and power marked the new corporate world. At the same time, the poor and working class struggled to survive in a world where those who controlled it sought to profit by exploiting the most vulnerable. Wendell Phillips, an abolitionist and supporter of labor and women's rights, feared that the United States was becoming an aristocracy of capital.[47]

This was the environment that greeted new immigrants in the 1860s and 1870s. German immigrants had fought for a more democratic republic in the German states, a fairer division of wealth, and greater political power for working people and would continue that battle in their new homeland. For the more radical among them, Marx's vision of the ultimate confrontation between the bourgeoisie and the proletariat seemed to have arrived. However, in the meantime revolution broke out in Paris, which served to terrify American capitalists and inspire workers both in Europe and the United States.

4

The Paris Commune

Some twenty years after the 1848 European revolutions, socialist revolution again broke out in France when the workers of Paris seized control of the capital and established the Paris Commune in 1871. That event captured the headlines of American newspapers and magazines, raising fears that the same thing could occur in the United States. The gap in wealth between the rich and the poor in the United States appeared to make the country vulnerable to the same social and economic unrest. The Paris Commune would come to characterize and in many cases to define the St. Louis Commune six years later.

When the French Revolution of 1848 ended, Louis Philippe was gone and Louis Napoleon, the nephew of Napoleon Bonaparte, was elected president of the Second Republic. He held that office until December 2, 1851, when he executed a coup and announced the beginning of France's Second Empire with himself the emperor. He held that position until 1870, when he was dethroned during the Franco-Prussian War, which gave birth to France's Third Republic. France's bourgeoisie had accepted the Second Empire, not because they preferred it to a republic but because of their greater fear of socialism. They could live with Louis Napoleon's empire; they could not live with a socialist government led by workers.[1]

France and Prussia viewed the Franco-Prussian War as necessary for their own reasons. Republicans and socialists were growing stronger in France;

Louis Napoleon had suffered a defeat in Mexico and was desperate for some success in order to unite the people behind him. Prince Otto von Bismarck believed a war with France would help to unite the German states under the leadership of Prussia. Both leaders sought to increase their power by inflaming nationalist feelings.

During Louis Napoleon's reign, the character of Paris was radically modified. He widened many of the boulevards in order to foreclose the possibility of street barricades in the event of another revolution. The new construction resulted in the destruction of some twenty thousand buildings and over one hundred thousand apartments, causing a shortage of living units. At the same time, the population of Paris had doubled during the decades of 1850 and 1860. Many residents were unemployed, and a quarter were indigent. There existed a large gap between the rich and the poor. Prices had risen while wages stagnated. The result of the new construction was higher rental prices, and the working class was thereby removed from the more expensive heart of the city and relocated to its outskirts. The eastern and northern parts of Paris became working-class ghettoes. The population of the working-class Saint-Denis neighborhood, for example, exploded from 41,000 inhabitants in 1841 to 356,000 in 1856.

While there were a few large factories employing workers in Paris, most industry consisted of artisans working in small workshops. Unions were prohibited, and skilled workers felt threatened by the new machines and the employment of unskilled workers to operate them. The use of unskilled workers resulted in lower wages. Industry had developed quickly, so that the number of machines used in industry in France increased from 5,332 in 1850 to 27,958 in 1870.[2] Police spies were everywhere, and the police force grew under Louis Napoleon from 750 to over 4,000. During 1870 there was growing demand for a republic and local autonomy in Paris, and Louis Napoleon was compelled to grant some constitutional liberties, primarily to the bourgeoisie.

There had been a feeling of unrest in Paris for some time. France's largest city was prohibited from electing a mayor, and Louis Napoleon appointed the representatives to the municipal councils. The mayors of the individual arrondissements were also appointed by the government. By 1870 there were demands for municipal autonomy and republicanism. Working-class members met with radical elements to discuss political change. These meetings drew massive crowds. Over twenty thousand attended one such gathering.

France declared war on Prussia on July 19, 1870. Unfortunately for Louis Napoleon, the French army was ill-prepared for the war, while the Prussian army was well-organized and well-trained. Just over a month after the beginning of the war, the French army was surrounded and surrendered at Sedan, where Napoleon was taken prisoner. In his absence, a governmental vacuum existed, and Paris proclaimed the Third Republic. There were demands in the city for free elections and more autonomy.

There was high unemployment in Paris as a result of the war, and in the absence of any French government the Parisians announced a moratorium on the payment of rents and debts and other social reforms. None but the rich had any money. The defeat of the French army and the siege of Paris weakened and ultimately brought down Louis Napoleon's regime. The stage was set for a confrontation between the bourgeoisie and the young proletariat.[3] With the breakdown of authority in Paris, the door was open for the creation of something new.

At the end of January 1871 the new provisional French government called for elections. On February 8 elections for a new National Assembly were held, and supporters of a monarchy were the primary winners. The new body chose Adolphe Thiers, who had the support of monarchists and conservatives, to organize the new government. The French Government of National Defense agreed to an armistice with Prussia, whereby France would pay an enormous war debt to Prussia and cede to it Alsace and a good deal of Lorraine. The agreement was abhorrent to the residents of Paris, who felt that the provisional government had sold out the country. In his *History of the Paris Commune of 1871*, Prosper-Olivier Lissagaray, who was a member of the Commune and fought on the barricades there, explained that it actually began as a patriotic movement against the Prussians and the surrendering French government.[4] When Parisians refused to surrender, the Prussians surrounded the city and began a siege on September 19, 1870. The working class of Paris viewed France's ruling class not only as exploiters but also as traitors in surrendering to Prussia.[5]

The siege of Paris coincided with an especially harsh winter. Adding to the problem was the spread of disease in the city. In one week 203 Parisians died from smallpox and typhoid; 64,000 died during the siege. The death rate of the working-class was twice that of the rich.[6] The siege destroyed Paris's economy, throwing thousands out of work. Even though there was almost universal unemployment in Paris as a result of the war and the siege, on March 7 the new National Assembly passed legislation ending the moratorium on rents, debts, and wages for the Paris National Guard. Eventually the seat of government was relocated to Versailles. The population of Versailles grew from 40,000 to 250,000 as wealthy Parisians relocated there along with French soldiers freed by Prussia.[7]

The Paris National Guard operated separately from the regular French army. It was made up of Parisians, 350,000 of them, primarily from the working class, whose purpose was to protect the city's people. During this period of economic distress, many working-class citizens of Paris joined the National Guard, which paid each member one and a half francs a day, together with an allotment for wives and children.

Vigilance committees in Paris, each consisting of thirty members, were elected at public meetings and sent delegates to the Central Committee of the Twenty Arrondissements. There was little doubt about the socialist leanings of these committees. Their Declaration of Principles stated, "All members of Vigilance Committees declare their allegiance to the Revolutionary Socialist party. They consequently demand and seek to achieve by every means the abolition of the privileges of the bourgeoisie, its elimination as a ruling caste and the advent of the workers to political power."[8]

In March 1871 the vigilance committees joined the Central Committee of the National Guard, whose meetings sometimes attracted up to two thousand people. Officers were elected by members of the National Guard. On February 24, 1871, the leadership voted to obey the orders of its Central Committee and to replace the regular army with a workers' militia. The National Guard possessed over two thousand cannon, which it situated in places that were safe not only from the Prussians but also from the Versailles troops. There were calls for the establishment of a Paris Commune led by the working class, and Paris moved in the direction of establishing its own government. Followers of the French anarchist Pierre-Joseph Proudhon, the father of "mutualism," the idea that individuals or cooperatives own property that is exchanged for commodities of equal labor value, were not interested in political matters so much as economic issues. In contrast, the Jacobins, radical leftists who looked to the 1789 French Revolution for inspiration, and followers of Auguste Blanqui, who favored small cells of professional revolutionaries, called for an insurrection.

In order to consolidate its power, it was necessary for the French government to disarm the Paris working class, which had refused to give up their arms at the time of France's surrender to Prussia. Consequently the new French government declared war on Paris and its radical element. On March 11 it suppressed six leftist newspapers and sentenced the revolutionaries Auguste Blanqui and Gustave Flourens to death. It also demanded that Paris turn over its weapons to Versailles. Paris refused the ultimatum, arguing that its National Guard had purchased its own weapons, which therefore belonged to it rather than to France.

Early on March 18, 1871, French troops attempted to seize the National Guard's cannon, which was situated on the hill of Montmartre. But they were delayed because they had failed to bring with them the horses that were necessary to move the cannon. Residents of the area who were on the streets early that morning saw the soldiers and sounded an alarm. Church bells rang throughout the neighborhood, bringing more residents into the streets. The working-class residents of Montmartre, Belleville, and Buttes-Chaumont resisted the French troops and built barricades in the streets. Many of the French troops fraternized with the people, and some of them actually joined the Parisians. One Communard, Louise Michel, described seven hundred women and children blocking the removal of the cannon while French troops stood and watched.[9] The French general Claude Lecomte ordered his troops to fire on residents three separate times, even threatening to shoot any soldier who refused. Yet the troops refused to kill other French citizens. The scene was described by a reporter for the *Times* of London: "The soldiers in the balconies and windows, where, I suppose, they had been placed to shoot the Guards, came down and embraced them instead; women shed tears of joy, and talked about their sons and brothers who were *sous le drapeau* [with the flag]; arms were intertwined, hands wrung, cheeks kissed and all the extreme demonstrations of fraternization to which Frenchmen are prone when they are not shooting at you out of a window."[10] The Paris National Guard took Lecomte prisoner, and he was later executed. The attack on Montmartre was the beginning of the insurrection and the establishment of the Paris Commune.

Twenty-thousand Communards gathered at the Hôtel de Ville with loaves of bread embedded on the ends of their muskets, representing the starvation of the people and their demand for bread. A red flag was raised over the building, the meeting place of the Central Committee of the new Paris Commune, while a band played the "Marseillaise." With only fifteen thousand troops at his disposal, President Thiers was forced to abandon the capital in order to gain time to rebuild his army. He had ordered all city employees to leave their jobs, so Paris was left with no government, except for the Central Committee of the National Guard, and no city services. The Commune was faced with the immediate challenge of organizing a functioning government and providing municipal services. Lissagaray described the scene: "The red flag floated above the *Hotel-de-Ville*. With the early morning mists the army, the Government, the Administration had evaporated."[11]

With Paris surrounded by Prussian troops, it was isolated and unable to bring in necessary supplies for its population. As a result, prices soared and Parisians suffered from a lack of food and other necessaries. In their desperation, the poor were compelled to eat whatever they could find, including dogs and rodents, while the rich butchered and feasted on animals from the Paris zoo. There were demands for the free election of municipal officials to lead the new Commune and to organize governmental services. At this time, most of the French army was still being held prisoner by the Prussians and played no part in the unfolding events in Paris.

The question then arose as to the Parisians' next move. Blanqui believed that a revolution was possible only if made by a group of dedicated revolutionaries. Three thousand of his followers were in Paris at the time, divided into separate cells of ten members each. They constituted the only organized revolutionary group in France.[12] The Blanquists called for an immediate attack on Versailles, before Thiers could prepare his government and army for an attack on Paris. At the time, Versailles was disorganized, and most of the French army, 250,000 troops, were still prisoners of the Prussians; it was doubtful that Thiers could fend off an attack by Paris National Guard forces. The Proudhonists, on the other hand, called for the establishment of a model community in Paris that would win the support of the rest of France. Others argued, however, that in order to establish legitimacy, it was necessary for the new Commune to hold elections. Leaders had arisen in the city, but not having been elected they had no legal right to hold specific leadership positions. This group insisted that Parisians were not a disorganized mob and that the holding of elections would show that the Commune was a legitimate decision-making body. The Central Committee of the National Guard chose to hold elections in order to establish a legitimate government before taking any other action. Later it would be argued that the decision to hold elections rather than immediately attacking Versailles sealed the fate of the Commune. In the meantime, eighty-five positions were filled on the Communal Council by an election. The Jacobins won forty seats; the mayors and their supporters nine; members of the International, primarily followers of Proudhon rather than Marx, won seventeen seats; and the Blanquists won only nine seats. Half of those elected were from the working class.[13]

The establishment of the Paris Commune was not planned in advance. It came about spontaneously as a result of the Franco-Prussian War, the fall of Louis Napoleon, France's humiliating terms of surrender, and the attack on Montmartre. Even then Parisians hoped for a compromise agreement that would establish a republic in France and more rights and autonomy for Paris. The Commune leadership sent an offer of settlement to the National Assembly in Versailles. It demanded that Paris be allowed to elect the mayors of the city's various arrondissements, that the prefecture of police be abolished, that the French army remain outside of Paris, that the Paris National Guard be empowered to elect its own officers, that the moratorium on rents be reestablished, and that the National Assembly declare a French Republic. The National Assembly refused the offer and instead blamed the Paris insurrection on socialists and the First International. The charge against the International was ridiculous. It was taken by surprise by the events in Paris, which were spontaneous and dependent on the factors discussed above. At the same time, workers in Paris began to think about more radical changes.

When word spread of the revolt in Paris, insurrections broke out in other French cities. Residents of Lyon declared a republic and demanded a continuation of the war against Prussia, their own autonomous municipal authority, and social reforms. Revolutionaries also seized power in Marseilles, Narbonne, Saint-Etienne, Le Creusot, and Limoges. Georges Clémenceau led a group of arrondissement mayors to Versailles in another attempt to end the standoff, but Thiers turned them away, hoping to buy more time for an attack on Paris. In Versailles's favor was the failure of the conservative rural areas to join Paris.[14] Versailles appeared willing to give everything to the Prussians but nothing to the Commune. Events were quickly transforming what began as a nationalist conflict into one based on social class. The now reigning bourgeoisie had no intention of empowering the working class.

The Commune desired a reorganization of the French government into a group of individual, autonomous communities that were part of a Republic. It also sought to enact serious social reforms to deal with poverty and unemployment. In March 1871 the First International announced its support for the Commune and called for social equality, free and secular education, the freedom to form associations, and autonomous municipal authority. Immediate social reforms were deemed necessary since at the time over three hundred thousand Parisians were unemployed.[15]

Most of Paris's population supported the Commune. On March 28 the birth of the Paris Commune was officially proclaimed at the Hôtel de Ville. The crowd there was immense, the people adorned in red and waving red flags, and the Paris National Guard agreed to cede its power to those who were duly elected by the citizens. But the Commune faced immediate existential challenges. It needed funds to get the city functioning; it was necessary to bring together the different political views among its supporters; and it needed to confront the fact that it was surrounded by French and Prussian forces. It had no money, and its supporters included anarchists, Marxists, Blanquists, and Jacobins, each of which held different opinions on what should be done.

The easiest challenge for the Commune to resolve was the raising of money since the headquarters of the Bank of France and most of its wealth was located in Paris. Some argued that the Commune should seize the bank and all of its funds, thereby solving its financial problems and also preventing

Thiers from financing his counterrevolution. Without funds from the Bank of France, Thiers could not fund an army or provide government services at Versailles. Later it was suggested that failure to take immediate control of the Bank of France was the second mistake of the Commune. But again those leading the Commune hesitated in the name of legitimacy. They were insistent that the Commune be seen as a legitimate and responsible entity and not as a group of outlaws or bank robbers. The Commune did request and was granted a loan and a line of credit from the bank in the amount of 16 million francs. Unknown to the Commune, however, was the fact that Thiers had secretly asked for and received a line of credit in the amount of 258 million francs, thereby providing him with sufficient funds to rebuild his army. When France signed the Treaty of Frankfurt in May 1871, agreeing to pay Prussia 5 billion francs, the Prussians released most of the captured French soldiers, and Thiers's army grew from fifteen thousand to approximately seventy thousand troops. Jules Favre was an official in France's Third Republic who was charged with negotiating a peace treaty with Prussia; he begged the Prussians for the release of more French troops, promising in return that the French government would "crush" the Paris Commune and Prussia would not have to expose its troops to the fighting. Said Favre, "We will crush it. We will take Paris by force. Thus we prove our good faith and our energy."[16] Because of the large number of Parisian National Guard troops, however, he was still not in a position to challenge Paris.

The Commune's defense forces were led by Gustave Paul Cluseret, who had military experience fighting with French forces in Algeria and for the Union in the American Civil War. His military plan was not to conquer Versailles and thereby assume control of France, but rather to hold off Versailles long enough to achieve a compromise agreement that would provide for greater Parisian autonomy. Men between the ages of nineteen and forty were required to serve in the Paris National Guard. Although the Guard's Central Committee had turned over its power to the Commune, it did interfere with Cluseret's orders, sometimes issuing its own contradictory orders, thereby causing confusion and a lack of organization. There was fighting between French, Prussian, and National Guard troops. By the middle of May, Versailles troops had moved to within a few miles of Paris, capturing fortresses at Moulin Saquet, Fort d'Issy, and Fort de Vanves.[17] Versailles had placed hundreds of spies in Paris, many of whom were found out and arrested by Commune officials.

Thiers set out to destroy Paris in order to teach a lesson. There would be no compromise or agreement. Now that the bourgeoisie was in power, Thiers's goal was to eliminate any danger of a challenge to that power by the working class. Beginning on April 2, he bombarded the city with cannon without regard to civilian casualties, residential areas, or hospitals. His artillery actually outdid the Prussians in causing death and destruction. Thousands of Paris civilians had been killed by the end of May. Hospitals were overcrowded, and, because of the siege, it was impossible to obtain medical supplies.

The Commune demanded that all prisoners be treated humanely, according to the Geneva Convention of 1864. In contrast, Thiers ordered his troops to execute all prisoners captured, including women serving as nurses. Those murdered included the Commune leaders Émile-Victor Duval and Gustave Flourens. In response, the Commune's Raoul Rigault called for the taking of hostages, including the archbishop of Paris, Georges Darboy, in order to stop Thiers's killings. In April the Commune passed the Law on Hostages and arrested approximately 300 of the city's 125,000 priests, monks, and nuns. There was a good deal of discussion and argument within the leadership of the Commune as to what should be done with the hostages. Eventually the Commune threatened to kill the hostages unless Thiers stopped killing his prisoners. But when the Commune failed to act on its threat, Thiers's killings continued. Commune leaders attempted to exchange hostages in return for Blanqui, who had been elected their president, but their offer was rejected. Thiers cynically planned to use any executions of hostages by the Commune as propaganda in order to turn the rest of France against the Commune and thereby justify his actions against Paris.

There existed a good deal of anticlericalism in Paris due to the Church's wealth, its support of the monarchy, and its hostility to the French Revolution. The Church had allied with the army to protect royalty and the rich.[18] The Commune, on the other hand, sought to create a secular society. It declared the separation of Church and state, ended government subsidies for religion, and confiscated the property of religious orders in Paris. And because education was seen as important to the new society, schools were to provide a secular education and end religious teaching. Adopting Enlightenment thought, the Commune believed that human progress was based on knowledge, not superstition. Marriage was made a civil procedure, and divorce, which had been illegal, was allowed. All children, whether or not they were legitimate, were to have legal rights. All of these changes enraged the Church, which considered them an attack on morality and family values.[19] The Commune also raised the pay of teachers, ordered the teaching of republican values in schools, equalized the wages of male and female teachers, created a professional school with a woman as its director, and ordered religious symbols removed from public schools and hospitals. After the Jesuits left the city, churches were converted into meeting places for the new political clubs.[20] The Church and Commune members ended up sharing Church buildings. Churches used the buildings during the day, and political meetings were held at night. Men respectfully removed their hats when entering the buildings and refrained from smoking in them.

Leaders of the Commune knew that what they were doing was important and was being watched by those in Europe and around the world. As a result, they were careful to show that working people were capable of creating a society that was much more fair and humane than the one ruled by capitalists. They called for a strict, revolutionary morality, honesty, and the participation of working people in government. Begging, prostitution, and gambling were prohibited. Meat and many other foods were sold at cost. The crime rate in Paris declined significantly, and not one murder was committed during the two and a half months that the Paris Commune existed.[21]

There was a huge gap between rich and poor in France and in Paris in particular, now exacerbated by the war and the siege. In response, the Commune immediately enacted social reforms. It prohibited the eviction of tenants who could not afford to pay rent, prohibited the sale of items at pawnshops, and granted debtors three years to satisfy their obligations. Restrictions on assembly and the media were lifted. Ninety new newspapers were published during the existence of the Commune, and political clubs were organized that were attended by women as well as men.

The status of women, who had endured second-class status by the Catholic Church and the French government, was also improved. Elisabeth Dmitrieff, a follower of Marx who had worked in cooperatives in Geneva, traveled to Paris and fought for equal pay for women. She brought women into the public sphere by creating the Union des Femmes, which boasted a membership of two thousand women and encouraged women to join in the defense of the Commune, to help at the barricades, to serve as nurses, and to leave the kitchen and bedroom behind by joining the men and participating in the public sphere.[22] Three thousand to four thousand women attended the meetings of the Women's Union, whose demands included the reduction of working hours, an end to competition between men and women workers, equal pay for equal work, and a call for all of its members to join the International.[23] A report on a meeting of two hundred women reflected their working-class consciousness. One speaker received applause and laughter after she remarked, "Let us do away with bosses who treat the worker as a producing machine! Let the workers form cooperative associations, let them organize their labour collectively and they will live happily. . . . We will only be content when there are no more bosses, rich men or priests."[24] While the Paris Commune was primarily concerned with working-class issues, it also sought to liberate or at least improve the position of all oppressed groups within French society.

The Commune also attempted to end monopolies and encouraged the creation of workers' cooperatives. The Commune's businesses would not be operated by capitalists, who had sought to squeeze out of workers the greatest profits possible and to pay as little as necessary. Proudhon's influence could be seen in their management. The cooperatives had a decentralized authority and were governed by the workers themselves. Managers and foremen were elected by the workers, who also had the power to recall them. Workers set their own hours and wages. Each day managers and workers would meet to decide production goals for that day and how to achieve them. Businesses that had been abandoned by their owners who had fled to Versailles were converted into cooperatives. Either rent would be paid to the previous owners or the value of the business would be determined by a jury and paid to them. Night work, which was always a complaint of bakers, was abolished. A maximum salary of 6,000 francs a year was established for all workers, including public officials. Regulations established for factory cooperatives specifically set out the new democratic rules for labor and management:

> The manager will be elected by all of the workers and will be liable to be revoked if found guilty of failing in his duty. . . . The shop-foreman and the charge-hand will also be elected by all the workers. . . . There will be a Council meeting every day without fail, after the shift ending at 5:30 p.m., to discuss the next day's work and the reports and suggestions submitted by the manager, the shop-foreman, the charge-hand or the worker delegates. . . . The Council will be composed of the manager, the shop-foreman, the charge-hand and one elected worker from each workbench. . . . The delegates will be completely replaced every fortnight; half of them will be replaced every week.[25]

Thus the workers were responsible for production, and every worker had his or her turn at participating in the governance of the workplace.

Attempting to regain a sense of normalcy, the Commune supported musical concerts and gave away tickets to the Comédie-Française. It established pensions for widows and children of Communards killed fighting, even those children who were considered illegitimate. The Vendôme Column, a symbol of Napoleon Bonaparte's greatness, which depicted him as a Roman emperor dressed in a toga, was destroyed. The Commune would not sanction a symbol of conquest and militarism.

While the leaders of the Commune planned a new world on a grand scale, those in charge of Paris's defense were both inexperienced and unorganized. A Committee of Public Safety was created. Soldiers in the National Guard, although numerous, were not well-trained or disciplined. The leadership of the Committee of Public Safety even disagreed with the Central Committee of the National Guard about who was in charge of defending the city. Spies for Versailles were active throughout the city, relaying information to the French troops.

On May 21, while fifteen thousand Parisians enjoyed a concert outside the Tuileries Palace, 130,000 French troops with artillery breached the city wall and entered Paris. Killing took place on a massive scale. Anyone living in Paris was considered by French forces to be a revolutionary and an enemy of the French government. There was fighting street by street throughout the city, while people built barricades in order to slow the advance of the Versailles troops. In response, Versailles forces entered buildings on parallel streets and fired down on the barricades while cannon blew them apart. The Commune was not prepared for the attack and was able to raise only about twenty thousand men to fight the invaders. Different orders emerged from different Commune offices. All the while, Versailles troops worked their way through the city killing anyone in their path, including women and children.

Consistent with Thiers's orders, the French troops took no prisoners. Five hundred men who had surrendered were shot to death in the Church of Saint-Eustache. Civilians as well as fighters were massacred, including pregnant women. Three hundred Communards were shot at the Church of the Madeleine, an incident made famous by Edouard Manet, who depicted the slaughter in a lithograph. Many of those killed had fought for France against the Prussians only a few months earlier. A soldier who refused to kill women and children was shot by a Versailles officer. A man, his wife and child, and the doctor attending the child were all shot. The streets of Paris were described as covered with blood like the floors of a slaughterhouse.[26]

Versailles troops continued the house-to-house killing. There was no rational plan as to who would live and who would die. Social class, however, often determined whether a person would survive. Foreigners were targeted. If a foreigner remained in Paris, it was thought that he or she must be an international communist and therefore a threat to the French government. One English student was killed because his name was Marx. Gen. Louis Valentin, Thiers's prefect of police, claimed that just remaining in Paris was a crime to be punished. Yet most Parisians had not worked in months and had no money to leave the city, even if they so desired. Anyone who wore working-class clothes or whose hands reflected manual labor was considered guilty and was shot.

The destruction of the Paris Commune was an attempt by Versailles to destroy the Parisian working class. Seven hundred Communards were shot near the Pantheon. Rigault was placed before a wall and shot. One Versailles soldier admitted that women, small children, and infants were killed by French troops, and rape often preceded the killings. In response, frustrated and angry French citizens broke into the prison holding Archbishop Darboy and executed him. During the course of the massacre, the Communards executed sixty-five hostages; the Thiers forces executed over thirty thousand men, women, and children.[27]

The murderous conduct of the Versailles troops was not designed simply to gain control of Paris. The killing continued for days after the Commune fell and after all of its leaders were dead. Thiers's goal was to wipe out as many people as possible and provide a lesson to anyone who thought of challenging those ruling the government in the future. Troops were brought in from the countryside and fed false stories of the Commune's horrors. The people of Paris had been presented to the rural troops as less than human animals, who were more like France's colonial subjects and not real French citizens. French troops even showed pride in their slaughter. Gen. Gaston Galliffet paraded in front of a group of captured working-class Parisians and announced, "I am Galliffet! People of Montmartre, you think me a cruel man. You're going to find out that I am much crueler than even you imagined."[28]

The immense amount of killing was planned in advance by Versailles, which specified that mass executions would take place at the Parc Monceau and the École Militaire. In the course of four days in May, three thousand men and women were killed in the Luxembourg Gardens. There was nowhere to run to escape the Versailles killing machine. The Prussians had the city surrounded and turned over anyone trying to escape. On the boulevard Prince Eugene, Versailles troops lined up and shot fifty-two women and sixty men. When some Communards were promised that their lives would be spared if they surrendered, they did surrender and were immediately shot. A British journalist estimated that in the Lobau neighborhood over 1,200 were killed in twenty-four hours. The *London Times* reported that even those caring for the wounded were shot. Communards were lined up and shot, their bodies falling into graves dug beforehand for that purpose. Thousands of bodies lay in the graves, and corpses littered streets all over Paris.

It was not enough to kill those who resisted the Versailles army. Thiers wanted anyone who supported the Commune to be found and punished. It did not matter if innocent people were caught up in his search. Reflecting the class nature of the killing, Versailles offered 500 francs to anyone who turned in a socialist or a traitor. Neighbors denounced each other, so that within the three-week period from May 22 until June 13 the police recorded 379,823 denunciations. Pierre Vesinier, a journalist, wrote, "The victorious bourgeoisie showed neither pity nor mercy. It had sworn to annihilate the revolutionary and socialist proletariat forever—to drown it in its own blood. Never had a better occasion presented itself; and it profited by it with ferocious joy."[29]

As French troops spread throughout Paris, National Guard members and others retreated to their own neighborhoods in a last-ditch effort to organize and build barricades of paving stones, sandbags, and mattresses. The defense of Paris, never well organized or coordinated, was at this time in a virtual state of anarchy. Each neighborhood fought its own war, isolated from each other. In Belleville, workers fought until they ran out of ammunition. At Parc des Buttes-Chaumont and Père Lachaise Cemetery, ten thousand communards were machine-gunned to death. Residents of the Rue des Rosiers were lined up against a wall and shot. All patients in a Commune hospital were killed. Communards made a final stand at Père Lachaise, with vicious fighting among the tombstones. The dead were buried along a wall of the cemetery in a mass grave. The killings continued long after there was any resistance. Twenty percent of those killed were women. More people were killed in the last week of May than in any battle of the Franco-Prussian War.

Repression followed the destruction of the Paris Commune and the slaughter of the residents of Paris. The punishment for the experiment in self-government, which had lasted only three months, continued for years afterward. Although Thiers had issued orders that no prisoners be taken from among the Communards, his directions were not always followed: thousands were taken into custody at the end of the fighting. Some forty thousand men, women, and children prisoners were forced to march the twenty miles from Paris to Versailles, many dying or being shot along the way. Military courts were established, held short hearings, and performed immediate executions. Twenty-six separate courts continued to hear cases until 1875, four years after the Commune's end.[30]

Not all of those convicted by the military courts were executed. Some were sent to French prisons in New Caledonia in the South Pacific, where France warehoused its political prisoners. One such prisoner was the French revolutionary Louise Michel, who at her trial told the judges that if they were not cowards, they should kill her, since every heart that beats for liberty has no right but to be shot.[31] Whether Michel, who had bravely fought on the barricades, sought death after witnessing the massacre in Paris or was simply deriding her judges as murderers of those who demanded liberty, is unclear. What is clear, however, is that she was among the bravest of the Communards. For years afterward the French government attempted to convince other countries to return Communards who had escaped Paris.

A French government estimate of the number of Parisians killed as a result of the attack on the Paris Commune was thirty thousand. The Municipal Council of Paris estimated the number killed to be closer to one hundred thousand. Versailles tried to cover up evidence of the extent of the killings. Bodies were removed from the streets and buried in mass graves, and those graves were camouflaged so that they were not recognizable as such. Versailles denied that it had murdered civilians, blaming those deaths on the Commune and the First International. The official government report on the Commune blamed socialists, anarchists, and the International for the bloodshed. Nevertheless Versailles was condemned by working-class and labor newspapers all over the world. The capitalist press, however, generally supported the destruction of the Commune, notwithstanding the overwhelming and unnecessary violence perpetrated by the Versailles government. The *New York Herald*, for example, opined, "Make Paris a heap of ruins if necessary, let its streets be made to run rivers of blood, let all within it perish, but let the government maintain its authority and demonstrate its power."[32]

After the corpses were cleared away and the fighting was over, there were remaining signs of the extent of the horror Paris had suffered. The city remained under martial law until April 1876, and the International was outlawed. Working-class leaders were either dead, in prison, or exiled. The labor movement had been completely broken.[33] For years there was a shortage of skilled workers in Paris; most had been killed by Versailles forces, while others were lucky enough to escape. It was estimated that half the house painters, plumbers, tile layers, shoemakers, and zinc workers of Paris had disappeared by the time Versailles troops had left the city. One observer remarked that only old women were seen in the streets of working-class

Belleville.[34] The Catholic Church returned to pre-Commune normalcy. It became even more conservative, and in 1875, only a few years later, built the massive Sacre-Coeur on the hill of Montmartre, the place where working-class Parisians had fought and died. The Church still called for a return of the monarchy in France.

Marx was opposed to the Commune from the beginning. He believed that the working class was not sufficiently developed and united to confront both the Prussians and the capitalists, and so he predicted its failure. The Paris Commune, he said, did not represent a revolution against capitalism by a developed proletariat. It was more of an alliance between small shopkeepers and artisans that had aroused the imagination of Paris's poor and working class. However, that did not diminish its importance. In a letter to a friend Marx wrote that even if it could not succeed, the Commune represented a new stage in the battle between the workers and capitalists of the world and was of historic importance.[35] The true secret of the Paris Commune, Marx wrote in *The Civil War in France*, completed just days after the fall of the Commune, "was this. It was essentially a working-class government, the produce of the struggle of the producing against the appropriating class, the political form at last discovered under which to work out the economical emancipation of labor."[36]

The Paris Commune existed from March 18 until May 28, 1871. Eight of those ten weeks was spent fighting off attacks by the French government. It was only in their spare time that members of the Commune were able to attempt to build a new society. The majority of the Commune were workers. Approximately 12 percent were petit bourgeois, small shopkeepers and such, so it had a real working-class character. Half were in the metalworking or construction industries, fewer from the older crafts, such as cabinet makers or shoemakers. Nevertheless it was largely composed of skilled workers, joined by a smaller number of the new industrial proletariat or factory workers. Skilled crafts were becoming industrialized, and artisans were in part making a last stand against the effects of that industrialization. At the same time, although not yet developed into a unified, class-conscious body, the young working class was making its first stand against the new industrialization. The Commune occurred at that moment in the transition of the working class from artisans to factory workers, when more workers were becoming wage earners than skilled craftsmen and therefore more proletarian. This new workforce was developing a political consciousness and an interest in socialism.

The laws passed by the Commune were not strictly socialist, but they were socialist in nature. They did not abolish private property, but the moratorium on rents and debts, the prohibition against night work by bakers, and the establishment of workers' cooperatives were in the interests of the poor and working class. The Commune could not be expected to construct a socialist society during the ten weeks that it existed. Building a socialist society is a process, not something that can be completed in two and a half months. Yet it is important to understand that the Commune was engaged in that process. Some, but not all, of the communards were socialists. Yet the policies that they instituted had a working-class character and socialist personality. Bakunin attempted to explain the socialist direction the Commune assumed: "We must realize, too, that the majority of the members of the Commune were not socialists, properly speaking. If they appeared to be, it was because they were drawn in this direction by the irresistible course of events, the nature of the situation, the necessities of their position, rather than through personal conviction."[37]

The Paris Commune did, however, represent a democratic and working-class experiment in government with a socialist perspective. It filled all important municipal offices by election, subject to recall by electoral means. It instituted universal suffrage and open debate on political issues. Different views were aired and tolerated, some of them diametrically opposed to others. Leaders compromised with each other, even when it meant supporting positions different from their own. Proudhonists, for example, agreed to allow workers to form unions, while Blanquists, who believed in small, conspiratorial revolutionary cells, supported the open and democratic nature of the Commune's governmental structure. At the same time, the Commune was a working-class attempt at self-government. Workers were in control of Paris; businesses and factories were transformed into workers' cooperatives, where no one person profited from an enterprise, but where the entire community benefited. The workers elected their foremen and determined their own hours of work, working conditions, and salaries and even set limits on their own wages. Social programs were organized to aid the poor. The people of the Paris Commune attempted to create a more humane civilization and to show the world what a city controlled by ordinary working people would look like.

Many leaders of the American working class supported the Paris Commune and aided its survivors. American labor had participated in the First International since its founding. The National Labor Union had declared its agreement with the principles of the International at its Congress in 1870. So there was a direct link between American labor and European socialism. Even the American abolitionist Wendell Phillips wrote in favor of the Commune, declaring, "The men who led the Commune were among the foremost, the purest and the noblest patriots of France, men who unlike Thiers and his assassins never bowed to Napoleon."[38]

The general strike in St. Louis was compared to the Paris Commune by both capitalists and socialists, businessmen and workers. To the capitalists of 1877, the strike represented a danger commensurate with the actions and violence that occurred in Paris only six years earlier. They feared a working class that was organizing and developing the consciousness of a united group that felt oppressed and that looked to seize power from the capitalists. To workers the Commune represented an attempt by working people to end their exploitation and to institute a new and fairer system that permitted them to live comfortable lives with dignity. Both groups called upon the memory of the Paris Commune to make their points. Whether the memory of the Commune was a boogie man that needed to be destroyed or an example to be followed depended on one's perspective.

The fact that the Commune had failed did not diminish its importance as a symbol for working people struggling for a better life. Eric Hobsbawm describes the Commune as a "heroic defeat."[39] According to William Morris, its material failure and destruction did not lessen its importance and effect on later events. Those who "believed that when the Commune was overthrown everything would fall back again into the old order of things" were wrong because they "could not understand that the great movements of history are not regulated by the chronology of defeats and victories, that its laws are accomplished by death and martyrdom as much as by success and triumph, and that the Commune of Paris, vanquished and drowned in blood, did yet spring from its ashes and, victorious in its own fashion, [became] the starting point of the irresistible Unity of Socialism in Europe and America."[40] The Paris Commune would inspire and encourage American workers and the Workingmen's Party of the United States during the St. Louis strike of 1877.

Occurring in 1871, the Paris Commune had a monumental effect on American society. The United States had only recently emerged from the Civil War; Reconstruction was in effect; slaves had gained their freedom; and African Americans were voting and occupying political positions in the states and in the federal government. The frontier war against Native Americans continued; movements led by women and labor were challenging the status quo; and a major depression battered the U.S. economy beginning in 1873. Change was in the air, and instability characterized the nation.

There had been a revolution in communication, so that Americans were able to follow what was happening in other parts of their own nation and around the world in record time. The number of newspapers and magazines quickly grew, and the invention of the telegraph and the growth of news services flooded society with up-to-date information from around the world. American readers were thus flooded with news and information about the Paris Commune, although the coverage was mostly unreliable.

Much of the news about the Commune that reached the United States came from Americans who were living in Paris at the time. Mostly of the upper classes, they reported the events in letters and interviews that were conducted by journalists and foreign correspondents. Americans were so numerous in Paris at the time that many were congregated in what was known as the "American Quarter." As a result, the information from that source that reached the United States was generally from the perspective of wealthy Americans who interpreted events in much the same way as did the French bourgeoisie. Tom Evans, one American then living in Paris, was a supporter of the French Empire and opposed to the French Republic, which was declared after the Franco-Prussian War. Evans blamed the Paris Commune on the communists who were active in the 1848 revolutions and the First International. Mrs. F. J. Willard, a Southern sympathizer originally from Louisiana, compared the fall of the French Empire to the defeat of the Confederacy and equated Communards with free blacks in the United States, both of whom, in her opinion, felt free to insult the better people of society. Willard considered the Commune to be primarily a conspiracy of cannibals. W. Pembroke Fetridge, who wrote guidebooks for the Harper publishing company, described the Paris Commune as criminal, bloody, and violent and its leaders as ruthless desperadoes, refuse, bandits, and atheists, who were under the influence of the communist International. Emmeline Raymond, who wrote for *Harper's Weekly*, described the Commune as terrifying and anarchic, committing crimes that she never thought possible. She would rather be eaten by cannibals, Raymond said, than live under the rule of the Commune. Even Elihu Washburne, a member of Grant's administration, considered the Commune anarchic and its leaders robbers, murderers, and assassins.[41]

Other Americans in Paris, however, described the Commune from a different perspective. Some were supporters and played an active role in its life. Some were French Americans who volunteered to fight in the American Civil War and then returned to France at its end. One Colonel Block commanded a volunteer corps of Communards; an American by the name of Witton was a surgeon in the Paris National Guard; and William Dugas Trammell, a native-born American, fought on the barricades against the French army sent from Versailles. John O'Sullivan, who is credited with coining the term "Manifest Destiny," was arrested while trying to make peace between France and Germany during the Franco-Prussian War, in which an estimated fifty French Americans died. An American journalist joined Communards in raids against the French army. Many Americans who had remained in Paris during the life of the Commune had helped build barricades and were arrested by Versailles troops as suspected sympathizers with the Commune. A St. Louisan named George S. Hanna was killed in a protest. Mary Putnam found the Commune to be peaceful and orderly, while an American astronomer, Simon Newcomb, claimed not to witness any violence or barbarism but rather found the Commune members to be well-behaved. The Civil War correspondent George Wilkes said that he did not witness any plunder or violence by Communards and accused Capital, Church, and State of distorting the facts about the Commune: "The Communists . . . on all occasions, exhibited integrity, morality, moderation, and respect for human life, while the track of their opponents was red with ruthless slaughter and characterized at every step by perfidy."[42] California attorney Frank M. Pixley asserted:

> The Commune is held up as the personification of misrule and destruction . . . and Paris of 1871 is described as a scene of frightful disorder, submitting to anarchy, pillage and murder.
>
> I was present in the city of Paris during the entire period that the Commune held sway. . . . And yet during the five weeks—weeks of menace from without and suffering within—I saw and heard of no single *act of pillage and murder.*[43]

Many American journalists in France sent reports critical of the Commune. Stories about violence, revolution, and political unrest contributed to the sale of newspapers and magazines. A Wisconsin publisher stated that his subscribers threatened to leave him unless he fed them a steady stream of conflict, calamity, war, revolution, and thrilling events.[44] Most reporters, however, were not in Paris during the life of the Commune but rather were stationed in Versailles and received their information from Thiers, and their reporting largely reflected the perspective of the Commune's enemies.

Even labor unrest in the United States was blamed on the Paris Commune. It was one way of explaining what was happening in the country without focusing on the inequalities and suffering of American workers, especially after the 1873 depression began. The famous nineteenth-century detective, union-buster, and red-baiter Allan Pinkerton blamed labor actions on agents of the Commune disguised as union members. The *Chicago Tribune* described demonstrations by the unemployed in that city as the work of the Paris Commune. The *St. Louis Globe-Democrat* declared that "every trade union and labor organization is infected with members of the American Commune."[45] The *Pittsburgh Commercial* equated the strike events in Pittsburgh in 1877 with the actions of the Paris Commune: "It was as though the French Commune had suddenly been vomited over us, and all the scenes characteristic of the Commune were re-enacted in the city of Pittsburgh."[46] There were so many news articles, pictures, and stories about the Paris Commune that it was impossible to ignore it in the United States, and it was used to characterize any labor unrest, such as the later events in St. Louis.

There was almost no important American issue at the time which could not be related to the Commune, whether the subject was slavery, freedmen, Indian wars, corruption, women, Reconstruction, labor, or the effect of foreign immigration. Even the Chicago fire was blamed on the Paris Commune and the First International.

Commentators linked events emanating from the American Civil War to the Commune. E. L. Godkin, the editor of the *Nation*, complained that the policy of Reconstruction was comparable to and just as bad as the Paris Commune. In an effort to legitimatize their rebellion Southerners pointed to the Commune's demand for municipal control as similar to the demand for states' rights. Later, white Southerners would attack Black legislators as akin to foreigners, communists, and European scum and refer to them as African communists. The former secretary of state of the Confederacy, Robert Toombs, argued that educating Blacks was preparing the way for the emergence of a Paris Commune in the United States. When a Black militia marched in South Carolina in 1874, locals complained that even the Paris Commune did not surpass such "subversion of God's law and order."[47] During the summer of 1871, when the Colored National Labor Union held a labor conference in Houston, a Galveston newspaper warned that the organization of Black labor would end like the Paris Commune, "with its sea of blood and its ocean of fire."[48]

Attacking the legitimacy of the Commune provided a weapon that could be used against corrupt political leaders. Equating the Commune with political corruption in the United States received tremendous press during 1871. In his cartoons, Thomas Nast compared the corrupt Tweed political machine in New York to the functioning of the Commune. The *Nation* claimed that Boss Tweed and the Paris Commune were both corrupt and only pretended to rule in the name or interest of the people.

The Paris Commune was even used to interpret uniquely American issues such as those involving Native Americans, women's rights, and the American working class. Godkin's editorials in the *Nation* referred to the "bloodthirsty Indian squaws" of the Commune. The *Chicago Tribune* compared Parisian workers to "Comanche hordes." One New Mexico newspaper opined that the murdering and plunder of the Commune would put the Apaches to shame.

Communards were compared to what were described as "savage Indians," and American workers were equated with Indians and Communards. The failure of Native Americans to recognize the concept of private property was said to be comparable to the views of workers and communists.[49] Such comparisons were especially cynical since it was the Communards who were massacred by government troops.

The struggle for women's rights was another example of the Commune's perceived harmful effect on American society. Even the clergy joined in blaming the social upheaval threatened by the issues of women's rights and religion on the Paris Commune. Reverend Charles Boynton linked the Paris Commune to the American women's movement and its danger for the practice of religion in American society. In a sermon given in Washington DC, Boynton denounced Charles Darwin and the International as other threats to religion. The Catholic Church referred to the Communards as enemies of God.

American labor unrest was not attributed to poor working conditions, low wages, or the greed of capitalists, but rather to the effects of foreign influences, especially communists. Attempts were made, even by men of the cloth, to dehumanize American workers by comparing them to Indians and to Communards. The 1877 labor unrest in the United States was specifically blamed on the Paris Commune. Henry Ward Beecher referred to the railroad strike that year as a very great crime induced by foreign elements. It was due to the importation of foreign ideas, which he called abominations, and was simply un-American. One Chicago clergyman called for hunting down striking workers as if they were mad dogs. The president of the Union Theological Seminary, Roswell D. Hitchcock, called "communism" the most hateful word in the English language. In Paris and in Pittsburgh, he said, it meant wages without working, arson, assassination, and anarchy. He added that society must smite it with the fury of lightning.[50] One commentator called for bullets and bayonets to be used against striking workers, just as Thiers had used them against the Communards, and the Reverend Joseph Cook suggested that the nation needed a Thiers in every city.[51]

The significance of the Paris Commune was recognized by both workers and capitalists during the railroad strike in 1877 and during the existence of the St. Louis Commune. For the workers it was an example of a democracy led by average citizens, which provided fair wages, safe working conditions, and a social safety net for the unfortunate. Capitalists, on the other hand, saw the Paris Commune as an entity that would deprive them of their power and property, under the rule of the most undesirable elements of society. References to the Commune and the application of its characteristics to American society have been made since 1871 and continue even today. Almost one hundred years after the fall of the Paris Commune, Mark Rudd, who led the Weathermen and the takeover of Columbia University in 1968, claimed to be following in the footsteps of "the Paris Commune and the international socialist revolutionary movement."[52] More recently the historian Philip M. Katz remarked that only "in St. Louis and a few other places did American strikers or their leaders act with the same political consciousness that the Commune displayed in its best moments."[53]

Both the Paris Commune and labor unrest in the United States were blamed on the First International, the worldwide labor organization founded by Marx. It was easier to deflect blame onto foreign influences than it was to focus on and attempt to resolve domestic problems and shortcomings. Nevertheless, while the First International played only a marginal role in the activities of the Paris Commune, members of the International did lead and influence the general strike in St. Louis and the St. Louis Commune.

FRANK LESLIE'S ILLUSTRATED NEWSPAPER

Entered according to the Act of Congress, in the year 1877, by Frank Leslie, in the Office of the Librarian of Congress at Washington.

No. 1,141—Vol. XLIV.]   NEW YORK, AUGUST 11, 1877.   [Price, 10 Cents. 1.75 Yearly. 2 Weekly, $4.00.

ILLINOIS.—THE RAILROAD STRIKES AND LABOR RIOTS—COLONEL AGRAMONTE'S CAVALRY CHARGING ON THE MOB, AT THE HALSTEAD STREET VIADUCT, IN CHICAGO, JULY 26TH.—SEE PAGE 385.

1. Sixth Maryland Division fighting workers in Baltimore. From *Frank Leslie's Illustrated Newspaper,* 1877. Library of Congress.

2. Franz Sigel, veteran of the 1848 German Revolution and a Union general in the American Civil War. 1860. Library of Congress.

3. Carl Schurz, veteran of the 1848 German Revolution, Union general in the American Civil War, U.S. senator from Missouri, and U.S. secretary of the interior. 1862. Library of Congress.

THE GREAT STRIKE—BLOCKADE OF ENGINES AT MARTINSBURG, WEST VIRGINIA.—From Photograph by D. Bendann.—[See Page 626.]

THE GREAT STRIKE—BURNING OF THE LEBANON VALLEY RAILROAD BRIDGE BY THE RIOTERS.—Drawn by Theo. R. Davis.—[See Page 626.]

4. Top: Blockade of engines at Martinsburg, West Virginia. Bottom: Burning of the Lebanon Valley Railroad Bridge. 1877. Library of Congress.

5. Meeting of the Paris Commune, held in a church, 1871. Library of Congress.

6. Communist brigade during the Paris Commune, 1871. Library of Congress.

7. The wealthy retake the streets. Veiled Prophet parade in 1878. Missouri Historical Society.

Market at 12th + Lucas
Enlargement from St. Louis Illus. ed of 1876.

DRIVING THE RIOTERS FROM TURNER HALL

8. Top: Lucas Market, St. Louis, 1878. Scene of meetings of thousands of workers held by the Workingmen's Party during the existence of the St. Louis Commune. Missouri Historical Society.

9. Bottom: Police attacking workers at Chicago's Turner Hall, 1877. Library of Congress.

10. North Carolina home of George Washington Vanderbilt II, 1924. Library of Congress.

11. Heinrich Boernstein, veteran of the 1848 German Revolution, publisher of the St. Louis *Anzeiger des Westens*, and colleague of Karl Marx. 1873. Boernstein led forces that captured the arsenal at Camp Jackson in St. Louis from Confederate sympathizers, thereby saving Missouri for the Union. Missouri Historical Society.

12. Henry Overstolz, mayor of St. Louis during the St. Louis Commune, ca. 1870s. Missouri Historical Society.

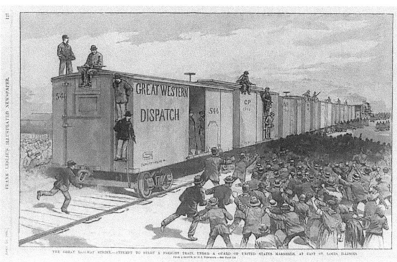

13. Top: Four Courts building, headquarters of the St. Louis Police Department, Missouri National Guard, municipal offices, and private militia during the St. Louis Commune. 1888. Missouri Historical Society.

14. Bottom: Railroad workers attempting to stop guarded trains in East St. Louis, Illinois, during the 1877 railroad strike. Missouri Historical Society.

5

The First International

Both leaders and members of the St. Louis Commune were active in the First International, an organization dedicated to uniting the working classes of all nations. It was a project of Karl Marx, feared by capitalists worldwide, and, together with the Paris Commune, was blamed for events ranging from labor unrest and the establishment of the St. Louis Commune to the fire that destroyed much of Chicago in 1871.

While capitalists organized the expansion of business and industry in the United States after the Civil War, another kind of organizing was occurring in Europe. There industry had also grown, and the number of workers was increasing. The British working class was troubled by the lack of American cotton for mills that employed textile workers, the deportation of the Italian revolutionary Giuseppe Garibaldi from England, the insurrection in Poland against Russia, and the use of foreign workers to compete with British labor. British capitalists imported foreign workers in order to break strikes and to work in England at lower wages than did British workers. It appeared to some that there was a need for greater communication and unity between the working classes of different countries so that the workers of one country could not be used to exploit the workers of another.[1] The solution to the problem seemed to be in the socialist organization of society. Only when the profit motive was removed could society end the exploitation that was part of it. The idea of socialism was not new to Europe. Saint-Simon, Fourier, Cabet, and other early utopian socialists had argued in favor of the collective ownership of property.[2] Socialists had also played an important role in the revolutions of 1830 and 1848.

According to Marx, the 1848 revolutions primarily had the effect of bringing the bourgeoisie or capitalists to power, replacing the feudal power of kings and aristocrats. The bourgeoisie had fought against European royalty in order to achieve certain rights, such as freedom of the press, the right to assemble, freedom of speech, freedom of religion, and republican government. But those, Marx explained, were merely bourgeois rights, which arose with the ascension to power of the bourgeoisie. Writing in *The German Ideology*, Marx explained that the "ideas of the ruling class are in every epoch the ruling ideas, i.e. the class which is the ruling *material* force of society, is at the same time its ruling *intellectual* force."[3] Human rights were different. Bourgeois rights empowered the capitalist class but did not guarantee working people the right to a living wage, enough food to eat and feed a family, or enough fuel to heat a home in the winter. They are rights, but the limited rights of a *bourgeois* society. Said Marx, "They do not free man from religion, but give him religious freedom. They do not free him from property, but give him the freedom of property. They do not free him from the indignity of trading, but give him freedom to trade."[4] According to Franz Mehring, Engels explained in *The Condition of the Working Class in England* that the development of large-scale industry gave birth to the modern proletariat, which the industrial system dehumanized and physically, morally, and intellectually crippled, and which would eventually overthrow the bourgeois system.[5] It would occur first on a national basis and later internationally. When the working class displaced the bourgeoisie and came to power, the nature of rights would also change. There would be no exploitation of man by man; workers would receive the true value of their labor, not what was simply necessary for them to survive and to work another day; everyone would have the right to a free secular education; and actual power would be exercised by working people.

London at the time was home to many of the radical political refugees from Europe's revolutions. The English labor movement was active and, perhaps more important, had an international perspective. The London

Trades Council in 1860 organized a demonstration of fifty thousand people to welcome Garibaldi to London. In 1863 it held a public meeting in support of Abraham Lincoln and against slavery. Also in 1863 George Odger, secretary of the Trades Council, wrote an "Address to the Workmen of France from the Working Men of England," proposing that they formalize their solidarity.[6] All workers, regardless of national boundaries, shared interests with each other instead of with the capitalists of their own nations.

On September 28, 1864, workers from various European nations met at St. Martin's Hall in London to create a new organization. Marx was elected to the General Council and charged with writing the Inaugural Address and to establish the organization's rules and program. The International Working-men's Association (IWA), also known as the First International, was to be governed by a General Council and consist of national federations and local sections. Marx's Inaugural Address and provisional rules focused on the growth of the bourgeoisie and the poverty of the working class. Workers, he explained, had not benefited from the growth of industry and commerce between 1848 and 1864. The only classes that did benefit were the propertied classes. That situation could be resolved only by the working class assuming power. Capitalism, wrote Marx, could not be defeated except by political means. The cooperative movement among workers showed that there was no need for bosses to govern workers, and cooperatives therefore should be created across Europe. Capitalists became rich, while the workers remained poor.[7] The working class could not depend on members of other classes to free them. In the provisional rules of the International, Marx announced that the emancipation of the working classes must be accomplished by the workers themselves. Further, a struggle for emancipation would result in the emancipation of everyone in society, not just workers. It was not a struggle for privileges for the working class but rather for the abolition of class rule. Marx also served as the International's corresponding secretary for Germany. Two followers of Marx, Hermann Jung, a Swiss watchmaker, and Eugene Dupont, a French musical instrument worker, became the corresponding secretaries for Switzerland and France.

Workers' concerns included the need for cooperation between unions of workers of different countries, stopping the capitalists' use of international

strikebreakers, and raising funds to aid in union organization.[8] Some of
the goals of the First International were specified in the Instructions for
Delegates to the first Congress in Geneva in 1866. According to Marx, the
working classes needed to organize on a national level in order to confront
capitalists, who already were organized nationally.[9] Aside from ending the
use of foreign workers to break strikes, the International sought to lessen
the workday to eight hours, limit the hours that children could be made to
work, guarantee recreation and education for children, support workers'
cooperatives in order to aid the transformation from capitalism to socialism,
and arm the people.[10] Delegates representing over twenty-five thousand
workers attended the Geneva Congress.

From its beginning, members of the First International sought to replace
capitalism with a more humane economic and social system, but they were
philosophically divided with regard to the manner in which capitalism could
be defeated and replaced. One disagreement involved a dispute between Marx
and Proudhon, who called for "mutualism," the establishment of producers'
cooperatives that would be financed by a People's Bank established for that
purpose. Society would consist of voluntary associations between working
people who would relate to each other by contract, and there would be no
authoritative government. Proudhon argued that socialism would be able to
triumph over capitalism by establishing workers' cooperatives within such a
system.[11] Marx rejected Proudhon's ideas as petit bourgeois ideology.

At the International's Congress in Geneva in 1866, Marx set out its program. The International would take up the struggle of the working-class in
its attempt to overthrow capitalism. In the beginning it was necessary to
support trade unionism and work to better the condition of the working
class. Unions strengthened working-class solidarity and enabled workers to
unite in their battle against capitalism. The International, Marx explained,
must support all movements that tended to emancipate workers. The purpose
of the International was to establish cooperation between working-class
organizations in different countries in order to aid in the emancipation of
all working classes around the world.[12]

The International supported workers in their struggles notwithstanding
national boundaries. When mine workers in Belgium revolted and were

crushed by the government, the International defended them and their cause. It supported strikes by building workers in Geneva in 1868 and weavers and silk workers in the fall of 1868 in Basel. When employers in Basel demanded that workers sever their relationship with the International, the workers refused, held a strike, and ultimately won. In the United States the National Labor Union, Washington Trades Assembly, Communist Club of New York, General German Workingmen's Association, striking transportation conductors and paper workers in New York, and other associations of workers all looked to the International for support. The General Council even resolved to stop the emigration of replacement workers from Europe to the United States in the event of strikes.[13]

Dissent within the association continued at the 1867 Lausanne Congress and the 1868 Brussels Congress. However, Marx's position finally prevailed at Brussels, and that Congress called for the nationalization of land, mines, and other private assets. The Congress also decided that the governing General Council would remain in London and that both individual workers and organizations were allowed to be members. The International provided information on the separate conditions and activities of the working classes in various countries, so that ideas could be exchanged and the actions of one could be supported by other members.

The International grew throughout the 1860s and served as a data clearinghouse, encouraged a solidarity of interests, confronted the problem of foreign strikebreakers, and supported strikes in different countries. In England members of the International generally came from craft industries rather than heavy manufacturing. The sections in France, Belgium, and Switzerland were especially strong and active. The organization was weaker in the German states and the Austro-Hungarian Empire, where repression after the 1848 revolutions was great. But there was still disagreement among some of the members.

Ferdinand Lassalle was active in the German Revolution in 1848, supported German unification, and was a member of the International. He and Marx later confronted each other with regard to the proper direction workers should take in the battle against capitalists. There remained, however, some tensions between workers of different countries. English workers viewed the

Irish as scabs who came to compete for their jobs, while the Irish felt that the English acted superior and arrogant toward those they saw as part of a British colony. Marx viewed that conflict as weakening the English working class and a reason to support Irish independence. The German revolutionaries Wilhelm Liebknecht and August Bebel brought workers from outside the Prussian state into the International.

As described earlier, in July 1870 Louis Napoleon, who established France's Second Empire, declared war on the North German Confederation and surrendered six weeks later, whereupon a republic was declared in France. The French Government of National Defense agreed to indemnify Prussia for the cost of the war and for the disarming and occupation of Paris and later transferred control of the Alsace Lorraine region to Prussia, resulting in the rebellion by workers in Paris. The Russian anarchist Bakunin appeared at an insurrection in Lyon, proclaimed himself the leader, and announced the abolition of the state.[14] The state, however, chased him back to Geneva. Revolts also occurred in Marseilles and Toulouse. By the end of September, Prussian troops had occupied France, outside of the city of Paris. Auguste Blanqui and his followers attempted to establish a revolutionary government, and the French government fled Paris and reestablished itself at Versailles, effectively turning the capital over to the workers.

The outbreak of the Franco-Prussian War saw working classes of different countries attempting to cooperate with each other on the issue of war. They saw themselves as having more in common with their working brethren abroad than they did with the rich of their own countries. European workers' organizations expressed their brotherhood with other workers across Europe. French and Prussian workers exchanged letters calling for peace between their countries. American workers supported their efforts. Section 2 of the International, located in New York, called upon French workers to turn away from war and instead to revolt against Louis Napoleon, and on November 19, 1870, some two thousand people attended an antiwar meeting at Cooper Union in New York, which was sponsored by the New York sections of the International. The meeting was led by Marx's friend F. A. Sorge, and speeches were presented in English, German, and French. Charles Sumner, a U.S. senator and abolitionist, sent his greetings, and Sections 1 and 2 of the North

American Federation of the International issued a joint antiwar statement alleging that the real purpose of the war was to weaken labor. The Cooper Union meeting passed a number of resolutions, including a condemnation of the war against the new French Republic, sympathy for both the French and Germans who were suffering as a result of the war and against the annexation of the Alsace Lorraine region by Prussia; it called on the U.S. government to act to end the war and for the establishment of a court for international arbitration, for an end to standing armies, and for unity against monopolists, speculators, and despots.[15]

Refusing to submit to Prussia, the workers of Paris remained in control of the city, threatened by both the Prussians and the new French government. Both blamed the establishment of the Paris Commune and the revolt by the Paris working class on the International, which they considered to be a communist revolutionary organization wreaking havoc throughout Europe. In fact, the International had virtually nothing to do with the uprisings in France. Marx was against the insurrection, arguing that the workers were not yet strong enough to confront the French bourgeoisie and the Prussians. In the meantime, Marx explained, the working class should make use of all of their civil rights gained in the 1848 revolutions, including the right to vote, assemble, and speak. Because the working class was becoming larger all the time, it could make use of those bourgeois rights in order to strengthen its position in society. It was even possible, he claimed, that socialism could be achieved in some countries where the working class was large and the civic and political institutions were strong, such as England and the United States, by peaceful means rather than by violent revolution. In any event, a working-class consciousness and an interest in socialism spread throughout Europe during the 1870s and 1880s. As a result, Bismarck passed the Anti-Socialist Law in Germany in 1879 in an attempt to stop the spread of socialism among the German working class.

Marx set out the requirements for a working-class victory against the bourgeoisie in a number of reports and resolutions. In his 1868 Report to the Brussels Congress, he insisted that in order for national workers' movements to be successful, only "an international bond of the working classes can ever ensure their definitive triumph."[16] As long as workers were divided by national boundaries, it was impossible for them to overthrow the bourgeoisie. He also warned of divisions within the working classes, which were being exploited by the capitalists. A resolution written by Marx and passed by the General Council explained how the bourgeoisie divides the working class, Irish against English, black against white, and by religion. Engels added to Marx's analysis by including rural elements against the urban poor. The reasons that the rural population was more likely to support the conservative bourgeoisie, Engels explained, was because rural people were more religious, less educated, and isolated in the countryside. Yet the rural proletariat, Engels insisted, must be brought into the workers' movements.

Marx and Engels also coauthored a resolution of the London Congress on Working-Class Political Action in September 1871 in which they stated that the working class must organize itself into a political party opposed to all the propertied political classes, thereby uniting its economic and political actions.[17] The purpose of the International was to link the different movements. In the United States the idea of socialism and a workers' party was not entirely new. Aside from myriad experiments by utopian socialists, an early Workingmen's Party in New York offered candidates for a number of offices in 1829. Its issues focused on the abolition of debtors' prison and a free public education.[18]

Reaction to the International by those in power was tremendous, and the repression of radicals and members of the International occurred throughout Europe. In July 1870 leaders of Austrian workers were charged with and convicted of treason, as were leaders of the Pest Working Men's Union in what is now Hungary. In September 1870 members of the German Social Democratic Workers Party were imprisoned, while in France Jules Favre called on all European powers to crush the International. Spain moved to suppress the International in the spring of 1871. Leaders of Austria and Germany agreed to coordinate efforts to smash the International in August 1871, and leaders of Austria's Social Democratic Party were arrested and charged with high treason. In November 1871 members of the Brunswick Committee in Germany were convicted and imprisoned; France passed a law in March 1872 that made membership in the International illegal; and Italy banned the Naples section of the organization. That month Bebel and Liebknecht were convicted of treason in Leipzig, and in May 1872 members of the Danish Central Committee of the International were imprisoned for holding a meeting. Even the pope felt the need to attack the International, calling it a "diabolical" organization and adding, "These gentlemen of the International, who are no gentlemen, are to be feared because they work for the account of the everlasting enemy of God and mankind."[19] The pope's opinion was probably based not so much on theology as on the International's attack on the Church's support of the aristocracy and monied property.

The International possessed nowhere near the power with which it was credited by political rulers and the capitalist elite. It was always short on funds and divided by factions. Yet it became the favorite target of governments throughout Europe and later in the United States, ultimately being blamed for the 1877 railroad strikes there and the St. Louis Commune, which were actually spontaneous events that caught members of the International by surprise. Any unfortunate event occurring anywhere in the world seemed to be blamed on the International. Marx summed up the situation: "When the great conflagration took place at Chicago, the telegraph round the world announced it as the infernal deed of the International; and it is really wonderful that to its demoniacal agency has not been attributed the hurricane ravaging the West Indies."[20]

Governments described the International as a secret revolutionary organization, though there was very little secret about it. Section meetings and goals were public; notice of the meetings were publicly announced; and results of proceedings were published. Members of the International posted and passed out broadsides on the street which set out its program, notices, schedules of the meetings of different sections, and resolutions passed by the organization. One leaflet, for instance, titled "Program of the Internationals" set forth the organization's goals:

> A reduction of the hours of toil. . . . Nationalization of Land and the implements of Labor, Railroads, Canals, Gas Works, Telegraphs, Expresses, &c., and the organization of every department of production and distribution; supplying the necessaries of life at cost, and guaranteeing direct employment to the people, on the basis of equal compensation. . . . Every

facility for the acquisition of useful secular knowledge, to be guaranteed by Government, and free to all. . . . Complete Political and Social Equality to all, without regard to nationality, sex or condition. . . . No interference with, or preference for religious opinions. . . . All persons subscribing to the above principles are invited to attend meetings and become members of the Association.[21]

The remainder of the broadside set out the different meeting dates and places of the various sections of the organization. It was hardly a secret, underground group.

With the suppression of working-class groups and the International, there again arose differences of opinion within the organization. At the Hague Congress in September 1872, half of the delegates were French and German.[22] Marx's leadership of the International was challenged by Bakunin, whose revolutionary activities had earned him years in prison and banishment to Siberia.[23] Bakunin had aided in the growth of the working-class movements in Spain, Italy, and Russia, but whereas Marx argued that revolution would be made by the working class, Bakunin argued that it would be led by young people, the peasantry, and the unemployed.[24] Bakunin agreed that the working class was being exploited but believed that any kind of authority was bad, even that held by workers. The Church and the state existed solely to control people. Instead, argued Bakunin, society should consist of independent associations, communes of individuals who would organize themselves at the provincial and national levels. Political power would be replaced by voluntary economic association.[25] Bakunin succeeded in obtaining membership in the International for organizations under his control, including the International Alliance of Socialist Democracy and the League of Peace and Freedom, and he also had influence in sections located in Switzerland, Spain, and Italy. However, police spies had infiltrated some of the sections.

Marx, on the other hand, argued that when the working class took power from the capitalists, there would be a temporary dictatorship of the proletariat, during which time society would be converted to socialism and class conflict would end since the mass of the people made up the working class. Bakunin responded that class conflict would not end when the working class took control of society because then it would simply be its authority over someone else. Whenever a state exists, Bakunin answered Marx, someone has the power of domination over others. If Marx's scenario came to pass, the rural peasants would be subordinate to the ruling urban proletariat. Those who were formerly workers would be in control and would not give up their power, so the period of the dictatorship of the proletariat would not be short, but rather it would be permanent. Bakunin's strength was primarily among the anarchists in Italy and Spain.[26]

At first the American press virtually ignored the First International. By 1871, however, the International and the Paris Commune were receiving a good deal of attention in the American media. The *Chicago Times* credited the International with the revolt of the Paris Commune, even though few members of the Commune were members of the International or followers of Marx. The Commune was primarily led by Jacobins, descendants of the ideology of the French Revolution, and followers of Blanqui and Proudhon. Of the ninety-two Commune leaders elected on March 28, 1871, only seventeen were members of the International.[27]

In any event, the newspapers exaggerated and distorted news of the Paris Commune. As a result of the publicity, the Commune made the International famous and appear extraordinarily powerful, so that some saw it as part of an international conspiracy determined to destroy society. The Paris Commune took on the appearance of merely the first step in a planned world revolution. The *New York Herald* claimed that the International was so powerful that it could grow and expand indefinitely, resisting any efforts by the rest of the world. The *New York Journal of Commerce* warned that the September 1871 demonstrations in favor of an eight-hour workday would end with a takeover of the country by communism. When Marx was interviewed by two American journalists, he responded that the International was only a union of workers with the common desire to liberate themselves by political means. The Massachusetts abolitionist Wendell Phillips chastised the press for its distorted reporting on the Commune, which, by refusing to submit to Prussia, he considered an example of French patriotism. Phillips was a supporter of labor and thought American workers could resolve their problems by organization, education, cooperation, and, most important, by voting.

As a result of news of the events in Europe, American employers, newspapers, and the Church were wary of what they saw as communist attacks on American traditions and institutions. Especially scary to them was news of the Paris Commune, as some saw the conditions that gave rise to revolution in Europe as being similar to those in the United States, where workers were exploited and barely able to survive. Others, however, believed that the labor situation was different in the United States. Europe, they felt, was marked by despotism and tyranny, while the institutions in America were more humane and fair. Any labor problems came from those misusing the system, so it was not necessary to destroy existing institutions in the United States as it might be to do so in Europe. While the most radical of the European radicals sought the elimination of private property, American workers were more likely to seek reforms within that system. Phillips saw no danger from communism in the United States. Strikes, he said, were not communism; they were merely the consequence of inhuman conditions imposed on workers by industry leaders.

Workers in the United States included those who were native-born and immigrants from Europe. The problems of the American working classes actually were similar in many respects to those experienced by Europe's workers. While there was never a feudal society in the United States, except perhaps in the South, capitalism operated similarly on both continents. Wealthy industrialists ruled their companies with iron fists and had a great deal of influence in government. During and after the Civil War, American labor conditions were marked by long hours, dangerous conditions, and subsistence wages. Women and children in the workforce tended to keep wages at a minimal level. A Senate committee reported that real wages fell by one-third between 1860 and 1865.

The depression in 1857 had badly weakened unions as a result of unemployment, but by the end of the Civil War they were making a comeback, with approximately three hundred unions representing sixty-one different trades. Unions during that period were composed largely of skilled workers and organized at the local level. However, by the late 1860s and early 1870s some workers' organizations were seeking to unite all members of a particular trade across the country. The National Labor Union was founded in

Baltimore in 1866 and called for the creation of international unions, the organizing of unskilled workers, and the eight-hour workday. Although the National Labor Union stressed cooperation between labor and capital, the General Council of the International did invite it to send a representative to its second Congress, and near the end of its life in 1870 the National Labor Union declared its support for the First International.[28] By 1873 there were thirty-two national unions in the United States with a total membership of some three hundred thousand workers.[29]

Some American labor organizations did view the labor problem with an international perspective. Those groups primarily consisted of immigrant workers. Approximately 1 million Germans immigrated to the United States during the 1850s, several thousand of whom had participated in the 1848 German Revolution. After 1850 most socialists in the United States were German immigrants.[30] Young America, which later became the Social Reform Association, was established in 1845 and claimed members in a number of American cities, including Philadelphia, Newark, Cincinnati, Baltimore, Milwaukee, and St. Louis.[31] Marx's friend Joseph Weydemeyer was active in the American Worker's League. The various organizations represented many different, radical views, including anarchism, socialism, and utopianism. Sorge was a member of the Communist Club in New York, which included refugees from the 1848 European revolutions. There were so many radical Europeans living in New York that they were able to celebrate revolutionary anniversaries with their own gatherings and parades. Over five thousand people participated in one such parade, while another one hundred thousand lined the parade route. Another ten thousand marched in December 1871 in support of the Paris Commune. When the Communist Club in New York joined the International as part of Section 1, it had only twenty members, mostly German immigrants. Section 1 of the American Federation of the International in New York grew and was extremely active in support of local unions and even unions in Chicago, Milwaukee, and St. Louis. According to Samuel Bernstein, the First International could be considered a training ground for "labor leaders who later participated in establishing the American Federation of Labor."[32] It also worked with African American workers, which many workers' organizations refused to do at the time. The National

Colored Labor Convention voted to send a delegate to the International's Fifth Congress in Paris in 1870, although it was postponed as a result of the Franco-Prussian War. The New York sections were the most active within the International. European radicals who escaped Europe mostly lived in New York, including those who fought in the revolutions of 1848 and some survivors of the Paris Commune, such as Eugène Pottier, who had composed the revolutionary song the "Internationale" in 1871. With the expansion of the First International, European and American workers connected over shared issues and interests.

The French community in St. Louis consisted of early French immigrants, creoles who moved there from Louisiana, and later French arrivals. In 1866 it established a French-language socialist newspaper, *La Tribune Française*. In 1868 the St. Louis section of the Union republicaine de langue française was formed, led by Georges Bauer, who had been a member of Cabet's utopian Icarian community. French sections of the International were also formed by the Union Republicaine in New York in 1870 and in St. Louis in 1871, and in July 1872 a German section of the International was formed in St. Louis. Otto Weydemeyer, Joseph's son, was the First International's St. Louis correspondent. An English-speaking section of the International was formed in St. Louis in 1872. The French Radical Club in St. Louis founded the Union republicaine de langue française in 1868, with branches of the organization in New York, Newark, Paducah, Kentucky, and San Francisco. While the organization generally supported Marx, it was also affected by the utopian ideas of Fourier and Cabet and some followers of Proudhon. The International eventually united the French American members into Section 2.

The International recognized the problems in organizing American workers. The United States was not a homogeneous country, as were the nations of Europe. The American working class was made up of many different ethnic groups, and the International organized sections based on ethnicity, primarily due to language differences. This, however, had the unintended effect of dividing the country's working class. Many of the immigrant workers did not speak English well or at all, and many groups had newspapers in their own languages. They could not hope to attract American-born workers that way. Added to that, many of the different ethnic groups felt that the Germans, who as a group were more educated than other immigrants after 1848, acted superior to the others. Yet the International made efforts to support workers from every different group. It supported all strikers, no matter their ethnicity. In 1871 it supported striking Pennsylvania miners. It was the greatest supporter of Irish independence outside Ireland. Sorge attempted to convince Irish workers that Ireland could not gain independence alone but required help from the IWA as an ally. The Irish became Section 7 of the American Federation of the International, which was impressive considering the Catholic Church's denunciation of the International.

The International in the United States grew larger and more successful. By September 1871 there were nineteen sections, three made up of American workers and the rest French, German, Irish, and other ethnicities. In New York there were French, German, Czech, and Irish sections. San Francisco had a French section, while St. Louis boasted German, English, French, and Bohemian sections. Sections were founded in New Orleans, Philadelphia, and Washington DC. Although workers made up a majority of its members, there were also teachers, lawyers, doctors, civil servants, journalists, and other professions represented. But the International still had problems enlisting American-born workers. It attributed the problem to the fact that most Northern workers were immigrants who had come to the United States for economic reasons, that workers in America generally accepted small reforms as progress, and that the leaders of American labor misled the workers for their own selfish reasons.

Some literature in the United States admitted to the poor working conditions and low wages that characterized the situation of American labor. The Civil War, some felt, had caused the concentration of capital and distorted the American economic system. But, many argued, it was only a matter of putting things back on track, and that could be accomplished by voting. Unlike Europe, they argued, the United States was a place that valued fairness, where everyone played a part in civic life and where all could participate in government. Some said that the United States was still a country where a person could get rich if he worked hard and didn't drink his wages. Theodore Banks, a member of Section 9 of the International, replied that laws were actually made by the rich in their own interest and not in the interest of the poor. The average person had no defense against giant corporations, which controlled the government.[33]

Divisions within the International continued to arise. There remained the fights between the followers of Marx, Bakunin, and Proudhon. In addition, members were divided between the positions of Marx and Lassalle. While Marx believed that it was necessary for workers to have their own political party, he felt that could occur only when labor was sufficiently united and strong. The International's primary task was to build labor organizations and to encourage and aid workers in coming together as a group and to recognize their common interests. Then it would be ready to engage in politics. Lassalle, on the other hand, argued that labor must immediately participate in politics and run candidates for political office. The state, he argued, could actually support the workers in attaining their goal of freedom. Lassalle actually did obtain expanded suffrage in Germany by working with Bismarck. With the working class growing in numbers, a workers' political party could be elected and take control of the government.[34] Although all supported the Paris Commune, they disagreed on its ultimate meaning. Followers of Proudhon and Bakunin viewed it as an anarchist experiment, while Marx saw it as an example of the dictatorship of the proletariat.

The extreme poverty that existed in both rural and urban settings after the Civil War resulted in the creation of social welfare organizations. The New England Labor Reform League, the Cosmopolitan Society, and New Democracy sought to educate the public about the problem of poverty and campaigned for equal rights for women, universal suffrage, currency reform, and the regulation of banks and large corporations. Conflict between socialists and reformers added another dimension to the divisions within the International. Socialists believed that concentrating on reforms removed one's focus from the primary problem of capitalism.

Those divisions were not limited to American sections of the organization; they even touched on the very mission of the International. A Swiss section demanded that the General Council limit itself to keeping records and corresponding with the various sections and not get involved with the merits of the different philosophies within the organization. Other sections argued that, following the Paris Commune, the International was under attack from all sides, and therefore the General Council required more, not less, authority to act in defense of labor. Marx complained that he would not be resigned to opening envelopes and forwarding mail. In Europe there was, of course, the same conflicts between communists and reformers, Marxists and Lassalle supporters, and utopians and anarchists that existed in the United States. In 1871 Marxists were in control of the organization, and the General Council was given more power at its Congress in London, resulting in the anarchists holding their own Congress in Switzerland, where they established the Jura Federation. James Guillaume, a Bakuninist, drafted new rules that provided for more autonomy for sections instead of what they viewed as Marxist authoritarianism within the International. Members of the International from Italy, who were largely anarchists, supported the move and held their own Congress in Rimini in August 1872 and called for abolishing the General Council, while sections from Germany, England, and Holland supported the General Council. In response the General Council attacked Bakunin and the anarchists, accusing them of conspiring to establish secret societies within the International.

There were even divisions within individual sections of the organization. Section 1 in New York, for example, contained both Marxists and followers of Lassalle. It originally was born as a result of the merger of Sorge's Communist Club with a Lassallean group. Section 2 harbored utopian socialists. A Fourierist group became Sections 9 and 12. Other sections harbored reformers among its communist members. Josiah Warren, a member of the First International, was an American anarchist who had lived in the utopian socialist communities of New Harmony in Indiana and Modern Times on Long Island. Another member was Stephen Pearl Andrews, who had also lived at Modern Times and viewed anarchism as the march toward freedom for the individual. A follower of Warren, Ezra Heywood, founded the New England Labor Reform League in 1869. Heywood believed in a society with a minimum amount of government that consisted of small property owners who created and exchanged products of equal labor value; he opposed labor unions and ultimately became an advocate of free love.[35] Section 26 in Philadelphia included followers of Fourier. The anarchist Lewis Masquerier was opposed to representative government and the nationalization of land, which he claimed diluted the power of the individual, and instead envisioned a society made up of small homesteads. He advocated a landowning society within a loose federation in place of government.

Divisions within the International became more complicated in the United States. Victoria Woodhull led Section 12 in New York, which experimented with spiritualism, atheism, and free love. Woodhull was a reformer who called for cooperation between labor and capital. Section 12 challenged the power of the Central Committee in the United States and requested that the General Council put it in charge of the American branch of the International. Section 12 represented a kind of radical countercultural movement, which was attracted by the International's desire to remake society but did not necessarily fit within the revolutionary working-class philosophy of the organization. Complaints against Section 12 alleged that its philosophy and conduct were not consistent with the philosophy or program of the International but rather that the group had its own agenda, that it was nativist, and that the advocacy of free love was not the purpose or mission of the International.

The Central Committee attempted to resolve the matter by requiring that two-thirds of any section within the International be composed of wage earners. The conflict with Woodhull went to the heart of what the International was supposed to be: was it a labor association or a multi-issue reform organization? Finally, the General Council ordered the two sections to unite, to abide by its decisions, and to draft rules that did not conflict with those of the International; it reiterated the two-thirds wage earners rule and suspended Section 12 from the International until the next Congress met and decided the issue. Unfortunately all of this occurred while the International was under attack by governments in Europe and the United States, resulting in a decline in membership in the American sections.

Matters ultimately grew even worse. Members of Section 12 called for a convention in New York in May 1872 for the purpose of nominating Woodhull for president of the United States. Five hundred delegates, made up of reformers, suffragettes, spiritualists, free love advocates, and temperance supporters, attended the convention, which gave birth to the Equal Rights Party and nominated Woodhull for president and Frederick Douglass for vice president. Included in the party's platform were women's suffrage, public ownership of mines, free trade, proportional representation, regulation of labor conditions, and public improvements. Some members of the International left the convention in anger, claiming that all of this was outside the mission and purposes of the International and would serve to alienate American workers. In June 1872 Woodhull's group finally left the International, evidencing its nativist tendencies by proclaiming that an American group should consist of Americans and not foreigners and not advance a political philosophy that was imported from Europe. In July 1872 they met in Philadelphia and established the American Confederation of the International Workingmen's Association, which anyone was welcome to join, even employers. That organization gained the support of some intellectuals but was not a part of the labor movement.

In the meantime, the North American Federation of the International held a Congress in July 1872, where twenty-three delegates represented twelve German sections, four French sections, and one each of Scandinavian, Italian, and Irish. It required all sections to be consistent with the rules of the International and prohibited workers from supporting any employers' political parties, whether Democrat, Republican, or other. The French sections were still divided between Proudhonists, utopians, Jacobins, and Blanquists. Followers of Marx were in the minority. Delegates to the Hague Congress of the International in 1872 were directed to support the General Council's strong central authority.

The largest delegations at the Hague Congress were French and German. Police infiltration was ubiquitous, and some of the delegates were police spies. Delegates from Section 12 attempted to attend the Congress and insisted that the emancipation of women had to come before the emancipation of labor, that capitalists needed to be members of the organization because they knew more about capitalism, that the two-thirds rule did not fit the situation in the United States, and that the General Council could not tell the Americans what to do. Marx responded that spiritualism and free love were not labor interests, that women's rights could not be placed above the interests of labor, and that the two-thirds rule was necessary if the International was to remain a labor organization. The Congress denied the credentials of Section 12. The Blanquists attending the Congress supported Marx over the anarchists but called for immediate revolution. They eventually left the Congress, and Marx won subsequent floor battles with the anarchists.

Then Engels shocked the Congress with a prearranged motion to move the location of the General Council to New York. London was the birthplace of the International and where the General Council had sat since its inception. The reason for moving the International's leadership to another continent was Marx's concern about the attempts of the European anarchists to take over the organization. He wanted to move its leadership and records to a safe place far from them. There was much discord in Europe; many European workers were emigrating from Europe to the United States; and there was less police repression in America. There was not yet the suppression of socialist organizations by the government of the United States as there was in Europe. As a result, American members were able to meet with workers, propagandize among them, and organize and educate them. The Blanquists opposed the move, claiming that leaving Europe would subject the working class there to repression with no one to defend them. Nevertheless, the General Council and therefore the leadership of the International was relocated to New York.

Responsibility for the International was now on the shoulders of the North American Federation. Bakunin's sections were expelled for leading a secret society within the organization.[36] Sorge, who was the leader of a German section of the International in New York and a follower of Marx, worked as a music teacher, organized workers, founded Section 1 in New York, and served as the general secretary of the organization from 1872 to 1874. Not all of the International's national federations agreed with the move, and the Belgian, Spanish, English, Italian, and French Swiss federations refused to correspond with the New York General Council.[37] The relocation of the International's leadership to New York would later directly lead to the founding of the Workingmen's Party of the United States, which led the general strike in St. Louis and established the St. Louis Commune.

Sorge continued the daily work of obtaining and distributing information regarding the working classes of different countries. The smallest details could prove to be important. For example, he wrote to the British federation requesting information on England's taxi drivers for use by those in Vienna: "Keep an eye on the workingmen's movement in England and give us authentic news about it. You are requested to collect at once . . . reliable information on the regulations, fares etc. of the hack and cabdrivers—if possible in German—for the use of the Vienna hackdrivers, who asked us for it."[38]

The move to the United States marked the beginning of the end of the First International. Financial problems became severe as a result of unemployment, the depression in 1873, and the failure of European members to pay dues in a timely manner. The great distance between the General Council and Europe and the loss of experienced European revolutionaries also weakened the organization. It needed to operate a socialist press, support family members of deceased Paris Communards, and support strikers in the United States and Europe, and it did not even have enough money to pay for postage. Letters from Sorge in New York to a St. Louis section, for example, described the need for funds to publish a paper supported by the International. They can sell all papers they are able to print, Sorge explained, but do not have the money necessary to continue to publish. He went on to describe fundraisers and festivals that were planned in New York in an effort to raise money and suggested that St. Louis sections do the same.[39]

The anarchists and Blanquists left the International, went their own ways, and set up their own organizations. In 1874 the London Trades Council broke with the International. The French and Italian governments suppressed whatever remained of it in their countries and imprisoned many of its leaders, and the Dutch Federation dissolved itself. The General Council could not even afford to send a delegate to a Congress in Geneva in 1873. Even the anarchists were divided among themselves over the issues of direct action, the general strike, and propaganda by deed.

In the meantime, St. Louis had a small but active membership in the International. Most of its members were French and German immigrants. The Germans were the most politically active ethnic group, many of them refugees from the 1848 Revolution. A German utopian, Wilhelm Weitling, formed a branch of the Arbeiterbund in St. Louis in the 1850s.[40] French utopians, followers of Cabet, also had a community in St. Louis. However, Joseph Weydemeyer, Marx's friend and his literary agent in the United States, is credited with introducing Marxist socialism to the city. When Weydemeyer decided to move to the United States, Engels had suggested that he avoid

Boston and Philadelphia as too provincial, and that St. Louis with its large German population, was a good place for him to settle. Weydemeyer arrived in St. Louis in 1861 and served as a captain of artillery during the Civil War under John C. Frémont and later as a lieutenant colonel of the Second Missouri Light Artillery, when he fought Confederate guerrillas in southern Missouri. He later became a colonel in the Forty-First Missouri Infantry and commanded an area that included St. Louis. He was active in Republican politics in St. Louis and edited *Die Neue Zeit*, a German-language newspaper. Marx sent him a copy of his Inaugural Address to the First International, and Weydemeyer had it published in the *Daily Press*, a St. Louis labor newspaper started by printers. The *Daily Press* was the first American paper to cover Marx's Inaugural Address. In 1864 Weydemeyer was elected auditor of St. Louis County and published an article in favor of the eight-hour workday movement. He died in the midst of a cholera epidemic in St. Louis in 1866.

James E. Cope was another International member active in St. Louis. An English shoemaker, Cope was a founding member of the First International and served as a member of the General Council in London. He settled in St. Louis during the 1870s, was active in the Marxist Workingmen's Party of the United States, and emerged as a leader of the St. Louis general strike in 1877 and the St. Louis Commune. Another friend of Weydemeyer, Hermann Meyer, had organized working-class groups in New York and settled in St. Louis at the start of the Civil War, where he continued his work.

Most important for the St. Louis general strike and the St. Louis Commune of 1877 was a Congress held in Philadelphia in 1876, consisting of remnants of the First International and various socialist organizations, which formed the Workingmen's Party of the United States. The St. Louis sections of the International were represented in Philadelphia by Albert Currlin.[41] The following year the WPUSA, led by Currlin, would take control of the St. Louis general strike and rule the city on behalf of its working people.

Dying not in a single event but rather more slowly, as by a thousand cuts, the International faded away in time, dissolving in July 1876. Its eventual death in the United States cannot be attributed solely to the American elements, since its end also occurred in Europe. Jonathan Sperber attributes its demise to the ideological struggle between Marx and Bakunin.[42]

However, there are certain American elements that did contribute to its death. Most members of the International in the United States were foreigners. They came from many different countries and spoke different languages; there was therefore a problem communicating with each other as well as with American-born workers. Most lived in their own ethnically based neighborhoods, further separating them. They attempted to convince American workers of a European philosophy, which was new and different from any with which American workers were familiar. As infrequently embraced as it may have been, there was a belief in America of class mobility, where one was not necessarily condemned to spend one's life in the class in which one was born, as was common in Europe. America was a place where oppressed people came to experience freedom, where people could start their lives anew. Everyone, including the poor and working class, had certain civil rights. There were expanding industries and vast, purportedly empty lands for settlement where one could own a farm free from oppression. There was the Horatio Alger myth, that anyone could become rich if he or she was willing to work hard and follow the rules. Some of these beliefs contained a modicum of truth, especially when contrasted with the more rigid class lines in Europe. But for the overwhelming majority of people, they were exactly that: myths. Most poor people would remain poor throughout their lives, and their children would continue to live in poverty. Most working-class people would work long hours in unsafe conditions for a subsistence wage, as would their children. That scenario would remain more or less the same for at least the next 150 years, but the fact that many American workers believed the myths made it difficult to convince them to participate in revolution.

In the mid-nineteenth century, the factory system and industry in Europe and the United States were young but growing and expanding. Independent artisans and skilled workers were finding it impossible to ply their trades. The growing use of machines in the factory reduced skilled workers to unskilled wage earners, resulting in less dignity for them as well as lower earnings. Their particular skills were no longer necessary to produce the goods. Peasants and farmers, not able to make a decent living in rural areas, moved to the cities looking for work in the new factories. A higher density of the urban population, together with lower wages, resulted in the growth of tenement buildings and urban slums. The new machinery was not constructed with the safety of workers in mind, and so factory work was dangerous. At the same time, the working classes in Europe and the United States were young and developing. Unions had existed earlier, but they were largely made up of craftsmen at a local level.

The First International was an attempt to unite and support workers on a national and international basis. As corporations grew into national and international organizations, it was necessary for labor to do the same. The International attempted to provide a way for workers in different countries to be aware of what was happening to others and to provide a means of communication between them. Its international congresses brought workers from different countries together on a regular basis. It supported workers' struggles wherever they occurred, often collecting money from workers of one country to aid strikes in another. It was the first time workers had organized on an international scale. The American branch of the International strongly supported labor's fight for the eight-hour workday. By May 1872 it had supported strikes by one hundred thousand workmen representing thirty-two trades in states in the East and the Midwest. It decided that even though workers were divided by crafts, they would unite over interests they had in common, such as wages and hours of work and that employers would conspire and unite against them.

Like all movements, there were differing views on what the ultimate goal should be and how to achieve it. Some argued for liberal reforms in the present, others for a workers' revolution. Communists sought a classless society, where there would no longer be exploitation of workers by capitalists. Anarchists such as Proudhon and Bakunin desired to do away with all government and replace it with voluntary, economic entities. Marx believed that the working classes must develop a self-consciousness as a separate class and build their strength in unions and workers' organizations before they could politically take control of society. Lassalle, on the other hand, called on workers to create their own political party immediately and begin running workers for public offices. The organization that attempted to unite all workers was itself divided.

Still, the First International did succeed in creating a mechanism for workers to come together and seek common aims, whatever their national origins. It aided in the organization of workers, supported their struggles, and provided an ideological basis for the labor movements. The First International served to connect American workers to those in Europe and with socialist philosophy and movements around the world. It linked European working-class struggles with those in the United States and provided an organizational structure for American workers to come together with other workers who had engaged in revolutionary activity. Its ideas were such that virtually every capitalist country in Europe feared it and sought to destroy it, wherever it existed. The First International would affect history long after its demise. Members of the organization were active in the American labor movement and served as leaders of the St. Louis Commune.

6

The Condition of the
American Working Class

By 1877 the American working class was desperate. Wages were low, many were unemployed, working conditions were unsafe, the United States was in the fourth year of a major depression, and large corporations strongly influenced or virtually controlled many states and the federal government. The situation was ripe for labor unrest.

Prior to the Civil War, the production and sale of commodities in the United States took the form of personal transactions between producers and consumers. Most producers were self-employed or worked in small shops. Many learned their trades from skilled artisans and later opened and operated their own businesses. Production was characterized by the independence of the shop owner and personal service. Consumers knew those who produced their goods, and the artisans were generally self-sufficient. Producers took pride in their work, which they created and produced from beginning to end. They were respected by others because of their skills and were able to earn a decent living. Those who worked for artisans were able to learn a trade and perhaps one day open and operate their own businesses, reflecting the social mobility possible for skilled workers.

The labor issues that emerged after the Civil War reflected the transition from individual artisan to factory wage laborer. In the 1860s and 1870s unskilled immigration from Germany, Ireland, and Italy aided in the growth of industrial workplaces and the transition to wage labor. With the growth of European immigration to the United States, especially the influx of unskilled labor from Ireland, the new factory system and urban poverty posed a problem for the working class. The skilled worker no longer created a finished product in which he could take pride, but rather was forced into the industrial system where he labored on only a small part of the production process and ultimately performed work that could be done by unskilled workers. As a result, he earned less and, perhaps more important, lost the pride of craftsmanship and his individualism and independence. With the rise of industrial capitalism came the factory wage earner, who experienced less community respect and who was entirely dependent on the factory owner for his wages and for his job. He no longer sold the product he created, but rather sold his labor and, in the end, himself.[1] In addition, journeymen artisans could no longer hope to one day be independent producers themselves.

The evolution from individual producer to factory wage earner brought with it a certain tension and resentment on the part of workers. An artisan with his own shop controlled his own working conditions. In a factory setting, that was no longer the case; the factory environment and conditions were determined solely by the owner. This was a major lifestyle change for the skilled worker and destructive of his independence. One worker who quit her factory job complained "about her 'obedience to the ding-dong of the bell.'"[2]

As a result of the factory system, great numbers of largely unskilled laborers massed together in the urban slums of the larger cities. The nineteenth-century depressions had taken their toll, leaving great numbers of workers unemployed or working for starvation wages. An 1850 investigation of working-class living conditions in New York City found that the average number of persons occupying one room was six and, in some cases, up to twenty. Individual houses in the Five Points neighborhood often contained three hundred residents. Two to four families often lived together in one room.[3] Writing in 1886, Norman Ware included a description of a house in Lowell, Massachusetts, in 1847, occupied "by one store and twenty-five different families embracing 120 persons, more than half of whom were adults. In one of the rooms, which was inhabited by two families, I found one of the families to consist of a man, his wife, and eight children—four of whom were over fifteen years of age—and four adult boarders."[4]

A number of solutions were presented to reduce working-class suffering, ranging from labor and urban reform measures to westward expansion and emigration from eastern urban jungles. Instead of the crowded tenements of eastern cities, workers could begin a new and independent existence on the western frontier. Many Republicans and labor organizations believed that encouraging the settlement of the West by offering free land to those willing to improve it was the answer to labor and urban woes. Those struggling financially in the East could create and build new lives in the West, which would act as a safety valve and release the growing labor tensions in eastern cities. In addition, as Frederick Jackson Turner was later to argue, settlement of the American frontier would be a boon to Americans' independence and the strengthening of democracy.[5]

The explosion in corporate and industrial growth following the Civil War was fueled by a philosophy of greed. No amount of profit seemed to be enough for those who owned or controlled the largest financial and manufacturing assets in the quickly expanding economy. The very purpose of corporations had changed through the years from the consolidation of capital to be used for public improvements and benefits to earning as much money as possible for shareholders. That latter purpose could be achieved by any means necessary, whether by hard work, new ideas, or exploitation and corruption. The 1870s were marked by wholesale greed and corruption that reached into the offices at the highest levels of government and business. The secretary of war, the ex-Speaker of the House, the president's secretary and brother-in-law, the vice president, members of Congress, a number of state governors and state legislators, and major corporations were all touched by scandal during that decade.

As industrial capitalism grew, workers were increasingly considered to be expendable appendages to the new machines, which created more and more profits for wealthy capitalists. The more hours workers labored, the fewer wages they earned, and the less money spent on safety measures guaranteed huge profits for the new capitalists. However, while the attainment of immediate profits for the large corporations may have looked good in quarterly reports, in the long run it was a losing strategy. The tensions between worker and capitalist grew stronger, which brought on strikes and labor unrest. But perhaps more important, such conduct deprived potential consumers of the money they needed to buy the goods capitalists were producing, thus causing the booms and busts that would characterize industrial capitalism.

As a result of the massive layoffs during and after the Panic of 1873, working people were desperate for jobs and were forced to work harder for less money and in more dangerous conditions. The alternative was starvation. Workers seemed to have no choice but to accept whatever terms management offered them. It was in many ways the Hobbesian world Spencer described as Social Darwinism, where life was a struggle to exist, and where those unable to sustain themselves in the new environment perished.

Many workers had suffered from inhumane working and living conditions since the eighteenth century, when machines began to replace skilled workers and the factory system began to dominate the workplace. Workers attempted to resist their exploitation by organizing unions. Early attempts resulted in the organization of craft unions, where workers of certain trades joined together. Later, attempts would be made to organize all workers in a workplace, no matter their particular skills or jobs. The depression in 1837 and those following it, however, hampered attempts to grow unions as workers were laid off, unable to pay union dues and unable to organize themselves. When economic conditions improved, so did union activity.

In Lowell in 1843 young women in the textile industry rose up against their working conditions. The workday for most girls and women began at 6:00 a.m. and did not end until 10:00 p.m., for which they earned $1.56 a week. The Female Labor Reform Association was organized in Lowell in 1845. A number of strikes followed, demanding a ten-hour workday.[6] Defenders of the longer workday argued that it was necessary in order to protect the morals of the young women operatives, who would otherwise be exposed to immoral attractions during their free time.[7]

In September 1845 in Pennsylvania, five thousand women struck for a ten-hour workday. Utopian socialists joined the ten-hour movement, and the New England Convention in Boston in October 1844 called for the freeing up of public lands, producers' cooperatives, and the ten-hour workday and endorsed Fourierism. Some states passed legislation limiting the workday to ten hours, but industrialists responded by requiring workers to sign contracts agreeing to work more than that even though they were not legally obligated to do so. In the midst of successive depressions, there was always a large pool of unemployed who would agree to submit to any capitalist demands.[8] When workers took over factories in protest of the forced work agreement, companies often answered by reducing wages accordingly. Although workers were being paid for the time they worked, wages were so low that families often could not survive on them.

Middle-class reformers began to support the position of labor in the 1850s. Labor issues then expanded from hours and wages to include child labor. Children were especially exploited in the textile mills. Samuel Slater's first mill was operated by seven boys and two girls, ranging in age from seven to eleven. Children were recruited from almshouses for work in the mills.[9] At a mass meeting in Trenton, New Jersey, in September 1847, workers demanded the ten-hour day and a limit on child labor. In the Rhode Island mills in 1853, there were 59 children under nine years of age, 621 between nine and twelve, and 1,177 between twelve and fifteen.[10] In 1851 New Jersey finally enacted legislation limiting the workday to ten hours.

One of several challenges to uniting the working class was that workers often had different interests. Skilled and unskilled workers were divided to some extent because skilled workers received higher wages, and most unions were still segregated by trades. However, unions began to accumulate strike funds and established the principle of collective bargaining, where the union would represent the interests of workers and contracts with companies would be between the union and the company rather than between the company and individual workers. Unfortunately union advances were reversed again by depressions in 1854 and 1857.

Another challenge to workers and one of the most important labor issues in the 1850s was the importation of immigrant labor as strikebreakers and for the purpose of reducing overall wages. Many of the new immigrants were unskilled workers who were willing to work for lower wages. The Contract Labor Law of 1864 allowed employers to bring to the United States thousands of immigrant workers. Between 1840 and 1850, over 1.7 million immigrants arrived in the United States, and another 2.6 million between 1850 and 1860. Immigrants made up a large part of American cities. In 1860, 47.6 percent of the population of New York City was foreign-born, as was 49.9 percent of the population of Chicago and 59.7 percent of St. Louis.[11] The issue of immigrant labor used to break strikes and lower wages was an important one recognized early by Marx and the First International.

One factor that apparently was not considered by capitalists who brought in foreign workers, however, was that many of them came with a European class consciousness and radical philosophies. This was especially true of immigrants from England and Germany. Many of the German-speaking immigrants who arrived in the United States between 1850 and 1860 were socialists as well as veterans of the 1848 German Revolution. The first miners' union in the United States was organized by a British trade unionist, and German immigrants included trade unionists, socialists, and those who had fought in European revolutions. Many of those immigrants became leaders in the American labor movement, the 1877 railroad strike, and the establishment of the St. Louis Commune.

The printers were the first trade to organize a national union in the United States. By 1860 they had been joined by upholsterers, hat finishers, plumbers, building trades, railroad engineers, stone cutters, lithographers, cigar makers, silver platers, cotton spinners, machinists, blacksmiths, painters, and cordwainers. However, national unions were, for the most part, weak or nonexistent in most trades in the mid-nineteenth century.

Once again labor advances were reversed by the depression in 1857, which threw over two hundred thousand laborers out of work. Yet the unemployed also attempted to organize themselves and demanded that cities invest in public works in order to create more jobs.[12] On November 5, 1857, over twelve thousand unemployed workers attended a demonstration in New York's Tomkins Square, a customary meeting place for left-wing radicals at the time, where the speakers reflected a growing class consciousness among the proletariat and the unemployed and attacked capitalists as responsible for the current situation. "Resolutions were then passed declaring sympathy with the strikers, and denouncing all legalized railroad, manufacturing and other corporations as the despotic enemies of the working classes and morally responsible by their tyranny for the acts of workingmen, who should form a party to make common cause against the common enemy."[13]

The Tomkins Square demonstration was peaceful until police waded into the crowd and beat people senseless just as the demonstration was ending. One witness remarked that everyone was treated equally, that the police clubbed both "the heads of the just and the unjust."[14] Several thousand workers and unemployed attended a mass meeting for the unemployed in Newark that same month. As more workers were replaced by machines and children, the number of strikes increased. Although many employers attempted to divide their workers by race or country of origin, many strikes were successful.

With few exceptions, workers' attention had previously centered on economic issues, such as working conditions, wages, and the length of the workday. By the end of the 1850s, however, they began to shift their focus to politics. In 1858 they organized the Workingmen's Union of Trenton, New Jersey, with the intention of affecting legislation. The Workingmen's Union demanded that public land be given to settlers and not to speculators or railroad companies and that workers have a lien on the property of employers in order to protect themselves against unpaid wages. Surprisingly, the major political parties endorsed their demands. Virtually all of these efforts by labor occurred in the North, not in the South. Slaveholders did not want factories in the South, as Blacks, they felt, were more suited for agricultural work, and no good could come from having class-conscious workers in their midst. The new Republican Party sought the support of labor by opposing the expansion of slavery into the territories, where slave labor would compete with wage earners, and called for the imposition of tariffs in order to protect growing American industry and jobs. Republicans also supported the 1862 Homestead Act, which promised 160 acres of western land to those who settled and improved it, thereby furnishing another option for the unemployed of the eastern cities.

Marx and the First International supported Lincoln during his campaign for the presidency, and Marx wrote to Lincoln after his election congratulating him on his victory. Marx viewed the American Civil War as a battle between Southern feudalism and Northern capitalism, much as he viewed the struggles in Europe in 1830 and 1848. According to Marx, feudalism was a reactionary system, which was bound to be replaced by the more progressive capitalism. A class-conscious working-class proletariat would grow under capitalism and ultimately overthrow it and institute socialism, at which time the exploitation of man by man would end. German radicals and Marxists supported, and in many cases fought for, the North in the Civil War, many achieving the rank of general in the Union army.

Workers' lives were especially hard during the Civil War. Northern businesses lost Southern products and markets, resulting in a reduction of the number of jobs available. Inflation was out of control, and prices for many goods increased 50 to 100 percent. Between 1861 and 1864 the price of butter increased from four cents a pound to twenty-five cents. The army was used to control the working class, as well as to fight the Confederacy and Indians. Workers who were engaged in war production were not allowed to picket; scabs were protected when there was a strike; union membership was prohibited; and those who did join unions were blacklisted. During the war, machinists and tailors in St. Louis were compelled to work at the point of a bayonet.

Later in and after the Civil War, unions restarted their organizing efforts, this time including women and African Americans. Because women were paid only half the wages paid to men, thereby lowering wages for everyone, unions supported the organization of women. Women umbrella workers earned less than one dollar a day, while working from 6:00 a.m. until midnight. They struck for higher wages, and the Working Women's Protective Union was formed in New York. Similar organizations appeared in Chicago, St. Louis, Indianapolis, Boston, and Philadelphia. The Ladies Cigar Makers Union was founded in Providence, Rhode Island, in 1864 and organized a boycott of employers who hired strikebreakers. In April 1864 women sewing machine operators in New York started the Working Women's Union. In 1867 the Cigar Makers' International Union began to admit women as members, and the National Typographical Union followed.

The National Labor Union called for equal pay for equal work, a slogan still relevant over 150 years later. Raising women's pay to the same level as men's was not only fair; it also denied capitalists the ability to save money—and thereby increase their profits—by hiring women instead of men. Women's right to vote was another issue raised by the labor movement. Susan B. Anthony and Elizabeth Cady Stanton attended the 1868 convention of the National Labor Union in order to advocate for labor's support for suffrage. While labor generally supported women on the issue of voting rights, Stanton was criticized for supporting women who accepted jobs while men were striking. Identity politics was thus another challenge to a united labor movement.

Employers also used race to divide workers, and so the National Labor Union called for organizing African American workers for much the same reasons as those applicable to organizing women. Owners of the Miners National Association in Ohio hired Blacks to break strikes in 1874 and 1875. In April 1877, 1,500 coal miners struck in Braidwood, Illinois, against the Chicago, Wilmington & Vermillion Coal Company over a third wage reduction within twelve months, which had the effect of reducing wages by 33 percent. The company brought in Black miners to serve as strikebreakers.[15] When corporate owners attempted to divide the working class by race, gender, and ethnicity, the National Labor Union responded by declaring that there were only two groups: laborers and those who lived off someone else's labor. Uriah Stephens, who was later to become the leader of the Knights of Labor, called for labor's support of both women and African American workers.

However, many unions themselves still discriminated against Black workers, refusing to admit them as members and thereby forced them to form their own, segregated unions. In 1870 the National Colored Labor Union called for a legislative lobby to work toward equality for Blacks, an educational campaign directed at white workers, and support for cooperatives and homesteads for African Americans. Reflecting its familiarity with and interest in European and German socialism, the organization even sent a delegate to the First International's Paris Conference.

Labor was even more active in the later years of the nineteenth century when strikes broke out in the textile, coal mining, and transportation industries. Between June and August 1877, two thousand ribbon weavers in Paterson, New Jersey, struck over a 20 percent wage cut. Joseph McDonnell, a radical Irish nationalist, organized textile workers in Paterson and edited the city's *Labor Standard*. McDonnell was a socialist, a member of the First International, an associate of Marx, and strongly supported the Paris Commune.[16]

There were two major lockouts in Pennsylvania in 1873 and 1874, when workers in mines attempted to join unions. One concerned the Cambria Iron Works in Johnstown and the other mine workers in Tioga County. The mine owners in Tioga County maximized their exploitation of the miners in several ways. Aside from paying low wages, the companies owned all of the housing for the miners and the company stores where miners were compelled to shop.

Workers who bought from other than company stores were fined, and the fines were deducted from their wages. Workers were also charged for improvements to the owners' properties, including the cost of roads and other development.[17]

In December 1874 coal operators declared a 20 percent reduction in miners' wages, and the governor of Pennsylvania sent in state troops against the miners. A strike broke out in 1875. Frank Gowen, who was president of the Philadelphia and Reading Railroad and owned the Philadelphia and Reading Coal and Iron Company, set out to crush the Miners' and Laborers' Benevolent Association and ordered pay cuts in order to stimulate a confrontation with the union. He then brought in imported scabs, spies, and a company police force to fight the workers' reaction. Pinkerton detectives infiltrated the Molly Maguires, an organization of primarily Irish coal miners who fought, often violently, the coal barons on behalf of mine workers. The strike was lost, and the Benevolent Association was destroyed.[18] Gowen accused the miners of being foreign agitators, communists, and members of the First International.

Railroad workers struck their employers at the same time. Between November 1873 and July 1874, workers on eighteen separate railroads struck. The only real union for railroad workers at the time was the Brotherhood of Locomotive Engineers. Nevertheless, not only engineers but also firemen, brakemen, track hands, and shop men struck. Most of the strikes occurred in small railroad towns along the line.[19]

During the Panic of 1873, the New York Central laid off 1,400 shop men, and a number of railroads reduced wages. The Pennsylvania Railroad violated a wage contract with the Brotherhood of Locomotive Engineers, and when the union sent a delegation to complain to management, the railroad fired them. Workers for the East Tennessee, Virginia and Georgia Railroad rebelled against a pay cut that did not include a reduction in work hours by removing coupling pins from freight cars. New Jersey Southern employees tore up track and telegraph wires, and workers for the New York and Oswego Midland Railroad tore up track and disabled switches when the company failed to pay them for a period of five months.[20]

On December 26, 1873, three thousand engineers and firemen of the Penn Central walked out in several large cities, including Chicago, Pittsburgh, Cincinnati, Indianapolis, and Louisville. The strike affected the Pittsburgh, Fort

Wayne, and Chicago Railroad, the Little Miami, and the Pittsburgh, Cincinnati and St. Louis Railroad. The Machinists' and Blacksmiths' International Union in Indianapolis refused to work on any Pennsylvania railroad engines. Four hundred workers struck the Erie Railroad in Susquehanna, Pennsylvania, and stopped trains in Hornellsville, New York, and refused to allow them to leave the city.[21]

The railroad strikes of 1873 constituted a preview of what was to occur in 1877. The issues raised by railroad workers during the two series of strikes were similar, and the actions of both labor and capitalists were virtually identical in both cases. The contradictions that existed between labor and capital were not confronted or dealt with in 1873, and were similarly ignored in 1877. As a result, according to the labor and social historian Herbert Gutman, "Three and a half years of severe depression ignited a series of local brush fires into a national conflagration."[22]

German, Bohemian, and French immigrant workers were especially supportive of labor organizations and included many radicals among them. Many had fought in the 1848 uprisings against the German, Austrian, and French governments. Pro-labor newspapers and German revolutionaries were responsible for the American publication of *The Civil War in France*, Marx's contemporary analysis of the Paris Commune of 1871. They worked with the First International in an attempt to stop the importing of strikebreakers from Europe, organized sections of the International in the United States, and founded socialist newspapers and organizations. In April 1869 the New York Compositors Union asked the First International for help against European strikebreakers, and the International called on its various sections in Europe to resolve the problem. In 1869 the National Labor Union sent a delegate to the Basel Congress of the International.

Much of the American labor movement was thus affected by European organizations and events. The German communist F. A. Sorge led the First International after Marx moved its headquarters to New York; in 1857 Sorge founded the Communist Club, which became a section of the International in the United States. By 1872 there were thirty sections and five thousand members of the First International in the United States, who were also active in the American labor movement. The German General Workingmen's Union was founded in New York in 1865 and two years later merged into the First

International. It primarily consisted of Lassalleans, who stressed political action by workers. It merged into the Communist Club in 1868, and Sorge became president of the Social Party of New York. At the end of 1870, ten American sections of the International formed themselves into the North American Central Committee of the First International. Section 1 in New York brought Black workers into the organization and held demonstrations in support of the Paris Commune, reflecting American labor's support for the French insurrection. When the Panic of 1873 threw thousands of workers out of work, the American sections of the First International attempted to organize the unemployed. They demanded public works to aid employment, and the First International supported huge demonstrations of the unemployed in New York and Chicago.

In 1875 the Irish United Workers of America affiliated with the First International. There was some tension between the German and Irish immigrants, especially with regard to the Catholicism of the Irish and the German radical free-thinkers. The German workers, however, were somewhat isolated within their own organizations and communities, and many did not speak English. German radicals were also divided between Marxists and Lassalleans. The Lassalle faction started the Labor Party of Illinois in the West and the Social-Democratic Party of North America in the East. Neither proved to be very successful at the polls. There was then a move to unite all socialist organizations in the United States.

In July 1876 the First International was dissolved at a meeting in Philadelphia. In its place the Workingmen's Party of the United States was established and directed its efforts toward economic matters, engaging in politics only when it believed it was strong enough to do so, which constituted a compromise between Marxists and Lassalleans. The Executive Committee of the Workingmen's Party was headquartered in Chicago.

In the decade following the Civil War, unions were being organized successfully and membership was growing. Twenty trades had organized into 79 unions by December 1863. Seven months later forty trades were reflected in 203 unions. In November 1865, 300 unions represented sixty-one different trades. By 1870 approximately 32 unions were organized on a national level.[23] William Sylvis was the head of the Iron Molders International Union and was active in organizing local chapters and bringing locals into the international union.

His union demanded higher wages, shorter hours, better working conditions, workers' cooperatives, political action, and international worker solidarity. The Iron Molders operated a successful cooperative that employed seventy workers and paid higher wages than were standard in the industry, and still it made a profit. The Knights of Labor, led by Uriah Stephens, was born in 1869 as a secret society that admitted only wage earners as members. The Knights called for the uniting of all workers, notwithstanding their particular trades, and advocated cooperatives and the end of racial discrimination within the labor movement.

But as the employees began to organize nationally, so did industry. Setting out to destroy unions, companies employed lockouts, blacklisting, and the infiltration of unions by spies who reported back to the employers. Anyone who declined to sign an agreement not to join a union was added to a national blacklist and was thereby unable to work in the industry anywhere in the country. Army generals from the North and South, who had fought each other during the Civil War, joined together to fight against workers' actions. Bills were introduced in state legislatures to outlaw strikes. Minnesota and Pennsylvania passed laws allowing striking workers to be evicted from company housing, and Pennsylvania allowed companies to hire private police forces.

A new issue emerged that led labor organizations to unite nationally. The eight-hour workday became a rallying cry for labor and its supporters. In Europe the First International had called for the eight-hour day as a first step in emancipating workers. By 1867 there were hundreds of eight-hour organizations in the United States. Aside from allowing workers to live better lives, part of the reasoning behind the demand was that Civil War soldiers returning to the workplace would result in higher rates of unemployment unless the workday was shortened in order to employ more workers on more shifts.

In August 1866 a national labor convention resulted in the formation of the National Labor Union, which by 1869 had eight hundred thousand members. Congress passed an eight-hour law for federal workers, and a few states and cities followed its lead. Employers again responded by forcing workers to sign contracts agreeing to work more than eight hours a day voluntarily or by cutting their pay proportionately. In New York, 20,000 workers marched in support of the eight-hour day, and in 1872, 100,000 workers struck for three months over the issue, followed by a parade of 150,000 workers.[24] Workers created trade assemblies to coordinate their actions within a trade, such as strikes and boycotts. Others organized cooperative groceries. A bill to outlaw strikes in New York was defeated only when fifteen thousand workers marched against it.

The Panic of 1873 caused another serious blow to union membership and effectiveness. While there were more than thirty national unions in 1873, only eight remained in 1877. Coopers' unions declined in membership from 7,000 to 1,500, and blacksmith and machinist membership dropped by two-thirds. In New York membership in trade unions dropped from 45,000 to 5,000. Nationally membership in trade unions dropped from 300,000 to 50,000.[25] In the building trades, wages fell by 33 to 50 percent and work hours were extended, and wages in the textile industry were reduced by 45 percent. Furniture makers' wages fell by 50 percent, and railroad workers endured several pay cuts constituting approximately 40 percent of their wages. One worker responded by way of a letter to the editor to an opinion that appeared in the *Missouri Republican* that claimed that St. Louis workers were well-treated and well-housed:

> In St. Louis to-day there is far more suffering among the laboring classes than ever heretofore. *They are not well . . . housed*. When families of eight or ten persons are forced to sleep, eat and occupy a room 12x14 for all purposes, huddled in on all sides by other rooms and families situated in the same way, with no opportunity for catching a breath of fresh air that is not impregnated with miasma and effluvia of water-closets, pools of stagnant water, piles of decayed and decaying vegetable matter, piles of filth and ashes surrounding the premises, you cannot call them well housed.[26]

Believing that the mainstream political parties were more concerned with the welfare of capitalists than of workers, labor established its own political parties and ran candidates for public office who workers believed would further their interests. The Labor Reform Party elected twenty-three of its candidates to the Massachusetts Legislature in 1869.

There was an active labor movement in St. Louis after the Civil War, but it was not able to more fully develop until later in the nineteenth century due to the frequent economic depressions. Employees were periodically laid off, and wages were reduced during those periods. Labor issues at the time included worker safety, child labor, and the long hours of the workday. Craft unions of carpenters, cabinet makers, and tin workers had organized locally in the city as early as the 1830s. The main issues for working people were wages, the length of the workday, which was then ten hours, and the need for a mechanic's lien law.

Immigration from Germany and Ireland in the 1850s had the effect of lowering wages as the new immigrants were often willing to work for less and increased the size of the available labor pool. In 1867 several local unions affiliated with the National Labor Union. Originally segregated, the National Labor Union voted at its 1869 convention to admit Blacks, who had previously formed and were members of their own unions, such as the levee workers in Mobile, longshoremen in Charleston, and dock workers in Savannah. However, the National Labor Union was more interested in politics than it was in organizing workers and ultimately became active in the Greenback movement to increase the supply of paper money in the economy.[27] Labor competition primarily affected the unskilled workforce until the Panic of 1873, which adversely affected all workers and virtually destroyed unions in St. Louis. That depression was a primary cause of the railroad strike which broke out in 1877.

Another action taken by labor organizations following the Civil War was the establishment of producer and consumer cooperatives. The idea of producer and consumer cooperatives was popular among working-class thinkers on both sides of the Atlantic. Cooperatives were part of the philosophies of European socialists and anarchists as well as a portion of the American labor movement. Rather than working and consuming at businesses operated by large corporations, workers would own and operate their own businesses and factories and purchase their necessities at stores also owned and operated by workers. By operating cooperatives, workers could control their working conditions, profit from the goods they created, and purchase goods at entities that were more concerned with serving the working public than amassing profits.

Thousands of cooperatives were established both before and following the Civil War by labor unions and organizations. Cooperatives were generally operated on a democratic basis, and all owners, investors and workers, usually had an equal voice in management. They were intended to solve the problem of low wages, employment insecurity, and poor working conditions. The shoemakers of Lynn, Massachusetts, and seamstresses of New York City opened cooperatives in 1845. Molders in Cincinnati organized a foundry in 1848 and showed a profit of almost $6,000 in just over a year.[28] In 1849 Boston tailors established a cooperative, which showed a profit of 4 percent on investment after operating for a year.[29] Shirt sewers opened a cooperative in New York in 1851 that boasted remarkable success. In 1850 and 1851 boot and shoe workers, hat finishers, book binders, carpenters, cabinet makers, and tailors established cooperatives in New York and Buffalo.[30] The Crispins of North Adams, Massachusetts, opened the North Adams Cooperative Shoe Factory, which was cooperatively organized and democratically operated. In 1865 labor activists in Philadelphia called on workers to unite in cooperative ventures: "Co-operation aims at elevating men morally, socially, physically and politically. This it does by freeing them from cankering cares of poverty and wretchedness which chain millions to a merely animal existence. . . . Men of America! Co-operate. Women of America! BUY YOUR GROCERIES AT THE CO-OPERATIVE STORES."[31]

In the 1860s and 1870s most cooperative experiments were operated by shoe workers, molders, carpenters, cigar makers, and machinists. Between 1866 and 1876 shoe workers operated over forty cooperative factories, and molders ran thirty-six foundries and cooperative stores. Most participants in the cooperatives were skilled craftsmen.[32] Over fifty cooperatives were formed in Massachusetts during and immediately after the Civil War. William Sylvis, the president of the Iron Molders' Union and the National Labor Union, was active in the cooperative movement in the 1860s.

The Sovereigns of Industry was founded in January 1874 with the support of Section 26 of the First International. It was especially concerned with establishing cooperatives. The organization bought goods at a wholesale discount, established cooperative grocery stores, set up warehouses to store goods, and used the profits from their enterprises to start other cooperative ventures. In the 1870s St. Louisan John Samuels was the editor of a Grange publication, an organizer for the Sovereigns of Industry, and the founder of a cooperative labor newspaper in St. Louis. John Sheldon, a tailor, was an officer of a section of the First International and later the president of the Sovereigns of Industry.[33]

By the 1870s cooperatives were an important part of the labor movement. John Best was the leader of the movement in Stoneham, Massachusetts. He started the Stoneham Cooperative Boot and Shoe Company. Stoneham had four cooperative shoe factories, two cooperative stores, and a cooperative tannery.[34] All were operated democratically; officers were elected by popular vote; and no action, no matter how small, was taken without a vote of all members. Some complained that cooperatives sometimes took the idea of democracy too far. Elections, for example, were often held to determine the membership of committees which themselves were charged with electing members of other committees. Still, wages were above the local norm, and workers were hardly ever punished for rule violations.

Producer cooperative ventures by workers aimed to improve wages and working conditions from those existing in factories at the time. The wages paid by cooperatives were generally 15 to 66 percent higher than those paid by factory owners.[35] Cooperatives operated by workers also provided more job security. For example, in the 1870s shoe manufacturers generally produced only items that had been specifically ordered. As a result, during slow seasons many workers were laid off. The workers' cooperatives, in contrast, continued to produce even through slow times, thereby providing steady work for their employees. Finally, cooperatives sought to end the exploitation of labor by removing the incentive to maximize profits.

Consumer cooperatives sought to provide necessities for working-class families at a lower cost than privately owned businesses. Again, they were not primarily interested in garnering the greatest profit possible. They were usually based in the working-class communities and served as meeting places for friends and neighbors, thereby contributing to the sense of working-class community.

Unfortunately most cooperatives eventually failed as a result of the depressions in 1857 and 1873. Most were undercapitalized, as workers simply did not have the extra money with which to survive financial crises. But while they existed, they provided workers with a decent living, the pride of ownership and labor, and the dignity that was absent from the factory setting. For a while they provided hope for the most vulnerable. A poem in the *Iron Molders' Journal* of May 1877 reflected that sense of mutual aid, cooperation, and community:

Brothers for years we've struggled vainly
In a hopeless uphill fight.
But at last the clouds are breaking
Before a gleaming light. . . .
For brothers 'tis the only way,
This co-operative plan,
By which labor may rule labor,
And a man may be a man. . . .
But the tyrants watch us keenly,
Us the men they so oft stung,
They hope to see our prospects blasted,
And to hear our death-knell rung.
But we have nailed our colors to the mast,
So we are bound to do our best,
And thus, the co-operators of the East,
Send a greeting to the West.[36]

The American working class during the mid- to late nineteenth century experienced a substantial change in daily life. Wage-earning factory workers largely replaced skilled artisans and small producers and shopkeepers. Machines replaced workers and destroyed individual businesses operated by skilled workers. Wages were low, and working conditions were poor and often dangerous. Both men and women worked long hours for little reward. Workers' unions and organizations were born, grew, and perished during the various depressions. Many workers were unemployed as a result of the booms and busts that characterized nineteenth-century capitalism and occurred both prior and subsequent to the Civil War. American workers were supported and influenced by European, especially German, revolutionaries and radical institutions, such as the First International, which ultimately led to the establishment of the St. Louis Commune.

7

German Immigration

One can argue forcefully that if it were not for German immigration to the city of St. Louis, there would have been no St. Louis general strike nor St. Louis Commune. The 1848 Revolution in Germany and the emigration of many of those revolutionaries from Germany to St. Louis provided the philosophy and leadership for the uprising there.

German immigrants came to St. Louis for economic, political, and religious reasons. Like most immigrants, they sought better lives where there was greater opportunity for those willing to work hard, free from European economic stagnation and feudal burdens. Some sought a place where they would be able to practice their religious beliefs freely, without restrictions by the state. Others, especially those who arrived after 1848, sought to live their lives in a republic and leave behind the remnants of monarchy and aristocracy. For the latter group, the United States seemed a model for republican civic engagement and civil and political rights, which they had attempted to attain in their native land.

Many of these so-called Forty-Eighters were free thinkers, radicals, socialists, and communists. They brought with them philosophies that at the time were virtually absent from mainstream American thinking. They opposed slavery and supported the Enlightenment ideals of humanism, individual rights, and dignity. A plurality of the best educated believed in socialism and were followers of Marx or Lassalle and brought those ideas to the forefront of the emerging battle between labor and capital in the United States. Many had participated in the 1848 revolutions, the Paris Commune, and the First International. They assumed leadership positions in the 1877 strike and the St. Louis Commune, causing those events to take on a radical and socialist character.

Prior to the German Revolution in 1848, most Germans had immigrated to the United States in colonial times and again in the 1830s. Those who arrived in the colonies came largely as the result of a depression following the Thirty Years' War in the seventeenth century and the War of Spanish Succession at the beginning of the eighteenth century, the famines that swept German-speaking Europe at those times, and because of religious intolerance. The Rhineland was devastated by the War of Spanish Succession, which was eventually won by England.[1]

In 1681 Quakers and Mennonites arrived in Pennsylvania, followed by over 100,000 immigrants from Europe at the beginning of the colonial period. Approximately, 250,000 Germans lived in the colonies prior to the American Revolution.[2] Most were so poor that they had to indenture themselves in order to pay for their passage or became farmers who lived on the eastern seaboard and the mid-Atlantic regions; they largely followed Lutheran and the Reform churches or were members of pietist sects such as Mennonites or other radical Reformationists. Many were illiterate and resisted secular education in favor of religious teaching.

Other waves of German immigration to the United States occurred after the revolutions of 1830 and 1848. Between 1831 and 1880, approximately 3 million German-speaking immigrants arrived in America. Some arrived at eastern port cities, while others landed in New Orleans, many then moving up the Mississippi River to St. Louis. Many were skilled workers such as bakers, butchers, tailors, machinists, cigar makers, and cabinet makers.[3] Approximately one-fourth of the immigrants were farmers; one-third were Catholic and the other two-thirds were Protestants. Most settled in what became known as the German Triangle, the cities of Cincinnati, Milwaukee, and St. Louis. The 1860 census reflected that in the city of Milwaukee, 38 percent of German-born heads of households were skilled workers, compared, for example, with 19 percent of Irish households.[4]

After the fall of Napoleon in 1815, there was a good deal of repression by Metternich in Austria and by the princes of the German states. Protest was ruthlessly crushed in German-speaking Europe. Consisting mainly of farmers and artisans, immigrants during the 1830s generally settled farther west in cities such as Cincinnati and St. Louis. They were sufficiently numerous to establish German-language newspapers and German cultural organizations and entities, including Turner societies, gymnastic clubs that supported German culture and progressive ideas such as abolitionism and republicanism. The St. Louis *Anzeiger des Westens*, a German-language newspaper, was established in the 1830s to serve the city's growing German community. It was a progressive paper, as was its later English-language edition, which became the *St. Louis Post-Dispatch*, and which at one time was led by Joseph Pulitzer.[5]

Some of the new arrivals were educated, but most were not. Most hoped to make their living by farming. Not all the Germans who settled in Missouri and southern Illinois had experience farming, however. They were attracted to the idea of free land in America and an opportunity to own and work their own property and live independent lives. Many came in groups, so that they could provide support for each other in a new country where they did not have jobs or property and did not speak the language. Members of the different groups had different interests and skills; some were skilled artisans. One immigrant described the different interests in his group that was planning to emigrate from Germany: "We shall bring along with us persons who will pursue different occupations, some Mechanics, some Waggoners, Husbandmen, all of whom wish to make a living."[6] Some immigrants had studied at or held university degrees. Those who were educated and sought to attempt farming were often referred to as "Latin farmers" by their rural neighbors because they were educated in the classics but had little or no knowledge of or experience in farming. Belleville, Illinois, across the Mississippi River from St. Louis, was one such German "Latin farmer" settlement.

Interest in emigrating from the German states and settling in Missouri and the St. Louis area was a result of both national and local factors. In the United States there appeared to be opportunity; there was no king or feudal class ruling the country; a person was not condemned to live his or her entire life as part of the class in which he or she was born; and there was the attraction of free land, free elections, religious freedom, and democracy, things that had been prohibited in Germany. And the landscape of Missouri, with its hills and rivers, reminded them of home. Many Germans were already living in Missouri and St. Louis, thus providing support for new immigrants. They were also attracted by the writings of Germans who had come to the area and advertised its benefits to those back home in letters and publications.

Gottfried Duden was one visitor to Missouri who spread word of its attractiveness as a new home to those in German-speaking countries who were interested in starting a new life somewhere else. Duden had held important positions in Prussia. He came to St. Louis in 1824, read about Daniel Boone and about westward expansion, and bought approximately a hundred acres in 1829 near the Missouri River, not far from Boone's last home. Bringing with him a farmer and a cook, Duden farmed for about three years, returned to Europe, and wrote about his experiences in his book *Report of a Journey to the Western States of North America*. He described Missouri's moderate weather and good farmland, the freedom to live wherever one desired, the religious freedom, and the absence of a king. As a result of his letters and books, Duden interested other Germans in immigrating to Missouri.

Duden suggested that those immigrating to Missouri travel and settle in groups instead of alone, so that they would have a support system when they arrived. A group of his followers set out to establish a community in Arkansas but ended up in Missouri.[7] Groups of Germans settled near Duden's land and organized their own villages. Some even spoke of creating a German state within Missouri. Many of those who chose city living over farming settled in the Carondelet area of south St. Louis.

Friedrich Muench also wrote about the joys and benefits of living and farming in Missouri. Muench was a liberal and a progressive, who was drawn to the United States by the promise of the freedoms of speech, press, and religion. Freedom from the feudal remnants still surviving in Europe, especially in the German states, was another reason to emigrate, according to Muench. In the United States one was limited not by the status of birth but only by the extent of one's willingness to engage in hard work. "Yet, I say as citizens of this country we are more fortunate than those in the old world. Here freedom of expression is tolerated. We have a far freer nucleus of sound citizenship than any other country. . . . Here no one is condemned because of his birth, or compelled to an humble position due to it. The field is open to everyone whose earnest efforts qualify him for it."[8] Another early Missouri settler, Paul Follenius, was a successful lawyer who desired to become a farmer. He ultimately became the editor of a German-language newspaper in St. Louis. So many German immigrants settled in Missouri that the names of its towns mirrored those in the German states: Berlin, Dresden, Frankford, Baden, and Wittenberg. Towns were also named Bismarck and Germania.

The 1848 revolutions began in France and spread throughout Europe. They posited the ideas of liberalism, republicanism, radicalism, and socialism against feudalism, monarchy, and royalty. Many of the ideas were a result of the 1789 French Revolution, such as liberty and equality, which had been spread in Europe by Napoleon's army and Enlightenment beliefs in rationalism, education, and social progress. Revolutionaries sought to overthrow the conservative forces that ruled Europe after Napoleon's defeat. The 1815 Congress of Vienna had returned monarchs to their thrones and established the German Confederation, a weak organization dominated by Prussia. Revolutionaries called for the establishment of republics, national unification, and more freedom and self-government. Liberals and radicals allied against the feudal elements but ultimately divided along class lines when their common enemy was defeated. The revolutions failed in overthrowing most governments, although they did result in greater powers for the new capitalist bourgeoisie.

Radicals, socialists, and the working classes of Europe were crushed by the terrific repression that followed the 1848 revolutions, and again many fled to other countries, including a massive immigration to the United States by members of Europe's working class. Many Germans also came for economic reasons. German-speaking areas were experiencing the early stages of the Industrial Revolution, and craftsmen were being replaced by machines and the factory system. Unions were as yet undeveloped. At the same time there was high unemployment and crop failures. Potato prices in the German states increased 425 percent between 1845 and 1847. There were food riots, and the winter of 1847–48 was unusually severe. Many Germans were attracted by the possibility of jobs, higher wages, and cheap or free land in America. The seemingly empty lands in the American West—that is, empty of European settlement—appeared to promise the individual freedom that was lacking in Europe. Others came for political reasons, the greater freedom and less governmental repression than in Europe.

Many of the later arrivals who tried farming failed in the endeavor and eventually migrated to the cities. The picture of a rural, independent existence was charming, but not necessarily a good fit for educated professionals, who eventually rejected the difficult physical work of farming. In the little time they had for recreation, their farmer neighbors did not share their desire for discussions about history and philosophy. Frederick Wittke described the Ohio Latin farmer who worked the fields in a dress coat and top hat, and Frederick Olmsted told of one Forty-Eighter who, in his country home, served coffee in tin cups placed on Dresden saucers and whose bookcases were filled with the classics and sweet potatoes.

Cities proved to be more popular places to live for those who gave up on rural life. German saloons in Milwaukee, for example, were said to witness political and philosophical discussions at a high intellectual level.[9] David Goebel, a German professor of math, found that farming was not for him and moved to St. Louis to take a job with the U.S. Land Survey Office.[10] Some who did not want to give up entirely on the dream of independence that farming promised became grape and wine growers. The hills and rivers of Missouri reminded them of home, and they started some successful wine production companies in the state. In a speech titled "The German Contribution to Missouri" before the Missouri Historical Society in January 1947, Judge Julius Muench spoke of the distinction between the earlier and later German immigrants to Missouri: "What distinguished the immigration after 1830 from any that had gone before was, of course, the large proportion of educated individuals, in the first instance."[11] Muench went on to say that St. Louis had as many German-language newspapers as English ones, reflecting the literacy of the new immigrants.

The total foreign-born U.S. population increased 85 percent during the 1850s.[12] In 1848, 62,684 Germans entered the United States; in 1854 that number grew to 229,562. The increase was supported by some of the German governments, which sought to rid themselves of those they viewed as troublemakers. Advertisements by American steamship and land companies attempting to increase their business attracted more Germans to American shores. The German Immigration Society of St. Louis was founded in 1859, growing out of the St. Louis German Immigrant Society, which was formed in 1847. The societies provided interpreters and aided immigrants in obtaining work.

The large German population of St. Louis was another feature luring Germans to the city. Immigrants arrived by train from eastern port cities and by boat from New Orleans. Between 1848 and 1852, over fifty thousand German immigrants arrived in St. Louis, many aided by the St. Louis German Emigrant Aid Society. In 1855 the Society found jobs for 283 Germans on the railroads, 192 on farms and in factories, 121 in workshops, 163 as female domestics, 35 artisans, 1 teacher, and 6 store employees and apprentices.[13] By 1850 one-third of St. Louis's population had been born in Germany.[14] The city took on a German personality, attracting new German immigrants to a place where they could feel at home in the midst of the German language, customs, and culture.[15] In his novel *The Crisis*, St. Louis's Winston Churchill described the city's southside German community:

> Richter took him across the Rhine. The Rhine was Market Street, and south of that street was a country of which polite American society took no cognizance.
>
> Here was an epic movement indeed, for South St. Louis was a great sod uprooted from the Fatherland and set down in all its vigorous crudity in the warm black mud of the Mississippi Valley. Here lager beer took the place of Bourbon, and black bread and sausages of hot rolls and fried chicken. Here were quaint market-houses squatting in the middle of wide streets; Lutheran churches, square and uncompromising, and bulky Turner Halls, where German children were taught the German tongue.[16]

In a letter dated July 4, 1847, Emil Mallinckrodt, the immigrant parent of the founders of Mallinckrodt Chemical Company, wrote home, "One hears much low German on the streets and markets, and all Germans are without exception, well off. They own one-third of St. Louis. . . . We live here as if in Germany wholly surrounded by Germans. Missouri is now becoming Germany for America."[17]

When the Forty-Eighters arrived in St. Louis, the city was an industrial and agricultural center. Agricultural products shipped east passed through, as did commodities going west and south. Additionally St. Louis was exploding as a manufacturing location as a result of its tremendous mineral deposits. During the 1840s and 1850s Missouri was second only to Pennsylvania in the iron industry due to its extensive iron ore deposits. The industry flourished during and after the Civil War, as Carondelet foundries built Union gunboats and steel rails for the expanding railroads. The city was also growing quickly in population and geographically, spreading farther and farther west from its eastern border on the Mississippi River. The population of St. Louis had grown from 74,000 in 1849 to 750,000 by 1880. In an April 1841 letter, Mallinckrodt described the riches to be made in real estate as a result of the city's phenomenal growth: "The City of St. Louis has grown within a distance of five minutes from our place and will soon be useful to us. In a few years we shall be living in the middle of the city and will earn a great competence through our property."[18] By the end of the 1840s one could almost triple one's investment in real estate within just a few weeks: "Last April I bought a place of seven acres for $3,700 and was offered $9,500 for it in six weeks. St. Louis will be greater than London."[19] Mallinckrodt was not the only one to recognize St. Louis's explosive growth and future. In a letter from Karl Bernays, a journalist and friend of Karl Marx, to Heinrich Boernstein, Bernays prophesied the city's future: "St. Louis is on the way to becoming the greatest city of the Union, it progresses with such giant strides. The greatest trading centers in Europe—Hamburg, Marseilles and La Havre—are trifles in comparison with St. Louis and its future."[20] Remarking on the future of the city, the *Mississippi Blatter* foresaw St. Louis as a unique success: "St. Louis will someday be the capitol of an empire of fifty million free people."[21]

Friedrich Hecker was a Baden intellectual who immigrated to the United States in September 1848. He tried his hand at farming in German settlements in southern Illinois, across the river from St. Louis. Hecker had been a democratic radical in Germany and brought those views to the American stage. He had participated in the German Revolution, seeking a democratic government, and he believed strongly in the American republic and its Constitution. He believed that landownership enabled people to become independent citizens, and he was one of the few Latin farmers who was successful at it. Hecker was one of the founders of the Republican Party; he was active in the Civil War, where he was a member of Franz Sigel's Third Missouri Volunteer Regiment and later served as a colonel in the Eighty-Second Illinois Volunteers, the liberal Republican reform movement, and a number of presidential campaigns.[22] While Hecker was not a revolutionary socialist, he did believe that the community should help the individual, that communities should associate with each other, share tools, purchase together in bulk, and act in a cooperative fashion. The *Democratic Press* in Chicago called Hecker, a frequent speaker on political matters throughout Illinois, "the most influential German in America."[23] In 1869 he helped Carl Schurz, a co-owner and publisher of the *Westliche Post*, get elected to the U.S. Senate from Missouri.

Although they no longer lived in German states, the Germans who settled in America followed events there carefully. They retained an interest in German unification and republicanism. The German-language newspapers were filled with news of German events. Money was raised in every German American community for political refugees and revolutionaries who remained in the German states. Dinners and benefit concerts were held to raise funds to send home. Weekly newspapers grew into dailies in order to satisfy the demand for news from the old country. Many Germans returned home in order to work for the establishment of a republic. Germans from Europe also toured the United States in order to raise interest in and money for another revolution. Gottfried Kinkel, who was wounded in the Revolution of 1848, was arrested and sentenced to life imprisonment, and then was freed by the efforts of Carl Schurz, traveled to America from London for that purpose. A crowd of five thousand listened to him speak in Philadelphia. In Cincinnati his speech was accompanied by a torchlight parade and a speech by the city's mayor. Another torchlight parade greeted him in Milwaukee. In St. Louis he engaged in a five-hour debate with Boernstein.

Parades and meetings were held in many cities that hosted a large German population. On May 8, 1848, over one hundred thousand attended a parade and service for those who died in the 1848 Revolution. In Baltimore the mayor, a senator, and Gen. Sam Houston addressed a German patriotic meeting. In April 1848 in Milwaukee a king was burned in effigy and Germans, Irish, French, and Scandinavians marched amid fireworks. Also that month St. Louis Germans, together with French, Italians, Poles, and Irish, participated in a huge demonstration which included a torchlight procession. Illinois's lieutenant governor Gustave Koerner spoke in Belleville, Illinois, and several hundred copies of his speech were sent to the German states for distribution. Resolutions were passed calling for a German republic and the unification of the German states. A crowd of twenty thousand cheered Hecker, the German republican and revolutionary, when he arrived in the United States in 1848. Hecker called for the establishment of a permanent revolutionary society to be located in St. Louis.

There did emerge divisions in German communities between the Forty-Eighters and the older German residents. Those who had lived in the United States for some time were referred to as the Grays, and the newcomers were known as the Greens. The Greens were more highly educated and wealthier. Many had been professionals in Germany, lawyers, journalists, or teachers. Unlike the earlier immigrants, the Greens came primarily for political rather than economic reasons. Having been leaders in Germany, they felt that they should lead the American German communities. Many of the Grays felt that the Greens were too arrogant and intolerant.

Other factors that affected the division among Germans were religion and politics. The lives of the more religious Germans centered on their churches, while radical Germans joined clubs reflecting their political interests. Older German residents were largely Lutheran and some Catholic. While the Catholics appeared to be more moderate, Missouri German Lutherans were very conservative. The Missouri Synod was led by Dr. C. F. W. Walther, an extreme conservative who referred to abolitionists as atheists, socialists, and communists. On the other hand, the Forty-Eighters were primarily free-thinkers, irreligious or atheists. The churches in the German states had largely supported the governments and their police states, so they were fervently opposed by the Forty-Eighters, whose membership included republicans, radicals, socialists, and revolutionaries. They viewed the earlier immigrants as uneducated, almost illiterate, and reactionary and believed that it was up to them to save German culture from the philistines.

While many German immigrants followed mainstream religions, the new arrivals contained a good many free-thinkers and atheists. The Free Congregation of North St. Louis was one such group. Its purpose was "primarily the education of youth by suitable school instruction from which was to be excluded all religious thinking. In the place of the latter, pure moral and ethical teaching was to be substituted."[24] Although it appears to be an oxymoron, during the American Civil War German soldiers had their own "atheist chaplain," who ministered ethics and morality to the troops rather than religious doctrine. The German writer Christian Esselen and many other German intellectuals were opposed to all faith-based religion, especially Catholicism, and sought to bring enlightenment to America by lecturing, operating newspapers, and writing pamphlets. The editors of the *Antiplaft of St. Louis* attacked both Catholics and Lutherans. A meeting of German freethinkers in St. Louis marched on a Jesuit monastery, where rumor claimed that a German was being held prisoner. Milwaukee's *Volksfreund* newspaper called for all Jesuits to be hanged. Boernstein's *Anzeiger des Westens* was consumed with opposition to the Jesuits, representing his personal views. A papal nuncio was sent to Cincinnati, where a thousand protestors who blamed the Catholic Church for the failure of the 1848 Revolution hung his effigy on a gallows. Historian Carl Frederick Wittke claimed that some German free-thinkers "out-know-nothinged" the Know Nothings in their prejudice against the Catholic Church.[25]

Forty-Eighters met in clubs, coffee houses, and saloons in St. Louis and Milwaukee to discuss politics. Before much time had passed, many talked about returning to Europe to fight in the next revolution. They organized militias in different cities, where they could train militarily and return to Germany at a moment's notice. They sought American aid in bringing about such a revolution, but such talk died down after a few years when they became more settled. They then turned their attention to reform in the United States. Their interests in reform extended from opposition to temperance and the Sunday Blue Laws to antislavery.

Many of the 1848 radicals had experience in journalism and started German-language newspapers in their new communities. By 1880 approximately 80 percent of all foreign-language newspapers in the United States were German.[26]

Those papers were generally liberal or radical in their political views. The leading German-language newspapers in St. Louis were the *Anzeiger des Westens* and the *Westliche Post*. Boernstein's *Anzeiger* was the oldest German-language newspaper west of the Mississippi. Boernstein was extremely anticlerical, especially with regard to Catholics, Jesuits in particular. But he had other interests in the German community in St. Louis, many of them related to German culture. When not editing his newspaper, he worked as an actor, playwright, theater manager, and hotel manager and ran a brewery and several saloons. He was especially struck by the materialism and individualism that he found when he reached the United States. It seemed to him that Americans were interested only in making money, that each person was on his own, and that there was a lack of community. A strong abolitionist, Boernstein was an early supporter of the Republican Party, served as the U.S. consul to Bremen under Lincoln, and eventually returned to Vienna.[27]

Other German revolutionaries settled in St. Louis and entered the newspaper business. Karl Bernays, a friend of Marx, was a lawyer and partner of Boernstein. He arrived in the United States in 1848, served as a colonel in the Union army, and later was U.S. consul to Zurich. Karl Dänzer (also known as Karl Daenzer) fought in the 1848 Revolution in Germany, became editor of the *Anzeiger des Westens*, and in 1857 founded the *Westliche Post*. Emil Praetorius came to St. Louis in 1853 after earning a doctorate in law. He worked as editor of the *Westliche Post* and later founded *Die Neue Zeit*, which eventually merged with the *Westliche Post*. He was an abolitionist and a Republican, worked to elect Lincoln in 1860, and supported complete equality for Blacks. In 1867 Carl Schurz joined Praetorius at the *Post*, which became one of the most important papers in the upper Mississippi Valley. Schurz had participated in the 1848 Revolution in Germany and would later become Grant's secretary of the interior, as well as a Missouri senator. Nevertheless, although Schurz traded the barricades for a more mainstream political life in the United States, many Americans, especially from the South, found it impossible to ignore his more radical past. An Arkansan named Joseph Elder wrote to attorney James Broadhead in June 1861, "Look at the appointments made by Lincoln; to name one, as a type, (& that one enough to damn him to eternal infamy in the eyes of a Christian) the appointment of the blasphemous red Republican infidel Carl Schurz."[28]

Like the Paris communards, the Forty-Eighters supported free secular education and sought to remove the teaching of religion from the schools. In the United States, they established German-language schools and evening schools for adults, as well as series of lectures on important subjects. Franz Sigel, who became a Union general during the Civil War, taught at such schools in St. Louis. They also brought the concept of kindergarten to the United States. Schurz's wife was active in the kindergarten movement; the first such school in the United States was opened in the Carondelet area of St. Louis by Susan Blow. They also instituted schools for the training of teachers.

St. Louis and other Germans made important contributions in other areas related to their interest in education. The suggestion that druggists should be trained in chemistry was raised by the Forty-Eighters. Enno Sander, a radical journalist, founded the American Pharmaceutical Society in St. Louis in 1858 and the St. Louis College of Pharmacy in 1863. In 1854 one-third of the doctors in New York were German immigrants who had received much more intensive training than did American doctors, who were required only to attend a year's worth of lectures. A St. Louis surgeon, Dr. Louis Bauer, founded the College of Physicians and Surgeons. Dr. Adam Hammer opened a German medical school in St. Louis in 1859. Dr. Philipp Weigel was the surgeon general of Missouri during the Civil War. Dr. Gustav Carl Erich was surgeon general of Ohio troops during the Civil War and later served as dean of what became the medical department of Western Reserve University. Dr. Ernst Schmidt served in the American Civil War, was chief of staff at Michael Reese Hospital in Chicago, ran for mayor in Chicago in 1879 on the Socialist Labor Party ticket, and was treasurer for the defense committee for the Haymarket anarchists.[29] Dr. Abraham Jacob was prosecuted in Germany for his participation in the 1848 Revolution; he was a socialist who, after immigrating to the United States, studied and wrote about the health of immigrant children living in tenements. He founded the *American Journal of Obstetrics*, was president of the American Medical Association, and received honorary degrees from Yale, Harvard, Columbia, and the University of Michigan.

The survivors of the 1848 Revolution in Germany contributed to still other fields in American society. Henry Villard was a journalist and war correspondent who married the abolitionist publisher William Lloyd Garrison's daughter and later became president of the Oregon and California Railroad and the Northern Pacific Railroad Company. He helped Thomas Edison establish his electric company. Heinrich Steinweg started a piano manufacturing company that grew to one of the largest in the world. Germans also held a virtual monopoly in the brewing of beer. Many Forty-Eighters owned breweries throughout the United States, including C. F. Kiefer in Philadelphia; C. W. Schmidt in Cleveland; Meinrad Kleiner in Cincinnati; Carl Gehm in Quincy, Massachusetts; the Lenk Brothers in Toledo, Ohio; and Mathias Frahm in Davenport, Iowa.[30]

The arts was another area in which the Forty-Eighters contributed to American culture and society. Theodor Kaufmann came to the United States in 1850 and opened and operated an art school in New York, where the political cartoonist Thomas Nast was one of his students. Henry Ulke fought on the barricades in Berlin in 1848 and later was chosen to paint a portrait of President Grant, which hung in the White House. Ulke's natural science collection resides in the Carnegie Institute in Pittsburgh. Julius Bien arrived in the United States in 1848 and gained fame for producing the plates for Audubon's *Birds of America*. He also prepared most of the maps issued by the U.S. government until 1900. John Gindele was a Chicago architect who served as chairman of the Illinois Board of Public Works and president of the Michigan-Illinois Canal Board. He designed Chicago's Lincoln Park.

German immigrants founded and operated some of the most important businesses in St. Louis: the Helmbacher Forge and Rolling Mills Company, the John J. Gandahl Lumber Company, the Regina Flour Mill, the William J. Lemp Brewing Company, the Nedderhuth Packing and Provision Company, the Mallinckrodt Chemical Works, the St. Louis Iron and Machine Works, and the Gast Wine Company.

Laboring six days a week, German workers looked forward to rest and recreation on Sundays. In the German states, Sundays were often spent socializing with friends and family at local beer halls, which provided food, drink, and music for dancing. St. Louis's Camp Spring Garden was filled with German families on Sundays. Beer and sausages were sold, people danced, and families socialized. Concerts were held on Sundays at Union Park in south St. Louis, and festivals were held at Concordia Park. One celebration that occurred after the end of the Franco-Prussian War drew hordes of people "celebrating the unification of Germany, and the victory of Germany over France. All the German element of St. Louis took part in it . . . all the singing societies, Turner societies, church organizations, without consideration of their faith, all German lodges, and other societies participated with complete unity of purpose."[31] The festival collected $20,000 for the Germans wounded in the war. In St. Louis the Gambrinus Society held a parade on May Day in 1858 in support of lager beer, and hundreds of Germans marched behind floats. Beer was synonymous with freedom, family, and recreation for the German immigrants and was therefore important to them.

However, partying and drinking on Sundays conflicted with the American Christian view of the manner in which a Sunday should be spent. Beer and spirits had no place on Sundays, a day set aside for church attendance and other activities more holy than drinking and partying. The cultural conflict was fanned by the St. Louis police, who had been placed under state control by a pro-Confederate governor and who were ordered to enforce Sunday closing laws against German recreational places. St. Louis mayor Washington King instituted policies supported by the Know Nothings in 1855 and closed Irish pubs and German beer gardens on Sundays. He did, however, allow hotel bars to remain open. Bigotry was masquerading as morality, a hypocrisy that did not go unnoticed in the German community.[32]

One Forty-Eighter described a St. Louis Sunday in the United States as the whole city in a cemetery. In St. Louis some Germans advertised their planned Sunday fun in Boernstein's newspaper, resulting in his arrest and conviction for contempt of court. In 1869 American Fourth of July celebrations were moved from Sunday, the actual day on which July 4 fell that year, to Monday, as it was considered sacrilegious to hold such a celebration on the Lord's day. But the Germans insisted on celebrating the holiday on the day on which it fell, not the next day. Parades of Germans accompanied by large bands paraded through the streets on a July 4 Sunday, drinking beer and celebrating the holiday, while others looked on in dismay.

Enjoying the discussion of philosophy and politics, the Forty-Eighters brought with them from Europe new ideas that would take root on American soil. They founded libraries that contained radical literature and lectured about politics, labor, and socialism. As radicals and socialists, they were strongly against slavery and supported a ten-hour workday, public education, and a progressive tax system. The German workers' movement was the basis for the first socialist parties in the United States.

An important cultural group for the German immigrants was the Turner societies. Founded in Berlin in 1811 as gymnastic societies, Turner groups existed in the United States earlier than 1848. However, they were especially popular with the Forty-Eighters. The Turner societies believed in the adage *mens sana in corpore sano*, a sound mind in a sound body. While primarily sports and cultural organizations, in the German states they were also used to hide certain revolutionary activities. Turner society members had trained revolutionaries in the German states in 1848 and had fought on the barricades with them. They had been suppressed by Metternich in the Austro-Hungarian Empire.

In the United States, Turner societies became the center for German radicalism and abolitionism during the 1850s. The Turners supported free public, secular education, and many Turner members served in the Union army. Every major American city with a meaningful German population hosted one or more Turner groups. A Turner group was started in Cincinnati in 1848, in Milwaukee and St. Louis in 1850, and in Chicago in 1852. By 1855 there were Turner societies in twenty-six states.[33] St. Louis was the main location for fostering Turner activity in the United States.[34] They sometimes had a difficult time functioning and attracting members in more Southern locations because of their abolitionist views.

The Forty-Eighters brought their radical views to the American chapters of the organization. Once again, their beliefs did not significantly differ from those who had supported or fought in the 1848 Revolution or the Paris Commune. The Turners demanded social welfare legislation, more rights for women, labor reform, secular education, an eight-hour workday, child labor laws, a progressive income tax, and public ownership of utilities. While they sought to reform certain parts of American society, they also admired it for its republicanism, lack of artificial class lines, and especially its Bill of Rights, all things they had fought for in the 1848 Revolution. In 1846 the national Turner Society supported the Free Soil Party. The Louisville Platform of 1854 called for an end to slavery, the end of racial and class privileges, anticlericalism, free land for settlers, equal rights for Blacks and women, a shortening of citizenship residency requirements, internal improvements supported by the federal government, prison and educational reforms, and more social legislation. One response to their demands was a riot by Know Nothings in Louisville in 1855.

The St. Louis Turners sponsored weekly lectures on progressive topics, had rifle drills, trained in Prussian military tactics, and formed the first companies of the First Regiment of the Missouri Volunteers. They established a library, a burial society, and a singing society. They began military drilling in 1861 in support of the Union, and their gymnasium was converted into a barracks. While most of Missouri supported the Confederacy, the St. Louis Turners were strongly antislavery and pro-Union and largely contributed to the defeat of Missouri's Confederate sympathizers. The movement of the Turners toward socialism was initially rejected as foreign to American thought and politics.

A German Workers Party was founded in Detroit in 1850, which was supported by many German-language newspapers, many of them published by German radicals. Gottfried Kellner was one such radical newspaper editor in Germany and later in New York and Philadelphia. Henry Meyer arrived in the United States in 1852, was influenced by Marx's friend Joseph Weydemeyer, worked in Milwaukee and St. Louis, and organized various sections of the First International in the United States. F. A. Sorge was a musician who fought in the 1848 German Revolution and arrived in the United States in 1852. In 1859 he joined the German Communist Club in New York and became the general secretary of the First International when it was relocated from London to New York.

Joseph Weydemeyer served in the Prussian army and later became a journalist. He was the assistant editor of the *Triersche Zeitung*, a German democratic and socialist newspaper. In 1845 he became editor of the *Westphaelische Dampfboot*, another socialist paper. Weydemeyer was a friend and follower of Marx and defended Marx's view of scientific socialism. He fled Germany for Switzerland, from which he later immigrated to the United States. He arrived in New York in 1851 with a letter of introduction from Marx to Charles Dana, the managing editor of the *New York Tribune*, a powerful Republican newspaper. Weydemeyer became an organizer for the Communist League, founded the Marxist newspaper *Die Revolution* in New York, and acted as the American literary agent for Marx and Engels. As such, he published Marx's *Eighteenth Brumaire of Louis Bonaparte* and *The Communist Manifesto* and carried on a regular correspondence with Marx and Engels.[35] Weydemeyer formed the Proletarian League in New York, which marked the beginning of the Marxist movement in the United States. He lived in Chicago, Milwaukee, and St. Louis. In Milwaukee he worked as a surveyor and was a regular contributor to the *Illinois Staats-Zeitung*, the leading German-language newspaper in the Midwest. He served in the American Civil War as a colonel, and after the war he wrote for the *Neue Zeit* in St. Louis and served on its editorial board. He was given command of the St. Louis District during the war. He started branches of the First International in the United States, was elected county auditor in St. Louis, and died of cholera in St. Louis on August 20, 1866.

Unlike European countries, the United States has, from its very beginning, consisted of different races, nationalities, and religions. As a result, the American working class was divided by those same factors. Weydemeyer sought to unite all working people in the United States as a class, irrespective of their other differences. The Proletarian League brought together German trade unions to form the American Workers League in an attempt to unite American workers. German unions such as the carpenters, shoemakers, tailors, painters, and cigar makers sent delegates to a meeting of the Central Committee of the American Workers' League. In August 1863 forty trades and over two thousand members met in support of striking house painters and called for the formation of a General Trades' Union. In a notice to workers in April 1853, Weydemeyer wrote, "It is . . . essential that we form one organization without distinction as to crafts and national origins, that we may rise up against our tyrannical oppressors, the capitalists and monopolists, in united fashion."[36]

The Forty-Eighters included not only revolutionary Marxists in their number. Several utopian communists came to the United States after the 1848 Revolution hoping to create intentional communities of like-minded people who would govern themselves democratically and share their assets equally. Utopian communism had a long history in the United States and included groups such as the Shakers, the Harmonists in Pennsylvania, the New Harmonists in Indiana, the Amana Colony in Iowa, Oneida in New York, Brook Farm in Massachusetts, Icarians in Illinois, and the various Fourierist colonies. With nineteenth-century Europe in an uproar, many sought new lives without conflict or exploitation in America. Dozens of utopian communist experiments were attempted from the east to the west coasts during the nineteenth century. Wilhelm Weitling was a member of the League of the Just, a French secret society; his vision of communism was a combination of primitive Christianity, French utopianism, and rationalism. Weitling organized the first German Congress in the United States, edited German-language newspapers, and worked for labor and social reforms. Other utopian communists in America were Joseph Stiger in Cleveland, Fritz Anneke in Milwaukee, Sebastian Seiler in New Orleans, and Franz Arnold in Chicago.

Plans to unite disparate groups often ran into trouble in America. During the 1850s, when many of the Forty-Eighters were attempting to settle into their new homeland, there was a huge influx of Irish immigrants as well as Germans. The British textile industry required more cotton with the introduction of the steam engine, and British absentee landowners converted their farms in Ireland to growing cotton. Already poor and hungry, the Irish were dependent on the potato for their survival. When the potato famine struck Ireland, hundreds of thousands died. But another 1.5 million, who were largely unskilled, immigrated to the United States. There they competed with free Blacks and other unskilled workers for jobs, causing friction between the groups. The Irish largely found work in mining and building the railroads.

Germans emigrated from Europe largely as a result of bad harvests, religious persecution, and the failure of the Revolution of 1848. The United States advertised itself as a melting pot of people from different countries and cultures, but despite its self-portrait of welcoming the oppressed, nativism has always been a part of American culture.[37] Many Americans were intolerant of those different from themselves and resented having to support poor immigrants who came from Europe owning virtually nothing. They accused the immigrants of taking American jobs, driving down wages, and importing communist ideas. There were therefore religious, political, and economic motives for their nativism and intolerance toward foreigners.

The 1850s witnessed perhaps the greatest period of bigotry and nativism in the country's history. The Know Nothings attacked foreigners, especially Catholics and anticlericals; they demanded voting restrictions on foreigners, a residency requirement of twenty-one years for citizenship, the prohibition of land grants to unnaturalized foreigners, anti-Catholic laws, a requirement that only native-born Americans could qualify to hold public office, and the reading of the Protestant Bible in public schools.[38] Some saw the Catholic Church behind the increasing political power of immigrants. A mob threw rocks through the windows of the *Anzeiger des Westens* newspaper in 1852; the next year a German group was attacked in New Orleans; and in Hoboken, New Jersey, German picnickers were attacked, beaten, and arrested. In 1855 Know Nothings took control of German Americans' polling places in Cincinnati in an attempt to keep them from voting, resulting in three days of rioting. Incidents occurred in Columbus, Louisville, Baltimore, and other American cities.

St. Louis Irish and German immigrants were divided along ethnic lines. By 1860, 16 percent of St. Louis was Irish, many of whom were pro-slavery since most Irish immigrants were unskilled and would have to compete for work against free Blacks.[39] Germans added to the ethnic tension by their attitude toward the Irish, who they felt were promiscuous, violent, and simple tools of priests and politicians. Catholic priests in turn viewed the Germans as infidels and anarchists. As a result, it was difficult to achieve unity between the two groups. This hostility caused the German and Irish communities to close ranks and to retreat within their own groups, thereby interfering with their assimilation into American society. The Forty-Eighters, however, generally fought against nativism, changing their political support from one party to another based on that issue. At the Republican Convention in 1860, the Republicans were led by Germans who demanded an antinativist position.

The issues of nativism and slavery enabled Republicans to take much of the German vote from the Democrats.[40]

German socialists and republicans were clearly against the institution of slavery. They tended to settle elsewhere than the American South, which was in any case not especially friendly to immigrants. They did not want to live in a place that many of them equated with the feudalism and royalty from which they had fled. Some refused to live in Missouri, which allowed slavery, and settled instead in southern Illinois, directly across the river from St. Louis. Belleville, in St. Clair County, Illinois, was a favorite place for those Germans to settle.

Religion was another relevant factor with regard to determining one's view of slavery. The Catholic Church was for the most part silent on the issue, while the Lutherans were divided into antislavery and pro-slavery groups. The Wisconsin Synod, for example, was against slavery, while the more conservative Missouri Synod supported it. Virtually all the free-thinkers among the German immigrants were against slavery, and the St. Louis *Anzeiger des Westens* and the Turner societies were strongly abolitionist. Most Forty-Eighters were against slavery and urged Germans to leave the Democratic Party over the issue, while most Catholics and conservative Lutherans refused to join the Republican Party. The Forty-Eighters would later be active in forming the new Republican Party, and by the 1856 elections most German immigrants were Republicans. German-language newspapers in St. Louis supported the Republicans; St. Louis stood alone as a Republican city in a Democratic state, largely because of its German population.[41]

In 1860 the first Republican ticket in Missouri included three Germans. Arnold Krekel, a newspaper editor, ran for attorney general; Henry Boernstein ran for superintendent of St. Louis public schools; and Friedrich Muench ran for the St. Louis Board of Public Works. Across the river, Gustave Koerner served as lieutenant governor of Illinois and was a founder of the Republican Party and a close adviser to Lincoln. He had refused to live in Missouri because it was a slave state. Koerner originally tried farming, but did not do well at it, hated the lifestyle, and soon tired of it. He translated the *Revised Statutes of Illinois*, the Declaration of Independence, and the U.S. Constitution into German and also worked for the *Belleville Zeitung*.[42]

As a result of the 1820 Missouri Compromise, Missouri entered the Union as a slave state, but slavery was prohibited in the territories to the west of it, which were north of a straight line drawn west along Missouri's southern border. Its admission enabled Maine to enter as a free state. The prohibition of slavery in western territories above the southern border of Missouri was to lead to violence and bloodshed in Kansas and a constitutional crisis involving Congress and the Supreme Court when the Court took up the *Dred Scott* case. In the meantime, while there were some slaves in Missouri, support of slavery was primarily limited to the southern and western portions of the state, while St. Louis remained strongly antislavery, especially among its German population.

In the 1850s Northern and Southern Democrats were divided over the issue of slavery. The Missouri Benton Democrats stood against the expansion of slavery, while others in the party supported its unlimited growth. The Northern and Southern Whigs were also divided and included elements of nativism. The Benton Democrats later formed the basis for the new Republican Party. In their early years German immigrants were largely supporters of the Democrats as a result of the anti-immigration position of the Whigs, but they broke with the Democrats at the time of the passage of the 1854 Kansas-Nebraska Act over the issue of slavery.[43]

Missouri was dangerously divided over the issue of slavery. While St. Louis as a whole was against the institution of slavery and was largely pro-Union, most of the remainder of the state supported slavery and the South. Western Missouri Confederate "bushwhackers" led raids into neighboring Kansas and burned the town of Lawrence to the ground. Their belief in liberty and freedom drove many Germans, especially Forty-Eighters, to enlist in the Union army during the Civil War, to the point that German enlistment was much greater than the German percentage of the population.

In 1861 there was a struggle for control of Missouri between pro-slavery and antislavery forces. Missouri's governor Claiborne Jackson was pro-Confederacy and sought to have Missouri join with the South during the Civil War. St. Louis, with its large German population, was anti-Confederacy and desired to remain in the Union. Outside of St. Louis, Missouri was overwhelmingly Democratic. In the election of 1860 the Republican Abraham Lincoln received only 10 percent of the vote in Missouri. Out of 2,600 votes cast in Boone County, Lincoln received only 12.[44]

From the 1830s the Democratic Party in St. Louis was largely supported by Germans and Irish. This support ended by 1860 when the Republican Party became active in St. Louis. The Republicans emerged in that city largely as a result of the split in the Democratic Party over the issue of slavery. Both the Benton Free Soil Democrats and the new Republicans were supported by St. Louis Germans. The pro-Southern Democrats were supported by the Irish in the city, and the nativists were supported by the American-born residents. One newspaper described St. Louis as similar to Caesar's description of Gaul, that is, divided into three parts. Because of its large immigrant population, St. Louis appeared to be a Northern city in a Southern state.[45]

Whether they were republicans or socialists, the German community as a whole rallied in support of the Union and against slavery both in their newspapers and through mass meetings. One typical broadside called on all Germans to unite in order to save their adopted country:

Germans Arouse!

There will be a German Mass Meeting, at the Courthouse on Tuesday Night, the 25th of October, 1864.

Hon. Fred Hassaurek, Carl Schurz and John Habermehl, Esq., Are expected to address you in the German language. Rally! To the rescue of Your Imperiled Country.[46]

The St. Louis Germans were largely considered responsible for causing Missouri to remain in the Union and not join the Confederacy. At the beginning of 1861 Republicans organized sixteen militia companies totaling fourteen thousand men, most of whom were German. The federal arsenal in St. Louis, under the command of Gen. Nathaniel Lyons, which was not well-guarded, contained approximately sixty thousand muskets and ninety thousand pounds of gunpowder.[47] The St. Louis Turner Society offered its services to Lyons in his attempt to hold the arsenal against pro-Confederacy forces. One Missouri regiment of volunteers, largely German immigrants, was commanded by Gen. Franz Sigel, another by Col. Heinrich Boernstein, and a third by Nikolaus Schutter. Frank Blair commanded the fourth regiment.

Sigel had been a professional soldier in the Prussian army but abandoned that career because of his progressive views. He joined the revolutionaries in 1848 and commanded four thousand men during the German Revolution. Sigel had been considering traveling to Italy to fight for its unification when the American Civil War broke out, so instead he volunteered to serve in the Union army. In 1861 new recruits in St. Louis were 80 percent German, and Sigel's Third Regiment consisted almost entirely of men born in Germany.

A Missouri state militia was ordered to St. Louis by the state's pro-Confederacy governor for the purpose of taking the city's arsenal. The militia was poorly trained and equipped both before and after the Civil War, a fact that would become important during the railroad strike of 1877. Troops from St. Louis City and County, on the other hand, were strong Unionists with substantial German populations, who had gained military experience in the Franco-Prussian War and the 1848 Revolution. The state militia that supported the Confederacy was no match against these more experienced troops.[48]

Seven hundred members of the state militia arrived in St. Louis for the purpose of taking the arsenal. Theodor Olshauson, an 1848 revolutionary and the editor of St. Louis's *Westliche Post,* compared the scene to Paris in 1848 and to Baden-Palatine in 1849.[49] Eight thousand men under Lyons's command, including the German regiments, surrounded the encampment of the state militia and other Southern sympathizers at Camp Jackson and forced them to surrender. Six hundred Southern sympathizers were taken prisoner, which resulted in a riot in St. Louis and twenty-eight deaths.[50]

While Sigel emerged a hero after the Camp Jackson confrontation, his subsequent military experience was not as successful. Sent to southwest Missouri to keep Confederate armies from consolidating, he failed in that mission and retreated from the Battle of Carthage. He later convinced Lyons to initiate a military maneuver, which again ended in defeat when Sigel lost control of his troops at the Battle of Wilson's Creek, resulting in Lyons's death. Nevertheless Sigel's military career was aided by political factors. Remaining popular with the large German community, he was promoted to major general when Frank Blair needed German votes during his run for Congress and was made commander of the Department of West Virginia when Lincoln required German votes in the election of 1864.[51] Although

Sigel was totally dedicated to the Union cause, he had little military talent. He also made a poor showing at the Second Battle of Bull Run, where he was accused of shooting another Union general. Gen. Henry Halleck wrote to Gen. William T. Sherman to argue that it almost constituted murder to give a command to Sigel. Finally, Grant removed Sigel from his command.

By 1862 Missouri had produced four German generals for the Union army, and Carl Schurz had raised a substantial number of German troops who fought for the Union at Chancellorsville and Gettysburg. The St. Louis troops were the most radical and revolutionary of any Union fighters, and their dedication assured that Missouri remained in the Union. According to Jonathan Sperber, "Of all these militias, the one in St. Louis was the most overtly revolutionary. Formed by émigré German democrats living in that city and manned by immigrant gymnasts, it disarmed secessionist forces, seized the St. Louis arsenal, and helped overthrow the pro-Confederacy governor of Missouri in April, 1861, saving the state for the Union."[52] The importance of and contributions by pro-Union Germans in St. Louis cannot be exaggerated. Robert E. Lee supposedly remarked that if it were not for the Germans, the Confederacy would have won the Civil War.[53] Grant added that if St. Louis had fallen into Confederate hands, the Union's Mississippi campaign would have been focused on taking that city instead of Vicksburg.[54]

Engels and Marx, living in Europe, also recognized the importance of the St. Louis Germans to the Union cause. In a letter to Marx dated June 12, 1861, Engels wrote, "The reconquest of Missouri by the Germans of St. Louis was the third success, and is of enormous importance, since the possession of St. Louis bars the Mississippi."[55] Writing in Die Presse on March 26, 1862, Marx suggested, "Without the considerable mass of military experience that emigrated to America in consequence of the European revolutionary commotions of 1848–1849, the organization of the Union Army would have required a much longer time still."[56]

The war that had united most Northerners against the South ended, and labor unrest again surfaced in St. Louis. The partnership between German revolutionaries and American liberals broke down over issues of social class, which eventually led to the St. Louis general strike and the St. Louis Commune.[57] Inflation caused prices to increase 56 percent between 1860 and 1864 and 68 percent by 1865. Railroad expansion quickly doubled the number of miles of track, machines replaced workers, and monopolies grew. Hecker viewed the consolidation of railroads and agreements between them as harmful to the interests of ordinary people and consumers and considered calling for a government takeover of the railroads. Strikes broke out throughout the North, including the city of St. Louis. In 1864 the city's machinists, blacksmiths, tailors, and shoemakers struck. Journeymen tailors struck for higher wages and recognition of their union. Reflecting the different nationalities united in the strike, speeches at a journeymen's rally were in English, German, and French. Molders struck against Giles and Oliver Filley's Excelsior Stove Works, which had produced iron armor for Union gunboats during the war. Filley fired the leaders of the strike, and Gen. William Rosecrans declared martial law against the workers.[58] The German press in St. Louis supported the strikers, and Karl Bernays, the editor of the *Anzeiger,* wrote a letter to Lincoln complaining of the actions taken by Rosecrans against the nonviolent strikers.

The social crisis that would explode in 1877 was emerging before the end of the Civil War. The Northern unity that had existed during the war broke down and workers replaced the Confederacy as the enemy of the newly emerging industrial class. Northern and Southern generals, who once fought against each other, were about to confront the working class together as allies. Those German radicals and socialists who courageously volunteered to fight for the United States and saved Missouri for the Union were about to be attacked as traitors, communists, and anarchists when they led the railroad strike in St. Louis and established the St. Louis Commune.

8

The Railroad Strike

Following the 1848 revolutions, the Paris Commune, the First International, German immigration, and the Panic of 1873, the national railroad strike of 1877 was the final event that gave birth to the St. Louis Commune. The poverty and harsh working conditions that beset the American working class equally applied to those employed in the railroad industry. Railroads emerged as the first and greatest national corporations following the Civil War. Speculators gained control of many railroad companies, resulting in rate wars, monopolistic practices, longer work hours, lower wages, and the termination of any workers who complained. It was no longer possible for employees to discuss problems with their bosses, since in most cases the bosses were now a board of directors thousands of miles away.

Some also saw the railroad as intruding into the myth of the American pastoral and the portrait of the quiet small towns and villages of the American countryside. The arrival of the railroad pierced that imaginary veil and brought with it noise, danger, pollution, and change. Ralph Waldo Emerson considered the whistle of the locomotive the voice of the nineteenth century announcing its arrival, and Leo Marx called the railroad the "industrial revolution incarnate."[1] Henry Adams saw it as replacing the Cross and the Virgin in American culture.[2]

Railroad track in the United States grew from thirty thousand miles at the time of the Civil War to almost two hundred thousand miles by the end of the nineteenth century. During the 1870s pay cut followed pay cut in the industry, as railroad workers were forced to work longer hours in a very dangerous workplace. Engineers were often forced to work up to twenty straight hours. Between 1873 and 1880 wages in the industry as a whole were reduced by almost half. Deaths and maiming were everyday occurrences in railroad yards and on city streets.

Because of the large number of unemployed desperate for jobs, workers were easy and cheap to replace.[3] They were expected to do as they were told and to be appreciative of having a job, no matter the conditions. Every worker was, according to the historian Robert Bruce, in competition with "his hungriest rival."[4] Writing in the *Railway Review* in 1880, Willard Smith remarked, "It seems to be generally considered that all that is necessary is that the men should keep quiet and obey orders."[5] People were so desperate for work that Jay Gould even claimed he could hire half of the working class to kill the other half.[6] During the depression in the 1870s, more than a million men were unemployed and would have worked for next to nothing. Those unemployed traveled from place to place looking for work; capitalists and Pinkertons considered them tramps, as if not having a job was a choice they had made. With more than one family sharing two or three rooms, the tenements were breeding places for crime and disease, and few working-class children attended school.

As a result of the 1873 depression, much of the working class was unemployed. They often met in mass meetings together with workers, demanding public works and social programs to create jobs. Trade unions and the American section of the First International in New York held a mass rally at Cooper Union in New York demanding an eight-hour day; a march of twenty thousand occurred in Chicago; and a parade and meeting held in Tomkins Square on New York's Lower East Side was broken up by police. There were strikes in Massachusetts textile mills and the coal districts of Pennsylvania, where nineteen members of the Molly Maguires, the organization made up largely of Irish coal miners, were executed.[7] In 1874 more than ninety thousand were homeless and forced to sleep in the streets and in police stations.[8]

Railroad work was an extremely dangerous occupation and often resulted in the loss of fingers, hands, and legs and even in death. The job of brakeman was the most dangerous in railroad work. In Massachusetts forty-two railroad workers were killed each year, half of them brakemen. There were so many accidents that insurance companies did not want to insure railroad workers. The *Ohio Railway Report* for 1877 contains some examples of the injuries suffered by railroad workers; note that blame is almost always attributed to carelessness by the worker and never to the negligence or fault of the employer:

Baltimore and Ohio and Chicago Railroad. January 3, 1877. D. W. Young, freight brakeman, Deshler: injured; hand crushed in coupling cars, so that two fingers and part of hand had to be amputated. Want of caution.

February 21. Thos. T. Ferril, freight brakeman, New Baltimore: instantly killed; fell from top of car and was run over. Train was moving slowly and gradually. He was setting brakes, and in passing from one car to the next, missed his foothold. Accident was witnessed by the justice of the peace and other citizens of the town, and an inquest was deemed unnecessary.

Central Ohio Railroad Company. November 14. Abram Rinker, carpenter, Bellaire: injured; was repairing cars on side track; another car was set in, striking the cars on which he was at work, throwing him down and breaking his leg. Want of caution.

Dec. 28. George Blizzard, yard switchman, Columbus: injured coupling cars; finger mashed, and was amputated. Want of caution.

January 17, 1877. Thomas Williams, yard switchman, Columbus: injured; one finger mashed while uncoupling cars. Want of caution.

May 16. Ira Bell, freight brakeman, near Campbell's Station: instantly killed by explosion of engine. Inquest by Elza Turner, J.P., Guernsey county, acting coroner, and verdict reached in accordance with the facts, attaching no blame to the company.

S. C. Baldwin, tonnage fireman: fatally injured by same explosion; died evening of same day. No inquest.

November 18. W. F. Holmes, brakeman, Dennison: injured; fell off train and run over; leg crushed and subsequently amputated. Want of caution.

Pittsburgh, Cincinnati and St. Louis Railroad. July 31. R. J. Tobin, brakeman, Dennison: injured; hand smashed while attempting to make coupling. Want of caution.[9]

In none of these instances was the railroad found to be at fault.

Railroad companies in the late 1870s were for the most part profitable enterprises. The Pennsylvania Railroad Company was the largest enterprise in America and employed over two hundred thousand. It exercised immense political power, as did other railroad corporations. When the Pennsylvania state militia suppressed a strike in 1874, a labor weekly referred to the Erie Railroad as George III and the Pennsylvania state government as Parliament.[10] Almost all materials were by that time shipped by rail. By 1877 only 10 percent of freight tonnage passing through St. Louis was by riverboat or barge; 80 percent of all grain that was shipped east came by rail. Railroads were given valuable real estate by state and federal governments, and many lines, such as those owned by Jay Gould and Jim Fisk, had a monopoly in certain geographic areas, setting prices as they desired without fear of competition.

Although the railroad companies blamed the need for pay cuts on the depression, the earnings of the Pennsylvania Railroad were higher in 1877 than they were in 1876, when they paid a very large dividend of 8 percent to stockholders. The B&O paid an even larger dividend of 10 percent at the same time as it cut wages by 10 percent for the second time in eight months. Engineers struck the Baltimore and Maine Railroad, which had cut wages 10 percent while paying a 6 percent dividend to shareholders and raising the compensation of officers of the company.[11] At the end of 1876, the Boston and Maine cut the wages of its employees by 10 percent, and the next month it raised the salaries of its president and superintendent.

Adding to the problems of low wages and dangerous working conditions was the fact that railroad workers sometimes worked only a few days a week, were required to pay for their own room and board at expensive company-owned hotels during layovers, and were not paid for travel back home from their destinations. So, for example, if a railroad worker went out on a run on

Monday and laid over Tuesday and Wednesday, then did another run, he was not paid for Tuesday and Wednesday and was forced to pay high prices for room and board for those days in a company-owned hotel. He was then required to buy a ticket for his return trip, so that his earnings for that portion of the week were negligible. Workers also were often paid in company scrip and forced to shop in company stores, where the products were of low quality and overpriced. Engineers and firemen often were required to pay for damage to their engines and were fired for failure to do so. The dangerous jobs of brakeman and fireman often paid less than that of an unskilled worker. Many railroad workers had their wages reduced by up to 50 percent by July 1877.

There were railroad strikes before 1877, but they were generally small and rural. They did, however, share many of the same characteristics as the 1877 strike. Although railroads were the largest employers, the Panic of 1873 had destroyed or weakened the railroad unions. The blacklisting of union members forced unions underground, where they were often infiltrated by company spies. Formed in 1863, the Brotherhood of Locomotive Engineers was the strongest railroad union in the 1870s. The Order of Railroad Conductors was founded in 1868, and the Brotherhood of Locomotive Firemen formed in 1873. Railroad workers' grievances included wages, the fact that wages were sometimes held up for months, the requirement to trade in company stores, and safety concerns.

Regarding the strikes in 1873–74, Herbert Gutman notes that there was no central direction but rather only local leadership; that there was immense local support for the strikers, who were members of the communities where the strikes occurred; and that the 1877 conflagration generally followed the same pattern as the earlier strikes.[12] Workers won some of the early confrontations. For instance, engineers won a strike against the Central in New Jersey, resulting in the rescinding of a wage cut, and the Grand Trunk Railway of Canada was forced to rehire union leaders it had fired.

As a result of the Panic of 1873, thousands of railroad workers were laid off, others were forced to work longer hours, and the railroads instituted more pay cuts. The Pennsylvania Railroad cut wages 10 percent on November 30, 1873, in violation of its contract with engineers and firemen. The East Tennessee, Virginia and Georgia Railroad cut the wages of its employees unilaterally by 20 percent. When the Pennsylvania Railroad union sent a delegation to discuss the wage cut with the railroad's western superintendent, the entire delegation was immediately fired. In 1874 New Jersey Southern Railroad workers protested working conditions by tearing up tracks, removing coupling pins, and disabling locomotives. Similar actions occurred on the New York and Oswego Midland Railroad and on the Louisville and Nashville Railroad. That same year in Hornellsville, New York, workers refused to allow trains to leave the yard, and a thousand workmen on the Erie at Susquehanna struck over the issue of wages. The B&O advised the U.S. Treasury Department that no freight trains were leaving Chicago for the North or the West because of the strikes.[13] Two hundred engineers and firemen stopped rail traffic in Logansport, Indiana, on the Pittsburgh, Cincinnati, and St. Louis Railroad.

In virtually all of the strikes there was strong community support for the strikers. David Stowell argues that not only those associated with railroads hated the railroad companies, but also ordinary residents of cities who had no direct relationship with the railroads. The railroads were disruptive of municipal activities and dangerous for ordinary citizens. In addition, they represented visible, uncontrolled industrial capitalism to those who lived or ventured into city streets. There was, Stowell writes, "spontaneous rebellion of urban residents against one of the most direct and damaging ways they experienced capitalist industrialization outside of the workplace, namely, the use of city streets by railroads."[14] In working-class neighborhoods, women and children used the streets for shopping and recreation. Because of the lack of storage space in tenements, more shopping trips to stores were necessary. A lack of parks in poorer neighborhoods made the streets a public play space for children. Peddlers and the pick-up and delivery of piecework done in working-class homes made traversing the streets both necessary and dangerous. By invading the streets, the railroad was the most visible part of capitalism and urbanization. The trains running through neighborhoods were both noisy and dangerous, especially as the urban population grew. From 1860 to 1880 Buffalo's population increased by 91 percent, Albany's by 46 percent, and Syracuse by 84 percent. From 1868 to 1880 deaths from trains increased nationwide by 59 percent and injuries by 178 percent.[15] Hundreds of non-railroad workers were killed each year in New York State alone. In addition, sparks given off by trains caused fires in neighboring buildings.

The railroad strikes unleashed people's frustration with the railroads in urban areas, accounting for the support railroad workers received in their communities. In Indianapolis, the mayor, a judge, and members of the city council attacked the Pennsylvania Railroad, and Gen. Daniel McCauley, the head of the Indianapolis militia, encouraged the engineers in their fight against what he denominated an oppressive monopoly.[16] In Pennsylvania the Lackawanna County sheriff refused the Erie Railroad's request to remove strikers, who were holding company buildings, until the railroad paid them their back wages. The sheriff also disarmed some two hundred special police the company brought in from New York. In an address to a town hall meeting, the district attorney for Blair County, Pennsylvania, showed his sympathy for the strikers: "You strike because of your necessities; because your wives and children cry to you for bread—for that which you are unable to give. . . . Every man not controlled by the Pennsylvania is with you heart and soul."[17] In Albany, New York, residents surrounded a work gang attempting to lay track in Steamboat Square, which resulted in the arrest of the work gang for tearing up the pavement and obstructing the street. Albany's, Buffalo's, and Syracuse's municipal indebtedness was a result of their investments in railroads by the issuance of bonds to pay for construction, thereby raising the rates of taxation in those cities.

Because state militias were made up largely of working people, they often sided with the strikers, and authorities were to learn that they could not be trusted to forcefully suppress strikers. The militias were caught in the middle. Many members were sympathetic to the strikers and did not want to fight them. Yet they were military entities, required to obey orders. The militias were unpopular almost everywhere they went, and morale was low among them.[18] Six hundred troops fraternized with strikers in Hornellsville, New York, and others in Lebanon, Pennsylvania. In Altoona, a crowd of five hundred took over a troop train, and the soldiers, not desiring violence, willingly gave up their guns.

By 1877 the Panic of 1873 was in the middle of its fourth year; millions of workers were still unemployed, and wages had been cut time and again.

In St. Louis there were runs on the banks, resulting in the closure of many financial institutions. The German Bank suspended business, and its assets were liquidated.[19] The Bank of Pike County suspended all payments.[20] There was a run on Boatman's Bank and Provident Savings Association, and the Bank of St. Louis and the North St. Louis Savings Association closed when they were met by a mob demanding their money immediately upon opening for the day.[21] Withdrawals forced the closing of the Bremen Bank at 10:00 a.m. on July 17.[22]

In June 1877 the New York Central announced a 10 percent wage cut. At the time, the railroad was earning a healthy profit and paid generous dividends to its shareholders. The Erie Railroad followed soon after with its own pay cut, while officials earned large salaries. In May 1877 the Missouri Pacific reduced the pay of engineers by 12 percent, and nine days later the Pennsylvania cut all wages by 10 percent, its second cut in pay since 1873. On the Baltimore and Ohio line, wages had dropped for firemen from $55 a month in 1873 to $30 a month in 1877. Brakemen's wages dropped in that period from $70 a month to $30. Conductors' pay was reduced from $90 to $50.[23] In July, the Vandalia, Indianapolis and St. Louis, the St. Louis and Kansas City, the Northern Lakeshore and Michigan Southern, and the Erie and Michigan Central railways all announced wage cuts.[24]

Because of the large pool of unemployed, railroad companies felt that they could impose whatever conditions they liked on their workers. If employees did not like the amount of wages paid or the working conditions, there were plenty of unemployed who would be happy to replace them. Nor did the companies have any real concern about a political backlash against their actions because they controlled a good many state legislatures and governorships and had an immense influence on the federal government. In addition, there was virtually no national leadership of railroad workers. Railroad unions were young, and they were divided by craft. Everything appeared to be in favor of the railroad companies.

Suddenly and without warning the explosion that had long been brewing occurred. The great railroad strike of 1877 began on July 16 in Martinsburg, West Virginia, and Baltimore, Maryland. Martinsburg was located approximately a hundred miles from Baltimore and was a major hub of the Baltimore and Ohio. The Pennsylvania Railroad also passed through Martinsburg. Almost all the railroad workers there were members of the Trainmen's Union. The B&O had cut wages 10 percent for the second time in eight months.

In 1877 a train usually had one locomotive and eighteen cars. A double-header had thirty-six cars with locomotives at each end. Doubleheaders required much more work and were extremely dangerous for the brakemen, who were required to move from car to car on moving trains in order to set brakes.[25] At the same time the pay cuts went into effect, the B&O and the Pennsylvania both announced that all trains would be run as double-headers, which resulted in twice as many railroad cars, more dangerous working conditions, layoffs, fewer crews, and an increased workload for those who remained. The Martinsburg workers responded with a demand for the restoration of the latest pay reduction, promising that no trains would be allowed to operate until that time. Baltimore and Ohio officials asked for the state militia to force the workers to return to their jobs. When the troops arrived the next day, many were in sympathy with the strikers, and some were railroad workers themselves. When attempts were made to run the trains, violence erupted, resulting in the deaths of both workers and militia members.[26]

When word of the Martinsburg strike spread, other workers along the B&O route also struck, many of them going to Martinsburg to lend their support. The strike began at Camden Yards in Baltimore, virtually simultaneously with Martinsburg, on July 16, 1877, also as a result of a 10 percent pay cut by the B&O. The firemen walked out and were immediately fired and replaced. By 6:00 p.m. box makers, sawyers, and can makers in Baltimore had also struck for pay increases. By midnight strikers were in control of the B&O property.[27] Fifteen thousand workers quickly struck in Maryland, Pennsylvania, West Virginia, Ohio, New York, New Jersey, Indiana, Michigan, Illinois, Kentucky, and Missouri.[28] The strikes were spontaneous, with no common leadership. All railroad workers were in similar situations with the same complaints, and Martinsburg was the spark that set off the other strikes. All freight traffic was at a standstill, but the railroad workers allowed passenger and mail trains to move. They were conscious of public feeling and did not want to alienate people from their cause by making travel inconvenient, and they did not want to interfere with the mails and thereby give the federal government an excuse to intervene.

When a militia arrived at Baltimore's Camden Yards, it was met by a crowd of several thousand hurling rocks and stones. Thousands of unemployed railroad workers and young people joined the crowd. When the militia tried to move the crowd back with the use of bayonets, the soldiers were chased into the depot, and the crowd physically removed from the train the engineer and fireman, who at that point had not joined the strike. The militia attempted to retreat to an armory, but only half the men made it, and twenty-five militia members were injured along the way. Once in the armory, they realized that their position was not sustainable. But they were trapped. The crowd surrounded the building, cutting off any escape. Whenever a militia member attempted to leave the building, he was pelted with stones. While the militia was unable to move, police patrolled the railway yards.

Finally, the surrounded militia attempted to break out of the armory, shooting as they exited the building, and marched down the street in an attempt to reach the railway depot. They were surrounded on the street, and rocks and bricks were hurled at them by the crowd and from windows of buildings along the way. Police were driven back by pistols and bricks, and tracks were torn up. A crowd of fifteen thousand surrounded the depot. A fire broke out, and when firefighters arrived their hoses were cut by the crowd. J. A. Dacus compares the scene in Baltimore to the Paris Commune: "The scenes of the night of the 20th of July, 1877, in the city of Baltimore, were not unlike those which characterized the events in the city of Paris during the reign of the Commune in 1870."[29] The B&O stopped all passenger trains as well as freight. Almost a thousand can makers and box makers joined the railroad workers and struck over wage issues. Governor John Carroll, after meeting with John Garrett, president of the B&O, ordered the Maryland National Guard into Cumberland and Baltimore, and five hundred federal troops were ordered to Baltimore.

Crowds gathered at the strike sites to watch. The railroads were unpopular in the cities and towns along their lines both because of how poorly they treated their workers and because the railroad workers were often residents of those towns. The workers moved railroad cars onto sidings and drove locomotives into the roundhouses. No trains would move, they said, until the latest wage cut was restored. When the mayor ordered the arrest of some strikers, a crowd surrounded them to keep away the police. People filled the railyards, too many for authorities to control. The company made attempts to move the trains, but each was stopped by the crowds.

At Martinsburg, at the request of the B&O, the governor called out the state militia and ordered it to the city. Significantly, much of the militia was made up of railroad and other workers, who were more sympathetic to the strikers than they were to the railroad companies. Many of them were residents of Martinsburg. The militia was led by Charles Faulkner, who told the strikers that he was sympathetic to their complaints but that he had to follow orders and move the trains. A striker changed a switch that would have directed the train back into the yard; he was seen by a member of the militia, who leaped off the train and attempted to restore the switch, was shot at, and returned fire, killing a worker. The engineer and fireman, who were not yet on strike, then walked off the train, claiming the working conditions were too dangerous. Faulkner called for volunteers to operate the train, and when he was answered by silence, he announced that he had done what he was ordered to do and could do no more; then he and his militia left the scene.[30] A cattle train was stopped by the crowd and the engineer and fireman removed from the train. Workers also removed the cattle from the train and led them to a pasture.

Governor Henry M. Mathews of West Virginia, a former Confederate officer, called out the Mathews Light Guards, which were based in Wheeling, over two hundred miles away. However, most of the Wheeling troops were also working class and had no love for the railroads. On the morning of July 18, Col. Robert Delaplain telegraphed the governor that the crowd was too large to control and that there was nothing he could do with regard to the situation. With the failure of the state militia to end the strike, Baltimore and Ohio officers asked the governor of West Virginia to request that the president order federal troops to Martinsburg, arguing that this was a domestic insurrection that could not be controlled by the state government. But Mathews was a former Confederate and had no desire to invite federal troops into his state. The immediate problem for the railroad companies was that commodities in the railroad cars were sitting and rotting in Martinsburg.

Finally, at the request of Mathews, President Hayes ordered three hundred federal troops to West Virginia because the strike had spread to other states. It was the first time that federal troops had intervened in a labor strike. By that time, conductors, brakemen, and engineers had joined the strike. Federal troops arrived in Martinsburg on the morning of July 19. The number of available troops was small because the entire U.S. Army had only fifteen thousand soldiers, most of them stationed on the frontier. At the same time, the railroad attempted to bring in replacement workers from out of town, but the crowds in Martinsburg blocked incoming trains and otherwise aided the local railroad workers. Virtually every family had a railroad worker on strike, so it was almost impossible for the company to hire scabs. The whole town supported the strike, and even the unemployed joined the strikers. Of the huge crowd in Martinsburg, many were not even railroad workers or their families. As a result of layoffs and a lack of work, there were many unemployed who directed their anger against those they felt were the bane of working people, in this case the railroads. Trains that managed to leave or pass through Martinsburg were stopped by miners and boatmen along the route. Workers took control of railroad property at Cumberland, at Grafton and Keyser in West Virginia, and other stations.

Governor Matthews agreed to meet with B & O officials in Grafton. As his train arrived in the evening, the railroad yard was filled with a hostile crowd. He immediately left for the meeting at a hotel, as the engineer and fireman from his train walked off, abandoning the train where it stood, to the cheers of the crowd. A vice president of the B & O ordered other railroad employees to replace the strikers, and when they refused, he fired them and the leaders of the strike. When he finally found someone willing to drive a train, the crowd pulled the driver off it.

On July 18 President Hayes ordered more federal troops from the Washington arsenal and from Fort McHenry to Martinsburg. The B & O provided transportation for the troops but billed the government for their passage. Col. William French arrived in Martinsburg on July 19. With the arrival of more federal troops, some freight trains began to move out of Martinsburg. However, they were often stopped along the way by miners and by canal workers on the Chesapeake and Ohio Canal, who joined the strikers. Of the sixteen freight trains that left Martinsburg on July 20, only one arrived at Keyser. At Grafton armed strikers threatened to kill an engineer who tried to run a train. Canal men and miners pelted another train with rocks as it moved along its route.

It was no longer necessary to stop all trains in Martinsburg since the strike was spreading to other cities, and freight trains could be stopped at a number of other locations. Strikers controlled the railroad yard in Newark, Ohio; brakemen and firemen struck the Erie Railroad in Hornellsville, New York, over wages and the price of renting shacks along the tracks for housing. Hornellsville was an important railroad center on the Erie line, where there were many unemployed, and most workers worked for railroads. Strikes broke out in Harrisburg, Altoona, and Reading, Pennsylvania, and the B&O stopped trying to run freight trains. Two hundred canal men joined the railroad strikers, and at Grafton and Newark trainmen blocked all freight. Miners at Summit Hill in Pennsylvania went on strike over pay cuts on July 27, marching with loaves of bread impaled on the tops of poles.

Strikers stopped a troop train near Buffalo, New York, on July 23, and after a fight the militia fled, leaving their weapons behind. That same day a militia in Reading, Pennsylvania, fired on a crowd, killing thirteen, and fifteen policemen were also shot. A crowd of two thousand attacked two hundred soldiers who were guarding the Lake Shore roundhouse in Erie, Pennsylvania, forcing the soldiers to withdraw. The Lebanon Valley Bridge in Reading was burned down on July 24, freight cars were burned, and tracks destroyed. At Wilkes-Barre, Pennsylvania, on July 25, railroad employees joined the strike, facing off against a thousand soldiers. Employees of the Delaware and Hudson Canal Company and the Pennsylvania Coal Company struck, and miners stopped a coal train on the Delaware and Hudson line. A number of people were killed in a gunfight between soldiers and a crowd in Johnstown, Pennsylvania. On July 25 all trains in Harrisburg were stopped in the rail yard by a crowd of four thousand. When the New York Central and Lake Shore railroads refused to send the mail through on their trains, the strikers told the postmaster to give them the mail and they would carry it. Also in Harrisburg, soldiers were disarmed by a crowd and twenty-three were taken prisoner. Realizing that they could not depend on local militias, the B&O asked that a militia from Baltimore be brought in since it would have no relationship to the Martinsburg strikers. When the Baltimore militia arrived, they were stoned by the crowd. In response the soldiers opened fire indiscriminately, killing ten. Not wanting to be part of what was occurring, half of the militia left and went home. A crowd of fifteen thousand kept any trains from moving.

The strike contributed to the development of class consciousness among the railroad workers. They began to see themselves as mere wage earners, a proletariat totally dependent on and vulnerable to the arbitrary decisions of capitalists, who were interested only in earning the greatest possible profit. Divided by craft, so that sometimes firemen would replace engineers when the latter struck, they realized that they needed unity, coordination, and leadership.

Railroad workers secretly organized the Trainmen's Union in June 1877. Thousands of workers joined, including conductors, brakemen, firemen, switchmen, and engineers. Within a few weeks the union had expanded to include railroad workers from Baltimore to Chicago.[31] Robert Ammons was elected leader. The B&O ordered that all members of the union be fired. Company spies infiltrated the union, and those who could be identified as members were discharged. The firings began only four days after the union was formed. The workers now viewed themselves as being in opposition to the owners and managers of the railroad. Although they all worked for the same company, they had no interests in common. Instead the interests of management were directly opposed to the interests of workers. As one worker explained while summing up their new class-conscious perspective, "I won't call employers despots. I won't call them tyrants, but the term capitalists is sort of synonymous and will do as well."[32]

Taken by surprise by the outbreak of the strike, by July 20 the Workingmen's Party of the United States began holding rallies in support of the railroad men. Dacus, a strike observer at the time, claimed that the Workingmen's Party was behind the upheavals in Baltimore and other cities.[33] In an editorial, the *Missouri Republican* recognized that the strike represented class conflict between what Marx designated the bourgeoisie and the proletariat: "The question in which they have their origin is one that society shrinks from grappling with. . . . It involves the whole relation between capital and labor, and is aggravating the hostility of that relation every day."[34] A few days later the paper again editorialized on the seriousness and the class nature of the conflict, a seemingly European experience new to the United States: "The strike of the employees of the Baltimore and Ohio railroad and of other lines to which the movement has extended is certainly entitled to the distinction of being designated as the greatest 'conflict between capital and labor' so-called, ever witnessed in this country."[35]

Pittsburgh was a heavily working-class city. Even its newspapers attacked the greed of the railroad companies. Much of its working class consisted of German and Eastern European immigrants, many of whom had experience with revolution and socialism in Europe. Most were factory workers, although some worked for railroads. The mayor of Pittsburgh, William McCarthy, was politically supported by the working class and had no love for the railroad companies. The city was hit especially hard by the Panic of 1873, during which half of the city's workers had lost their jobs. In July 1877 even half of the police force had been laid off.

On July 16 Robert Pitcairn, the superintendent of the Pennsylvania Railroad's Pittsburgh Division, ordered that all freight trains traveling east from the city would be doubleheaders. That would mean more layoffs for railroad workers and double duty for those who remained. Only half the brakemen and conductors would be needed, and the situation was much more dangerous for brakemen, who had to move from car to car to set brakes while the train was moving. Additionally, the railroad had reduced wages 10 percent on June 1. On July 16 crews refused to take out freight trains, and no eastbound trains were able to leave. Pennsylvania strikers joined with those of the B&O, and all trains arriving in Pittsburgh were stopped. The demands of the Pennsylvania Railroad workers were similar to those of the B&O workers. They called for the end of doubleheaders, the restoration of the wage scale prior to the announced wage cuts, and the rehiring of those workers who had been fired. In the meantime, workers took control of the train yards. No trains, except passenger trains and those carrying mail, were allowed to leave Pittsburgh.

The railroad company requested help from the mayor, who refused their plea. He was dependent on working-class votes for his position. State militias were called out in Pittsburgh, but many did not show up and others threw down their guns. Soldiers mingled with the crowds. The railroads made use of private police forces, including Pinkerton detectives and other paramilitary forces, against the strikers. The Coal and Iron Police, a private police force in Pennsylvania, was supervised by the Pinkerton Detective Agency.[36] However, the entire city of Pittsburgh seemed to be on the side of the strikers. Over two thousand freight cars and locomotives were idle, and squatters moved into them. With no working transportation with which to bring in necessities, the army informed the president that the city of Pittsburgh had only enough provisions for about three days. Thomas Scott, head of the Pennsylvania Railroad, sought a presidential declaration that Pennsylvania was in rebellion, not only against the Pennsylvania Railroad but also against the United States, and the president's cabinet met three times in a twenty-four-hour period in order to consider the matter. On July 25 the cabinet decided to treat the strikes as an insurrection.

Railroad officials, recognizing that the Pittsburgh troops were not reliable, asked that other state militia troops be brought from Philadelphia. The Philadelphia militia would have no family among the Pittsburgh strikers and would contain no members from Pittsburgh. Along the way the Philadelphia militia stopped at Harrisburg to pick up two Gatling guns and ammunition. When the Philadelphia troops arrived, they were met by a crowd of six thousand to seven thousand protesters. Because the crowd included workers from industries other than the railroads, many of Pittsburgh's industrial plants and dependent businesses were effectively shut down as well. The Philadelphia militia moved into the crowd with bayonets pointed forward, while rocks were thrown at them. When some of the troops were struck by stones, they fired on the crowd, killing twenty people, most of whom were spectators.

A later grand jury investigation referred to the shooting as "murder," and an investigation by a coroner's jury found "an unauthorized willful, and wanton killing . . . which the inquest can call by no other name but murder."[37] The *St. Louis Globe-Democrat* reported, "Three of the killed were women, and of the wounded a large proportion were women and children who were among the spectators on the hillside."[38]

Enraged, the crowd attacked the militiamen. Workingmen poured into Pittsburgh from neighboring cities, and workers took guns from gun shops and from the local armory; four hundred rifles and five hundred pistols and ammunition were looted from one gun store, and two thousand rifles were obtained from other sources. The Philadelphia militia moved into the roundhouse for protection. The railroad company attempted to run trains again but were stopped by the crowd, as the militia with its Gatling guns watched from the roundhouse. There they were surrounded by the crowd and had no way out and no way to bring in food. Stones, bricks, and gunshots rained down on them. After many hours, the militia was scared and hungry.[39]

As a result of the shootings, the entire city turned against the Pennsylvania Railroad and authority collapsed. A good deal of blood had been shed, and the crowd was angry. At various times the size of the angry crowd was estimated to be between fifteen thousand and thirty thousand. Dacus wrote that it looked as if the entire city had joined the strikers. At about 10:00 p.m. the crowd set oil tank cars on fire and pushed them into the roundhouse. Firefighters were threatened at gunpoint not to interfere, and their hoses were cut by the crowd. The fire spread from railcar to railcar and from building to building. The crowd somehow obtained a cannon, probably from the armory or the militia. Some of the militia members threw down their guns, changed their clothes, and tried to run away. Railroad cars were broken into, merchandise was stolen, and railroad cars were burned along with other railroad property. Over 2,000 railroad cars and 104 locomotives were destroyed, and another twenty miles of railroad cars sat silently. Although the crowd blocked firefighters attempting to save the railroad's property, it aided efforts to keep the fire from spreading to other properties. The *St. Louis Globe-Democrat* reported, "The situation at the roundhouse is still critical. The soldiers inside are becoming desperate, and threaten to cut their way out. The mob are frantic. At least fifty oil and freight cars have burned or are burning. A report just in says the stockyards at East Liberty have been fired. All the stock, many thousand herd, have been turned loose. The fire is approaching the roundhouse. It will almost certainly be destroyed, and it is doubtful if any of the 1,500 soldiers will escape."[40] Policemen were throwing loot from the train cars to the crowd in hopes that they would take the merchandise and go home. Four hundred trains, many containing perishable goods, were held idle in Pittsburgh.[41]

The militia finally left the roundhouse and marched toward the railroad depot, aiming their Gatling guns at the crowd. Rifle and pistol fire was directed toward the militia along its way, some from windows and some from around corners as they approached. They headed for the arsenal in an attempt to find cover and protection. But they were turned away there, either because there was no room for them or because of fear of the mob, and they continued their retreat. They finally stopped about twelve miles outside of the city. Their remaining number at that time was so small that they were ordered to disband.

The railroad depot was set on fire, and it and the accompanying hotel went up in flames. The fires ultimately destroyed 104 locomotives, 2,152 railroad cars and other railroad property, twelve tenement buildings, several businesses, and a dozen houses.[42] The freight depot and offices of the Pittsburgh and St. Louis Railroad were burned. The focus of the crowd appeared not to be limited to the railroad companies. A grain elevator, owned not by a railroad but nevertheless by a monopoly, was also burned to the ground.

Twenty-four people were killed that Saturday and Sunday. Only three of the dead were railroad workers and four were militia members. The rest were ordinary citizens. According to the *Globe-Democrat*, the trouble had started

> when the Philadelphia troops, who had been sent here to suppress the strikers, fired upon the crowd. The terribly fatal effects of the shots fired by the troops exasperated the citizens as well as the strikers, and in less than an hour thousands of workingmen from the rolling-mills, and coal miners and various manufacturing establishments hurried to the scene of the conflict, determined to have revenge on the troops and railway officials. It was stated that Gen. Pearson, commander of the 6th Division of the State Guards, had directed the troops to fire before any resistance had been made, and the fact that many of those killed and wounded had gathered on the hillside merely as spectators, served to increase the bitterness of the crowd.[43]

When a call went out for volunteers for a citizens' army or committee of public safety to confront the strikers, only a hundred men appeared, though more joined later. As a result of the pressure on authorities due to the extreme violence, the city armed these volunteers with guns and baseball bats. Some of the city leaders suggested that the railroads offer at least a token concession to the strikers, but railroad officials refused, believing that they could expect unlimited help from the federal government. The Pennsylvania Railroad's Thomas Scott had been an assistant secretary of war during the Civil War and was largely responsible for the compromise that placed Rutherford Hayes in the White House. In 1876 the Texas and Pacific Railroad needed $300 million from government bonds, and Hayes agreed to support the measure if Scott could make him president. It was Scott who delivered the Southern states that elected Hayes.[44]

The railroads were determined to win the strike and destroy the unions, whatever the cost. The companies refused to meet with workers' organizations or discuss any kind of settlement. An officer of the Erie Railroad said that "any demonstration would be speedily put down even if it should be found necessary to sacrifice life."[45] This was to be a showdown between capital and labor, and the railroads intended to teach the workers a lesson. In the future, the railroad companies argued, workers would abide by terms determined by the railroads and no one else. The immense price being paid by the railroads in loss of property would therefore be worth it in the long run.

The roundhouse riot in Pittsburgh resulted in the arrest of 139 people, almost all of whom were working class. Over half were unskilled or semiskilled; most of the others were unemployed. Pittsburgh, like Baltimore, according to Dacus, was the American version of the Paris Commune: "The fiendish spirit of the Commune had taken possession of an incredibly large proportion of the people of Pittsburgh."[46] As if confirming the effect of European socialism and revolution on American workers, the Paris Commune was repeatedly cited as an example of what was occurring in the United States.

Younger workers appeared to be more radical than their elders. For instance, engineers were older and made more money than most other railroad workers, and it required two engineers to work a doubleheader, so they were not as adversely affected financially as were others. Therefore the engineers' union had not originally joined the strike.

The strike and violence continued to spread. In Allegheny, workers broke into an armory and gun stores, stole guns and ammunition, dug trenches, and took control of the railroad and telegraph offices. In Columbia County and Meadville in Pennsylvania and Chenango County in New York strikers seized railroad property. Women in Altoona stopped trains by pouring grease and soap on tracks leading up a hill, so that the trains skidded and slipped back downhill. Also in Altoona troops surrendered to a crowd, stacked their arms, and went home. In Reading crowds tore up track and burned bridges and railroad property. A crowd stoned seven companies of national guard troops, and eleven were killed when the guard opened fire on the crowd.

The militias were divided in their loyalties. Some arriving troops turned their guns on the national guard and threatened to shoot them if they again fired on the crowd. A national guard company mutinied in Lebanon, Pennsylvania. In Reading the railroad was two months behind in the payment of wages. When two thousand people tore up tracks, derailed railroad cars, and set fires, some national guard troops fired into the crowd, killing six. Others refused to fire and went home. Even Washington DC was thought to be endangered, and more federal troops were moved there. The Lake Shore and Michigan Southern Railroad ordered trains to stop carrying mail after a crew abandoned a train at Erie, Pennsylvania, on July 24. The strikers wired President Hayes that it was the company, not the strikers, that refused to move the mail. In almost every case, violence was initiated by the railroad or troops.

By the end of 1873, Chicago was in the midst of a serious depression. Approximately 25 percent of the working population was unemployed. In December that year, four hundred members of the German Socio-Political Workingmen's Union and other immigrant groups held a mass rally demanding "work or bread." The next night about ten thousand workers and unemployed marched from Turner Hall to Chicago's City Hall demanding work. Chicago's more elite citizens referred to the group as communists, robbers, and loafers.[47] Union organizing at the time was largely carried on by members of Turner societies and German radicals. In Chicago 70 percent of factory workers and unskilled workers were immigrants. Labor leaders came primarily from the group of skilled artisans, who saw their way of life dying as a result of machines, factories, and mass production. By 1876 the Social

Democratic Party had merged with the Workingmen's Party of Illinois to form the Workingmen's Party of the United States. The Chicago anarchist Albert Parsons, who would be hanged as a result of the Haymarket affair, represented Chicago at its founding convention.

The 1877 railroad strike spread to Chicago, a center for freight and passenger transportation. Skilled and unskilled workers joined with the railroad workers in the city. On July 21 over a thousand men gathered at Twelfth and Halsted streets demanding work. On July 23 almost thirty thousand gathered at Market and Madison to listen to speeches, while another five thousand convened at Madison and Canal, where they were urged to join the WPUSA. The next day Parsons was threatened with assassination by Chicago's police chief unless he left town. Workers shut down the B&O and the Illinois Central in Chicago, and on July 25 workers marched in the streets to the sound of the "Marseillaise," the French anthem of revolution.

There was a meeting at Chicago's Turner Hall called by the WPUSA. A large crowd filled the hall, and the sidewalks and streets surrounding it. Police broke in and indiscriminately clubbed people who were peacefully attending the meeting. One person was killed. Thereafter more than six thousand citizens attended a rally organized by the WPUSA and demanded the nationalization of the railroads.

The next day crowds closed down the rail yards and called out factory workers to join the strike. A crowd of five thousand gathered at South Side Rolling Mills, where they stopped all work and then proceeded on to other establishments, shutting down brickyards and tanneries. Police, supported by the national guard and federal troops, fired into the crowd, killing three. The next day an armed crowd of five thousand fought police in the streets. On July 26 a street battle between police and five thousand workers and sympathizers around the Halsted Street Viaduct resulted in a police cavalry charge in which eighteen people were killed. A squad of mounted soldiers attacked the crowd, firing on them with cannon and rifles and waving sabers. Seven thousand workers within a five-block radius fought with and threw stones at police, who fired on the crowd until they were almost out of ammunition, and then retreated while the crowd chased after them. Police reinforcements arrived and fired into the crowd, while the cavalry charged. The *Globe-Democrat* described Chicago as an armed camp, controlled by armed workers, in the midst of a revolution: "The busy hands of trade are transformed into stockades. The dry goods stores are arsenals. The grocery stores are fortresses, and everybody is a militia man for the time being. There is absolutely nothing but riot and disorder going on. These have taken possession of the city, and although they have been to a certain extent held in check up to tonight, they have managed to control the city during the day, and promise to control it during the night."[48]

Federal troops were called away from fighting Indians in the West in order to fight workers in Chicago. Gen. Philip Sheridan was recalled from fighting Sioux on the frontier to face workers in Chicago.[49] "General Sheridan was to meet Gen. Sherman to-day at the mouth of Little Big Horn River, and he there received notification to return to Chicago without delay."[50]

It was a time of growing political consciousness as well as one of action. People who were not formerly involved in labor issues suddenly became politicized. Many people, including Lucy Parsons, the wife of the Haymarket martyr Albert Parsons and a labor agitator in her own right, became educated in radical politics in those days in Chicago: "It was during the great railroad strike of 1877 that I became interested in what is known as the labor question."[51]

Unlike the B&O, the Chicago and Northwestern, weary of the strike and attendant violence, agreed to the demands of the strikers.

One issue that would continuously arise was the status of railroad companies that were bankrupt and in receivership, such as the Erie Railroad. Legally those lines were owned or controlled by the federal government, and after courts issued restraining orders enjoining strikes or interference with the operation of the trains, strikes against them were considered to be actions in contempt of federal courts, a decision that would be used in many localities against strikers.

In Syracuse, Albany, and Buffalo, militia appeared on the scene even before workers voted to strike. On July 23 railroad workers in Syracuse voted to send a letter to William Vanderbilt, owner of the New York Central, demanding that a July 1 pay cut be restored, and warning that a strike would begin if it was not. The workers also voted that the property of the railroad was not to be damaged, that there would be no drinking during the strike, and that a committee meet with the Brotherhood of Railroad Engineers in order to coordinate future actions. When Vanderbilt refused to negotiate with the workers, the strike in Syracuse began, with strikers patrolling and guarding the railroad's property.

Machinists in East Syracuse also voted to strike. While the workers promised that no trains would leave Syracuse, that threat added little to the conversation, since most trains were stopped before ever reaching the city. The strike was called off when Vanderbilt promised to sit down and discuss matters with the railroad workers as soon as calm was restored. Of course, he had no intention of doing so. The New York Central was his railroad; no one was going to tell him how to run it, and so he would not give in to labor's demands. Bargaining with workers was not in his interest, nor in the interest of the United States. After interviewing Vanderbilt, one reporter wrote, "The owners of the road could not consent to let the employees manage it. There [are] great principles involved in this matter, said Vanderbilt, and we cannot afford to yield, and the country cannot afford to have us yield."[52] The policy of not allowing workers to have any say or any power in matters of their wages or working conditions was not limited to Vanderbilt. In a letter from railroad trustee J. H. Wilson to Carl Schurz, Wilson made clear that only he would determine the conditions in which the railroads under his command would be run: "I am managing property now in the custody of the U.S. Courts, and I shall certainly not permit my employees to fix their own rate of wages, nor dictate to me in any manner what my policy shall be."[53]

Over a thousand people attended a railroad workers' meeting on July 23 in Albany. Their demands were similar to those in Syracuse and elsewhere: restoration of the pay cut and a raise in wages. They voted to send the demands to Vanderbilt. The next day half of Albany's workforce failed to appear for work. Six hundred workers walked through the rail yards encouraging others to join the strike, while military forces were called in. The governor was a stockholder and director of the Erie Railroad. That afternoon a thousand people, most of them not railroad workers, met outside the capitol, marched to the rail yards, stopped men from working, destroyed switches, stopped trains, and removed rails. During the afternoon the crowd doubled in size. By Wednesday, July 25, hundreds of soldiers had arrived in Albany, and together with federal troops, the police, citizen patrols, and Civil War veterans from the Grand Army of the Republic, took over the rail yards and crushed the strike. Vanderbilt continued to refuse to negotiate, and under the threat of two thousand troops and eight pieces of artillery, the railroad workers went back to work.

Workers in Buffalo struck on July 21. The next day crowds joined them as 1,500 congregated at a roundhouse. The crowd stopped all freight trains but allowed passenger trains and the mail to pass. A ninety-car train with livestock was stopped and disabled. The crowd grew as the day went on, and the police were greatly outnumbered. Authorities tried to move a freight train at 4:00 p.m., but it was stopped by the crowd. On July 23 a large crowd met at the East Buffalo rail yard. The strike by firemen and brakemen on the Erie Railroad spread to include the New York Central and the Lake Shore and Michigan Southern. Engineers joined the strikers, and all work in the railroad shops was stopped. A Buffalo and Jamestown Railroad train was halted by workers, until they realized that the company had not reduced their wages, at which time it was allowed to proceed with railroad workers protecting it. Workers stopped a train full of militia members on its way to Buffalo, and armed workers forcefully took their weapons from them. Gunfire erupted, twelve were injured, and an eighteen-year-old boy was killed. One of the cars was set on fire, and when the crowd attempted to push it into the roundhouse, railroad workers stopped them.

Buffalo police asked for citizens' help as the strike grew on July 24. Members of a workers' committee who tried to negotiate with railroad management were fired. A crowd of five hundred attacked car shops of the New York Central Railroad, where a militia was housed. The crowd pushed its way in through the front of the building, while the militia escaped through the back. A number of the New York Central's railroad cars were burned. Thousands of troops occupied Buffalo, weakening the strike. Interestingly, the majority of the crowds were not railroad workers, demonstrating the anger of residents against railroad companies. The speed with which the strike spread to so many locations made it impossible for state and federal troops and militias to respond effectively. When Gen. W. F. Smith, the president of the New York Police Department, requested that certain regiments be sent to New York

City, Gen. A. Shaler, who commanded the First Division of the New York National Guard, responded, "It will afford me pleasure to comply with said demand, except that I shall be compelled to substitute the Twelfth Regiment for the Eighth, which is now en route for Buffalo."[54]

As the railroad strike spread, workers in other industries walked out in support or over their own issues. Even newsboys joined the strike in Detroit when the *Evening News* raised the price it charged them for papers. They stopped selling the newspaper and destroyed all the papers they could find until the company reduced their cost to the prior amount.[55] In McKeesport, Pennsylvania, National Tube workers joined the strike, then a mill and car works company, and Carnegie workers and Braddock car workers also joined. Miners struck, as did Jones and Laughlin steel workers. In Buffalo crowds called out workers; factories were closed in Harrisburg; and in Zanesville, Ohio, the unemployed joined in and shut down factories and stopped building construction. A crowd of two thousand marched and called out workers in Columbus, Ohio. Four thousand workers attended a mass meeting in Cincinnati, where "the speaking was in German, [and] a Communist flag was displayed."[56]

Black and white workers struck together in the South. The Texas and Pacific Railroad workers struck over a 10 percent pay cut. In Louisville, Kentucky, Black and white sewer workers struck, and a crowd of five hundred stoned the Louisville and Nashville Railroad depot. Crowds shut down most of Louisville's factories. Seven thousand people responded to a Workingmen's Party rally in San Francisco, which demanded an eight-hour day and government operation of the railroads. The movement in San Francisco was weakened by racism against Chinese workers, which resulted in rioting.

At a low ebb in 1877, cigar makers were inspired by the railroad strikes. Workers at the deBary cigar factory in New York lay down their tools and struck for higher wages. Samuel Gompers, then president of Local 144, led the strike and negotiations for cigar makers, winning a wage gain of 15 percent. "A unique feature of the relief program was the operation of a cigar factory by the union. The factory was purchased by the Central Organization of Cigarmakers to provide work for some of the strikers. . . . About 2,400 workers were employed in the shop, a percentage of their wages being deducted to pay for the factory."[57]

Marx and Lassalle had fought for many years over the correct course to take with regard to the proletariat's battle against the bourgeoisie. Marx believed that emphasis should be placed on organizing unions around economic issues in order to strengthen working-class organizations and class consciousness among workers. Only when that was successful should workers create their own political party. Lassalle, on the other hand, thought that workers should enter the political arena immediately with their own labor parties. At the 1875 Gotha Congress, followers of both theorists came together, and in the United States they formed the WPUSA, a communist organization, which ultimately sought to overthrow the capitalist bourgeoisie in the United States. The WPUSA made some electoral gains in Chicago, Milwaukee, and Cincinnati and published twenty-four newspapers, only eight of them in English.[58] The party was not responsible for the railroad strike in 1877. In fact, the spontaneity of the strike and the speed with which it spread took the party by surprise. It did hold mass meetings in a number of cities, including Philadelphia, Newark, Paterson, Brooklyn, San Francisco, and New York, in support of the strike once it broke out, some of them attracting upwards of ten thousand people. However, only in St. Louis did it take over leadership of the strike and of the city itself.

The railroad strike of 1877 shook American society to its core. Not only was it the greatest strike by workers in American history, but it also introduced and spread European revolutionary and socialist ideas throughout the American labor movement. Capitalists' fear that their world was on the brink of disaster cannot be exaggerated. The strike constituted a confrontation between labor and capital that had never been seen before in the United States. According to Philip Foner, the 1877 railroad strike brought the United States closer to a social revolution than anything other than the Civil War.[59] The *St. Louis Globe-Democrat* stated that "the very life of the nation was threatened."[60] The *Pittsburgh Leader* editorialized that the strike appeared to be the beginning of a new civil war, this time between labor and capital.[61] Writing in 1877, Dacus said that "it seemed as if the whole social and political structure was on the very brink of ruin."[62]

Altogether there were more than fifty killed and one hundred wounded as a result of the railroad strike.[63] In the end the railroads withdrew some pay cuts, and the strikes led to some regulation of the railroads and contributed to the unity of labor. The strike did not, however, destroy the capitalist foundation of American society, nor did it result in a socialist revolution. The railroad strike reflected the frustration of American workers with nineteenth-century industrial capitalism, but it did not have the leadership or focused revolutionary drive to overthrow the system it so overwhelmingly rejected.

In one place, however, the strike resulted in the only moment in American history when a major city was ruled by followers of Karl Marx and a communist party. The St. Louis Commune was born as a result of, and directly descended from, the 1848 European revolutions, the Paris Commune, and Marx's First International.

9

The St. Louis Commune

The effects of the 1848 revolutions, the Paris Commune of 1871, the First International, the 1873 depression, and the railroad strike of 1877 all came together in St. Louis in what could be described as a perfect storm. Each of those events affected the next, and together they resulted in the St. Louis Commune.

Following the Civil War, the expanding economy in the United States brought tremendous wealth for some, but it also caused hardships for small businesses and for the common worker. Much of the economic instability was a result of the expansion of the railroads, which overbuilt as a result of speculation. The railroads had laid miles of track in the western territories without commensurate consumer demand. The result was a loss of investment capital, a failure of confidence in banks, an unstable stock market, bankruptcies, and ultimately the Panic of 1873. Before the Civil War there was little federal regulation of businesses and banks, and panics had previously occurred in 1819, 1837, 1857, 1860, and 1861. The National Banking Act was consequently passed in 1863.

The Panic of 1873 was international in its scope. It began when the Vienna stock market collapsed in May of that year. But in the United States the Panic was primarily attributed to the financing of railroad construction; the country was especially vulnerable to the economic downturn since it was both recovering from the Civil War and embarking on tremendous and unregulated industrial growth. In 1873 the collapse of a New York banking house caused a lack of confidence by depositors everywhere and consumer runs on banks. Banks reacted by restricting withdrawals, which caused businesses, which were unable to purchase inventory or to meet their payrolls because of a lack of cash, to fail. By September there were suspensions of business by sixteen national banks, eleven state banks, seven savings banks, fifty-nine private banks, and four trust companies.[1] Most failures occurred in New York, but they had a ripple effect throughout the country. Working people experienced the banking instability by suffering from late or nonexistent payments of earnings, an inability to obtain loans, and a general lack of money. Short of cash, manufacturers often issued scrip instead of payment in dollars. There was a downturn in business expansion, manufacturing and production, and consumer spending and consequently employee layoffs. The lack of cash led to less buying by consumers, followed by less production, less manufacturing, and therefore fewer jobs.

Those businesses that had invested in or loaned money to railroad companies were especially hard hit by the depression. The Brooklyn Trust Company, which had made loans to the New Haven and Willimantic Railroad, closed in July 1873. On September 8 that year the Mercantile Warehouse and Security Company failed, and Kenyon, Cox and Company followed on September 13. The Mercantile Warehouse had advanced money to the Missouri, Kansas and Texas Railroad, which was unable even to make interest payments, and Kenyon and Cox had endorsed $1 million of the Canada Southern Railroad. Jay Cooke and Company, one of the most prominent banking houses in the country, failed on September 18. Its Philadelphia branch had advanced $15 million to the Northern Pacific Railroad. The First National Bank in Philadelphia, which was owned by Cooke and E. L. Clark and Company, suspended operations, and the First National Bank of Washington DC, in which Cooke also had an interest, failed.

The day following Cooke's failure the brokerage house of Fisk and Hatch suspended operations. Stock prices fell, and more than thirty brokerage houses became insolvent. There were runs on the Union Trust and the Fourth National Bank in New York, the Freedman's Bank, the Washington DC Savings Bank, and the Fidelity Trust and Safety Deposit Bank and Union Banking Company in Philadelphia. The closing of the Union Bank caused the suspension of the operations of the Keystone Bank, the Citizens Bank, and the State Bank. The National Bank of Commonwealth, National Trust, and Union Trust suspended operations on September 20, and on September 23 there were runs on virtually all banks in Manhattan and Brooklyn. Most banks had long lines of people who were attempting to withdraw funds. It was estimated that $30 million was withdrawn from banks in New York, Philadelphia, and Washington DC within a period of three days.[2] The stock market closed for ten days in an effort to maintain some stability in financial markets.

In late September the financial unrest spread throughout the Southeast, the Midwest, and the upper South of the United States. There were runs on eight of nine banks in Petersburg, Virginia. The Merchants National and First National banks were insolvent, and receivers were appointed; the People's Bank and the Planters and Mechanics banks were also closed, as was the Citizens Savings Bank. In Richmond, Virginia, the Dollar Savings Bank, the Mutual Loan Company, the Lancaster Bank, and Isaac, Taylor and Williams, a private bank, failed. On September 25 the Merchants and Planters National Bank and the Planter's Loan and Savings Bank suspended operations in Augusta, Georgia. The next day there were runs on banks in Savannah, Georgia, and three banks in Charleston, Virginia, suspended payments. Real estate and grain prices fell in Chicago, where the Franklin Bank closed and the brokerage house A. C. and O. F. Badger failed. Large runs on the banks in Chicago led to the closing of five national banks, including Union National, which was the largest bank in the West. Runs on the Memphis banks began on September 24, resulting in the closure of the First National Bank and the Desoto and Freedman's Savings Bank. The bank closings brought about a serious downturn in the economy.[3]

A study of six economic areas found a decline of 32 percent between 1873 and 1878. Railroad stock prices fell by 60 percent. Dun and Company reported that the number of bankruptcies increased from 5,183 to 10,478 during those years. More banks failed in Rhode Island in 1878 than in the entire history of the state.[4]

The poor, of course, were especially vulnerable to and harmed by the depression. They had no money or cushion of any kind to live on during times of crisis, so the loss of employment could mean the difference between life and death for destitute families. Yet there appeared to be no sympathy for them from the wealthy or those who exercised power in American society. It was, after all, the time of the Social Darwinist philosophy, according to which society evolved by the dying off of the weaker of the species and the survival of the fittest. Such, it was argued, was the law of nature. It was better for society as a whole if its weakest members were allowed to fail than to offer them help. Society was better off without them. Thus New York's governor opined that too much money was spent on educating the poor since it made them discontented with their situation in life.[5] William Graham Sumner, a staunch supporter of free markets and Social Darwinism, testifying before a congressional committee, argued that government should not interfere with economic markets and that society owed no one a living, except perhaps those in prison.[6] And the New York Society for Improving the Condition of the Poor declared that one should not accept the "foreign idea" that a person has a right to work or to receive subsistence if unable to work.[7]

The American labor movement was still young at the time of the depression and had been ravaged by the Civil War and later financial crises. Business failures led to the loss of jobs, and therefore a fewer number of workers were financially able or eligible to join unions. Following the Civil War, Marxist influence due to the efforts of German radicals and the First International grew and spread within the American labor movement. Early efforts to radicalize labor included the organization of the American Labor Union, which was started in 1853 by five German immigrants and was led by Joseph Weydemeyer, Marx's friend. Weydemeyer served as a colonel in the Union army, fought Confederate guerrillas in Missouri, and was later appointed by President Lincoln to command the military in the Union's St. Louis District. The Communist Club of New York was organized in October 1857, and other Communist Clubs were started in Chicago and Cincinnati. All opposed slavery and encouraged African Americans to join as full members, which was unusual given the blatant racism at the time. The leader of the clubs in the United States was F. A. Sorge, who supported Marx in his conflict with Lassalle on the importance of building working-class consciousness and unions prior to engaging in political activity.

The First International grew after the Civil War and spread through Europe and then across the Atlantic to the United States. By 1871 there were twenty-seven separate sections of the First International in the United States, most consisting of foreign-born workers in the largest cities. Of those twenty-seven sections, only six were made up of American-born workers, while ten sections were German, eight French, one Czech, and two Irish. The French sections contained many survivors of the Paris Commune, which had only recently shaken the confidence of European and American capitalists.[8]

Due to the Panic of 1873, the American sections of the First International raised three primary demands, which were not unlike the policies called for or instituted by members of the Paris Commune: (1) an eight-hour work-day at decent wages for all workers, (2) the guarantee of a week's worth of food or money in times of distress, and (3) a six-month moratorium on the collection of rents.[9] Industry, it was claimed, should provide workers with that relief, and if it was unable to do so, then the government should step in and guarantee it. Those demands by a communist organization were not especially radical during a period of severe economic troubles, but the fact that they were rejected in their entirety does exhibit the lack of sympathy for the poor at that time among the rich and powerful.

While union activity was suppressed during the Civil War, the harsh working conditions afterward increased interest in union organization. Sorge became the general secretary of the General Council of the International, which Marx had relocated from London to New York out of his concern about a potential coup within the organization by anarchists and Blanquists in Europe. When the National Labor Union was founded in August 1866, many members of the First International joined, and Sorge was the International's delegate to the new union. The National Labor Union, like the First International, recognized the need to organize workers internationally and to unite European and American workers, emphasized the need for the organization and growth of trade unions, and supported labor's demand for an eight-hour workday.

The first labor organization in St. Louis was the St. Louis County Agricultural Society, which was formed in 1822. It was primarily a social and educational association for farmers, but it did serve to unite them in their common interests and efforts. By the 1830s labor organizations in the city included the Typographical Society, the Society of Carpenters and Joiners, the Cabinet Makers Society, the Tinners Society, and the United Journeymen Cabinet Makers Society. Some of those unions would later be especially active in and supporters of the St. Louis general strike and the St. Louis Commune. In December 1835 the United Benevolent Society of Journeymen Tailors instituted the first strike of unionized workers in St. Louis, established a cooperative, and three months later declared their strike a victory.[10] In October 1836 even the city's barbers struck, demanding ten cents for a shave.[11]

Issues of race plagued early attempts at organization, a problem that continued for many years. Although the labor-related interests of Black and white workers were identical, free Blacks were perceived by some white workers as wild and undisciplined, and thus race was used by employers to divide white and Black workers. Employers themselves, however, did not distinguish between Black and poor white workers, but rather showed disdain for all members of the working class by considering both Black and poor white workers lazy, drunken, and violent and possessing no stake in a civilized society.[12]

Between 1830 and 1840 the population of St. Louis increased dramatically, and there was considerable building of both factories and housing, resulting in a shortage of workers; consequently, wages temporarily increased. The pay of common laborers increased from seventy-five cents to $1.75 per day, and the wages of iron workers and carpenters rose almost 50 percent.[13] Also, the ten-hour workday had become a national issue in the 1840s, and St. Louis labor organizations began demanding a ten-hour day in 1837 and showed an interest in politics in order to affect national and state legislation. In St. Louis, journeymen carpenters began demanding a ten-hour day in 1837, masons in 1838, and journeymen house carpenters in 1839.[14] In July 1840 representatives of approximately twenty-four trades met and established a committee to determine which candidates for public office were sympathetic to labor concerns, especially with regard to the ten-hour day.[15] A shorter workday had a positive effect on workers' health, enabled them to spend more time with their families, and allowed them time to improve themselves and to become better and more participatory citizens. The Mechanics and

Workingmen's Party was active in the 1841 election; it called for a ten-hour day and the removal of restrictions for holding public office. The mainstream political parties began to seek support from labor, and while unions were not yet strong enough to elect their own people to public office, they were often in a position to affect the outcome of some elections.

Unions were not especially active in St. Louis during the 1850s, but the Panic of 1857 caused a renewed interest in labor organization. The St. Louis printers formed a union in 1859 but were crushed by the newspaper owners. St. Louis unions were represented at the National Labor Convention in Baltimore in August 1866 by the Ship Carpenters and Caulkers Protective Union, the Molders Union, the Journeyman Painters, and the General Workingmen's Union.[16]

The Panic of 1873 had a tremendous effect on union activity. Unemployed workers arrived in a growing St. Louis looking for jobs, but employers were at the same time reducing their workforces. As a result, there were fewer jobs in St. Louis and a growing pool of unemployed labor. The rich of the city lived on private streets, for which St. Louis was famous; the poor lived in the wooden firetraps that made up urban slums. On Washington's birthday in 1874, over 1,200 members of the Societies of Bricklayers, the Stonemason's Union, and the United Order of Ancient Plasterers marched in a parade in the city. That same year the Mechanics and Blacksmith's Union suggested combining into an organization with the Grangers, while another proposal called for the unionization of the entire working class.[17] Although the national labor movement was young, there were signs of a growing class consciousness among workers.

In 1874 the followers of Lassalle left the International and started the Workingmen's Party of Illinois in the western states and the Social-Democratic Workingmen's Party of North America in the East. The issue again was whether the working class should enter the political arena immediately or, as Marx insisted, only after it had first succeeded in building strong labor organizations and unions. The primary purpose of the Lassalleans was to attain political power in order to ensure, among other goals, government financing of producers' cooperatives. However, between 1874 and 1876 Marxists and Lassalleans did engage in a working cooperation in Europe, which did not previously exist. European Marxists and Lassalleans agreed on a common program at the Gotha Congress in 1875, out of which grew the German Social Democratic Party. In the United States, Lassalle's followers unsuccessfully participated in the 1874 elections, and Marx's followers gained control of the Social-Democratic Workingmen's Party at its 1875 convention. The Marxists were successful in passing a resolution stating, "Under the present conditions, the organization of working people into trade unions is indispensable."[18] At the same time, the Workingmen's Party of Illinois successfully supported workers in strikes against a reduction of wages. At an April 1876 convention in Pittsburgh, a "Declaration of Unity" called for the unification of socialists and for the establishment of the Socialist Labor Party of the United States of North America.

It was in this political environment that the Workingmen's Party of the United States, the first Marxist political party in North America, was born. In July 1876 delegates from nineteen sections of the First International met in Philadelphia for the purpose of dissolving the International and establishing a united socialist party in the United States. The so-called Unity Congress met for four days and established the Workingmen's Party of the United States. It adopted many of the ideas of the First International, established a national executive committee in Chicago, and decided to allow local sections to engage in politics when the conditions were favorable. It also endorsed the Lassallean goal of establishing workers' cooperatives. Marx's ideas were also supported, as the organization's positions were clearly a compromise between the followers of the two theorists. While it was permissible to sometimes participate in politics, as the Lassalleans desired, the party would engage in political activity only when "it was strong enough to exercise a perceptible influence," as Marx proposed.[19] The stated purpose of the new organization was to "work for the organization of trade unions upon a national and international basis to ameliorate the condition of the working people."[20] Its demands included an eight-hour workday, the sanitary inspection of workplaces and housing, the end of prison labor, the end of labor for children under fourteen, free educational institutions, employer liability for workplace accidents, the abolition of conspiracy laws, the nationalization of all transportation companies, and equal rights for women in the workplace.[21] The *Labor Standard* was designated the official newspaper of the WPUSA.

The philosophy of the WPUSA and its political program was not unlike that of the First International. In *Papers for the People, No. 1*, wherein it set forth some of its philosophy, the party denied the justice of the present system of labor in the United States: "That a system of society that gives to the masses excessive toil and excessive poverty, and, to the few, leisure and wealth, is systematized injustice; and an iniquity that must be abolished."[22] The Executive Committee of the WPUSA published a pamphlet by Dr. A. Douai which sought to explain the reason for the lack of jobs and the suffering of working people in the United States. The reason, according to the WPUSA, was the institution of capitalism:

> This one cause is called *Capitalistic Production*. What does that expression mean? It means that those who produce all the goods and merchandise are not the owners of their means of labor. (Lands and real estate, mines, factories, machines, means of transportation, etc.) but must sell their working force to some owner of those means of labor; the former one called wages laborers, the latter capitalists. The capitalist does not pay to the laborer all the earnings of the labor of the latter, but only a portion thereof; he keeps the rest to reward himself for the loan of the means of labor—or, in other words, he makes the laborer work more hours a day than is needed to refund the outlay of capital and the outlay for wages.[23]

Such a system, explained Douai, creates wealth for a few by paying workers less than the value of their labor, and it creates misery for the many. There was no hope that the two different interests could ever come together and operate in harmony: "Private capital is a beast of prey that lives and thrives solely on human flesh and blood, or the substance of wages laborers. How can beasts of prey live in harmony with their victims?"[24] The WPUSA, Douai continued, supports and accepts the same principles as the International Workingmen's Association, the First International, and is not dismayed by being labeled a communist party by its adversaries: "Our party has been (reproachfully) called the *Communistic* party. We do not indignantly repudiate that name, it is in our view no title of reproach, but rather an honorable name."[25] Notwithstanding the allegations thrown at it by its adversaries, Douai went on to state that the WPUSA did not seek the violent overthrow of the U.S. government but instead advocated peaceful change. Violence was acceptable only in self-defense. The battle against capitalism had to be won on moral grounds. "It is for that reason," he continued, "that we deprecate and shun all violence, all wanton disregard of existing laws, how bad so ever they be, and all bloodshed, unless we be provoked and wantonly attacked, and forced to resist."[26]

The WPUSA's Constitution set forth its program, which included the demands listed above as well as free access to the courts and the nationalization of railroads, telegraphs, and other means of transportation and industry and the establishment of cooperatives.[27] Any two members speaking the same language were eligible to establish a section of the party, so long as three-fourths of the section consisted of wage earners.[28] The compromise between Marxists and Lassalleans is also codified in the Constitution: "The political action of the Party is confined generally to obtaining legislative acts in the interest of the working class proper. It will not enter into a political campaign before being strong enough to exercise a perceptible influence, and then in the first place locally in the towns and cities."[29] The party prioritized the emancipation of women, but as part of the emancipation of labor generally, similar to its position with regard to African Americans. When working people gained control of society, women would be free and equal to men: "The emancipation of women will be accomplished with the emancipation of *men*, and the so-called women's rights question will be solved with the Labor question. . . . By uniting their efforts they will succeed in breaking the economical fetters, and a new and free race of men and women will rise recognizing each other as peers. We acknowledge the perfect equality of rights of both sexes and in the Workingmen's Party of the United States. This equality of rights is a principle and is strictly observed."[30]

Notably, there was no specific mention of African Americans in the party's statement of purpose or demands, although its program on behalf of all workers certainly included them as well as white workers. However, the party did not set out demands specific to issues affecting African Americans. The end of racism, it was believed, would occur with the achievement of socialism.

Although African American workers were not a specific focus of the WPUSA, they did constitute a group that could not be ignored. African Americans were an important part of the workforce in the United States, especially in the South. In 1865 there were one hundred thousand Black mechanics in the South compared to twenty thousand white mechanics. In addition, many Black workers moved to the North after the Civil War. While neither the WPUSA program nor its papers dealt with issues specific to Blacks, it took the position that Black and white workers had the same common enemy: capitalism. Issues specific to Blacks would be resolved by socialism, which stood for justice and equality for all workers. The social battle was between economic classes, not between races.

While definitely a small minority within the group, African Americans were active members of the party. One well-known member was Peter Clark, a Black high school principal from Cincinnati, who later taught at Sumner High School in St. Louis. At one time Clark had attempted to move to Liberia but was stopped in New Orleans.[31] He had been a Republican, but became disillusioned by the Republican Party's failure to protect Blacks in the South after 1876 and the growing power of the capitalists in the party. He announced his support of the WPUSA in March 1877 and described the plight of poor Blacks and whites in the South as attributable to capitalism: "Capital must not rule, but be ruled and regulated. Capital must be taught that man, and not money, is supreme, and that legislation must be had for man."[32]

Sorge called for labor unions to work for a decrease in working hours and an increase in wages, consistent with Marx's belief that focusing on everyday issues would unite the working class and develop its class consciousness. The WPUSA also sought to organize unemployed workers and demanded public works programs in order to create new jobs. Women's issues were also targeted since women made up half of the workforce. The party grew quickly and by October 1876 boasted fifty-five sections, including thirty-three German-language sections, one Scandinavian, and one French. Less than a year later, there were seven thousand members of the WPUSA with eighty-two sections, twenty-three of which were English-language sections. The party operated three newspapers, two in the German language and the English-language *Labor Standard*. The WPUSA was especially strong in St.

Louis, where it boasted a local membership that was approximately 20 percent of the national membership. In St. Louis the WPUSA contained adherents of all stripes, including Marxists, Lassalleans, anarchists, and utopian socialists, who were followers of Cabet. While its numbers were increased by such inclusion, philosophical divisions continued strong within the party.

The depression was in its fourth year in July 1877. Fifteen million people were unemployed, wages had fallen, and layoffs had increased. It had only been six years since the Paris Commune, which was still in the minds of the propertied classes in the United States. According to Philip Foner, the United States was then closer to a workers' revolution than at any time in its history.[33] Labor's anger was primarily focused on the railroads, which had become a symbol of the corporate control of the U.S. government and society. The railroads generally suffered a downturn as a result of the depression, overbuilding, and rate wars, most of which were of their own doing. However, by laying off workers, reducing wages up to 50 percent, and doubling the amount of work employees were required to perform, some railroads were able to increase profits. In a letter from the Chicago, Burlington & Quincy's Robert Harris to a Mr. Griswold, Harris boasted that at the end of the third week of July 1877, the company was some $80,000 ahead of the prior year in profits. Harris did recognize, however, that it might not be in the long-term interest of the railroads to pay their desperate employees the least amount possible: "I dare say men can be hired at the rate of $30 per month or perhaps less, possibly at a price that will simply buy their necessary daily food. I do not think the Company should confine its observations to the single point: What is the least price at which labor can be had?"[34] Starving workers may have been a way to maximize short-term profits, but it was not a long-term winning strategy for railroad companies.

When the railroad strike broke out in the summer of 1877, the First International had been gone for a year, and the WPUSA was a relatively new organization. By July 22 over 1 million men had struck the railroads, and the strike had become national in scope, not as a result of the actions of any national labor organization but rather by a growing series of local actions that came together in a giant wave spreading across the country. The strike caught the WPUSA unprepared for the mass action by railroad workers throughout the United States. Although the executive committee in Chicago called on all its members to support the strike and put forth demands for an eight-hour day and the nationalization of railroads and telegraph lines, the WPUSA played no active part in the early events in Martinsburg, Baltimore, Hornellsville, Buffalo, Terre Haute, Indianapolis, or Pittsburgh. However, by July 22 it did recover sufficiently to organize rallies in various cities, such as the Tomkins Square demonstration in New York, and in Boston, Philadelphia, Louisville, and Cincinnati. In Philadelphia a meeting called by the WPUSA numbered upwards of five thousand and was broken up by the police. In Cincinnati the approximately four thousand attendees at one rally waved the red flag of communist revolution and the Paris Commune, and Peter Clark called for the nationalization of all industry and for the replacement of capitalism by socialism. A mass meeting of workers in Chicago attracted over twenty thousand people, and WPUSA members George Schilling and Albert Parsons addressed the crowd. Members of the party were arrested and its offices destroyed by police. Still, the party attempted to contain or to minimize violence and the destruction of property.

Although unions had made an early appearance in St. Louis, they were strongly affected by the arrival of new immigrants. Craft unions, including cabinet makers, carpenters, and tinners, had been organized in St. Louis since the 1830s. While the major issues concerning those unions were the ten-hour workday, wages, and the desire for a mechanic's lien law, the massive immigration that characterized the 1850s brought with it a number of German intellectuals, who provided the labor movement with new ideas and theorists. Although many of the new German immigrants were skilled workers or educated, most of the new Irish arrivals were unskilled, and the resultant larger labor pool had the effect of lowering wages generally. In the 1860s many St. Louis unions were affiliated with the National Labor Union. Like workers in the East, they eventually won the eight-hour day, but the victory was dulled by the use of contracts that were purportedly voluntary and required workers to labor longer hours. Refusal to sign such contracts resulted in an inability to find work or in blacklisting within the industry.

The Panic of 1873 dealt a serious blow to St. Louis unions and its working-class citizens. The overcapitalization of the railroads and the power of the new huge monopolies, together with blacklists and the infiltration of unions by Pinkerton detectives in the employ of the railroad companies, for a time virtually destroyed union activity. But the pay cuts instituted by the eastern railroads in the summer of 1877 resulted in the national railroad strike, immense violence, and a terrific destruction of property. Just six years following the Paris Commune, major American cities were marked by strikes and violence, and many Americans saw visions of the recent Paris Commune in the United States. Wendell Phillips warned of what he saw as revolutionary ardor existing below the surface of American society: "Scratch the surface of New York society, and you will find the Paris Commune."[35] Although there was a great deal of violence in some eastern cities, it was only in St. Louis that the railroad strike expanded into a general strike led by socialists, who ultimately ruled the city.

Most of the railroads around St. Louis came together in East St. Louis, directly across the Mississippi River in Illinois. St. Louis and East St. Louis were second only to Chicago as a railroad center. David Burbank, in *Reign of the Rabble*, has put together an excellent account of the strike events in St. Louis during the summer of 1877. Following the outbreak of spontaneous strikes in the East, on Saturday, July 21, railroad workers in East St. Louis met and announced their support of those workers on strike. The next night a number of East St. Louis railroad workers, representing different lines, elected an executive committee, which issued what was known as General Order No. 1, which directed workers to stop all freight traffic in East St. Louis that day at midnight. Passenger and mail trains would be allowed to run so that the traveling public was not inconvenienced more than was necessary and so the federal government had no excuse to intervene. A huge meeting of a thousand workers was held at the railway depot in East St. Louis, where four hundred St. Louis workers joined them, having ferried across the Mississippi River singing the "Marseillaise."[36] American workers singing the anthem of the French Revolution appeared to relate American labor to European revolution.

Peter A. Lofgreen, Albert Currlin, and Henry F. Allen, members of the Executive Committee of the WPUSA in St. Louis, spoke to the crowd at the East St. Louis meeting. Luke Hite, a prominent lawyer in St. Clair County,

Illinois, also spoke and declared that a war was being waged between labor and capital.

The radicalism that had emerged in the American working class was evident at the meeting. According to one speaker at the meeting in East St. Louis, capitalists, including their children, despised members of the working class and considered them to be of lesser worth.[37] The decision to strike was spontaneous, with no existing railroad-related organization calling for or supporting a strike at that time. The WPUSA in St. Louis immediately declared its support for the strike and the restoration of the 1873 wage scale, which was about 50 percent higher than that following the wage reductions.[38]

As described earlier, also on July 21 Lofgreen and Currlin spoke at a meeting of workers in Carondelet, and the WPUSA came out in support of the national railroad strike. The St. Louis papers on Monday described the violence in Pittsburgh, called on former Civil War generals to aid in the suppression of the strike in St. Louis, and asked for federal troops to be moved to the city.

The city of East St. Louis was largely working class, and the villages immediately surrounding it included several company towns. The city was a haven from the municipal regulations that existed in St. Louis. According to Walter Johnson, from the moment it was founded in 1861, "the city of East St. Louis was a municipal shell for unbridled capitalist extraction and unchecked governmental corruption."[39] Because of the weakness of the municipal authority and the large population of railroad employees in the city, it was not difficult for workers to take control of the city.

The mayor of East St. Louis, John Bowman, supported the strikers, even appointing many of them as special police to protect railroad property. Bowman did not want to alienate the workers, who constituted a good share of East St. Louis's citizens and voters. Although he was more of a nationalist and a republican than a socialist, Bowman had participated in the 1848 Revolution in Germany and had belonged to a conspiratorial group in London, which was made up of former revolutionaries. The strikers' executive committee trusted Bowman and authorized him to meet with the railroad managers and owners in order to reach an agreement, but the owners refused the invitation to discuss a settlement of the strike with him. The strike then spread to other industries throughout East St. Louis as the population was strongly in support of the railroad workers.

Mayor Henry Overstolz of St. Louis, the first German-born city official, asked the railroads to reinstate the wage scale prior to the pay cut in order to avoid violence in the city. The Missouri Pacific Railroad agreed, and the Union Railway & Transit Company agreed to postpone a planned wage cut, but the other companies refused the mayor's request. There was no question that the wages paid by the railroad companies were hardly sufficient to ensure survival. Even the attorney for the Ohio and Mississippi Railroad Company admitted that the strike was a result of the pay cuts and that wages were entirely too low.

The strikers then made a decision whose wisdom and strategic value could later be questioned. East St. Louis strikers discovered Missouri Pacific employees working in St. Louis, since the railroad had acceded to their demands. The East St. Louis workers asked the St. Louis workers to walk out anyway, in support of the other strikers, and the Missouri Pacific workers agreed to do so.[40] It had been decided to continue the strike against all railroads, whether or not any particular one had agreed to the strikers' demands, until each and every company had agreed to restore the pay cuts. Rather than allowing those railroads that reinstituted the prior wage standard to operate, thereby providing an incentive for companies to come to an agreement with workers and putting those companies who refused at a disadvantage, the strikers decided to continue to strike against all railroads unless and until all acceded to their demands. Under the all-or-nothing situation, there was no incentive for a railroad to reach an agreement with workers unless all did so. Workers would continue to strike whether or not an individual company agreed to their demands. Therefore, instead of dividing the railroad companies by allowing those that rescinded the pay cuts to operate to the disadvantage of the others, the strike committee instead ensured that the railroad companies would all unite. It was the strikers, especially those from East St. Louis, who in fact made it not only possible but also necessary for the companies to act together.

The strike soon spread to other areas of Missouri, and, as a result, train schedules were seemingly worthless, with some trains running a regular schedule, others more infrequently, and still others completely shut down. In Carondelet, a mass meeting on Monday between railroad workers and employees of the Vulcan Iron Works was a sign that the railroad strike had the potential to become a general strike and spread to other industries.

Even though there had been little to no violence in St. Louis, merely a work stoppage, J. H. Wilson, the receiver for the St. Louis and Southeastern Railroad, telegraphed Secretary of the Interior Carl Schurz, a veteran of the 1848 German Revolution, in Washington DC on July 22 to request the intervention of federal troops: "The railroad employees met at East St. Louis tonight and have resolved to stop all freight trains and switching engines after midnight. No violence yet. Are there any troops at arsenal here the situation is alarming."[41] By admitting that there was no violence, Wilson sought to enlist the power of the federal government in favor of the railroad companies and against lawful strikers. It is also clear that he desired an immediate confrontation with workers, with the railroad companies and state, federal, and municipal governments united against the strikers. He had no interest in discussing a settlement but rather sought to crush the strike as soon as possible. Interestingly, it was as if Wilson agreed with Marx that the battle between capital and labor was inevitable. In a letter to Schurz written on the same day he sent the telegram, Wilson wrote, "I write today, that in my opinion, the fight ought just as well be made now as at any time."[42]

On Monday night several thousand people attended a mass meeting called by the WPUSA at St. Louis Market. The crowd was so large that it was necessary to erect three separate speakers' stands. Lofgreen was elected to serve as chair of the meeting, and speakers included Currlin and Curtis of the WPUSA and Glenn of the Knights of Labor. As workers from each railroad company announced that they were joining the strike, there was loud cheering from the crowd. But perhaps more important, the working-class anger was directed not only against the railroad companies but also against the capitalist monopolies. One speaker specifically identified monopoly as the enemy of the working class: "Monopoly has us by the throat, and it will crush us if we show it that we will allow it to do so."[43] Another speaker pointed out that the violence against working people was being perpetrated by large corporations, which enacted policies and procedures that caused the deaths of workers in the absence of any consequences. In effect, the meeting served as a basis for an attack on capitalism and its control of the state. One reporter summarized another speech: "He said the papers told them that the rights of property ought to be maintained, and that those who shot anybody ought to be hung. But monopolies stole railways and starved their workmen, and in this way took life, but they were not hung. This state of things had been going on for years and was getting worse. The rich corporations stole our lives, and when they did that they stole the most valuable property in the possession of man."[44]

Then Lofgreen asked the crowd, "Why should we allow ourselves to be trodden upon by a few monopolists, who having the reins of government in their hands, are using the organized assassins to crush us?"[45] Corporations had taken control of the government and were using its power to enslave the working classes. Another speaker was cheered when he explained that workers were taxed "to sustain a standing army to be used to repel invasions by foreign powers, but the army is now used as a tool to oppress and slaughter innocent men, women and children."[46] Another speaker pointed to the grand buildings of the city and stated that the poor had built them, yet the rich owned them. They used the social superstructure, as Marx had explained, to control and oppress workers: "Why this state of things? Because it's so, according to the law. Well, if that's law, then d—n the law. [Prolonged cheers]. If that is the rule that governs society, then the sooner it is broken the better."[47] It was clear that a movement that originally was directed against railroad corporations over the issue of wages was expanding its focus to include all capitalist monopolies and the governmental forces they controlled. The WPUSA Executive Committee had experience with strikes, international labor organization, and socialism. For example, Cope had been involved with the London Trades' Council, many members of which were active in the First International, and Currlin was a delegate to the Philadelphia convention that disbanded the First International and founded the WPUSA.

As an antislavery city located in a slave state, St. Louis was uniquely affected by racial matters. Although there was still a good deal of racism in the city at the time, a Black worker also spoke at the meeting and was applauded by the crowd. He asked whether white workers would stand together with Black workers, and the crowd thundered, "We will!" The meeting then elected a committee of five, including WPUSA members Currlin, Curtis, James McCarthy, and Cope, and a Black worker to meet with the mayor to request that he ask the president not to send federal troops to St. Louis.

While the workers in St. Louis met, strikers were active all over the country. That same day some workers in Reading, Pennsylvania, were killed by a militia, thousands of workers attended a mass meeting in Chicago, and railroad workers in Kansas City went on strike. Pennsylvania's governor wired President Hayes on July 23 warning of an insurrection: "I repeat application of this morning and hourly the situation is growing worse and spreading all over the state and the whole country will soon be in anarchy and revolution unless you can save it by prompt action."[48] The next day John Welsh, president of the North Pennsylvania Railroad, wrote Hayes from Philadelphia: "It is not one part of the country but all parts of it, and it is not one class of the community but all classes whose interests are involved and the fact cannot be disguised that if the violations of law which have occurred are not checked & punished not only individual rights but the government itself may be sacrificed."[49] In St. Louis the national guard transferred a hundred rifles and men to the city's Four Courts Building, where it set up its headquarters. In Chicago on July 24 a vice president of the Illinois Central, W. K. Ackerman, sent his daily report to the president of the line describing the situation there: "Between 100 and 200 outside men came down to the freight House this morning and ordered the men to quit work and demanded that the switching engineers should be sent back to the Round House whereupon all of the men at the Freight House quit work. . . . This will necessitate the stoppage of all passenger trains out this evening and this seems to be the general action of all the lines centering here. The crowd is now going around forcing men to quit work in all directions. . . . We have stopped all our freight trains outside the city."[50]

The reduction in pay was not the only financial hardship experienced by railroad workers. Work was unsteady, and a regular work week was infrequently scheduled. After having experienced two wage reductions, the engineers, firemen, and brakemen of the Missouri Pacific Railroad demanded a restoration of wages to the level in effect prior to January 1, 1877. The railroad responded that it was willing to restore wages only to the rate before May

15, 1877, whereupon the strikers replied that they would accept that offer if they could at least be guaranteed a full day's work. Rather than promise a regular work schedule, Missouri Pacific then agreed to restore wages to the amount paid workers prior to January 1, 1877, as the strikers originally requested.[51] Another meeting was held Monday night at Market Square in south St. Louis, where deafening applause followed speeches in favor of the strikers. The class nature of the strike was clear from the speeches: "Capital had overridden and violated the Constitution, and was bringing down labor into serfdom. Workingmen must either fight or die."[52] It was better to die from bullets, some remarked, than to die from starvation.

By Tuesday, July 24, the railroad strike had spread across Missouri. In Sedalia, workers for the Missouri, Kansas and Texas Railroad had struck over the wage cuts and the back pay owed them. Workers employed by the St. Louis, Kansas City and Northern and the Missouri Pacific at Kansas City also struck. Engineers for the Missouri Pacific refused to haul U.S. troops farther than Sedalia, and on one occasion had abandoned them on a side track. The Chicago and St. Louis, the Cairo Short Line, Ohio and Mississippi, St. Louis and Southeastern, Chicago, Burlington & Quincy, and the Vandalia Line all stopped running trains through St. Louis.[53] In Hannibal there was a strike against the Chicago, Burlington & Quincy lines and the Hannibal & St. Joseph, the latter being three months behind in the payment of wages. All railroad lines in East St. Louis were closed down, and virtually no freight moved east. J. H. Wilson, the federal receiver, asked Mayor Bowman of East St. Louis to arrest the strikers, even though they had broken no laws, but the mayor refused to do so. At this time the workers had only struck and withheld their labor, without violating any laws.

Recognizing the validity of the workers' complaints, the *St. Louis Times* called on the railroad companies to agree to the strikers' demands. That day the East St. Louis strikers' Executive Committee issued Order No. 2, which officially provided that only the Committee could agree to a settlement on behalf of the workers and that there would be no settlement unless all railroad companies were part of it. The management of some railroads themselves stopped all passenger service, although such traffic was not otherwise affected by the strike, in an attempt to turn the public against the strikers. That tactic was attempted by companies elsewhere, but the traveling public appeared to recognize that the companies, not the strikers, were responsible for any obstacles to passenger travel. In a letter to the *Missouri Republican*, seventy-one travelers in Erie, Pennsylvania, accused the railroad companies of causing their inconvenience, while exonerating the strikers:

> We, the undersigned passengers who have been detained on the trains in this place the past twenty-four hours, wish to express the indignation we feel towards the railroad companies for what we have every reason to believe has been an uncalled-for abandonment of their trains at this point. The strikers here have been remarkably peaceable and orderly, and show every mark of kindness to the passengers, and have used every exertion in their power to forward all mail and passenger trains from this point. . . . As an example of the kindness of the strikers toward us, at their meeting last evening a contribution was taken to defray the expenses of passengers who were unprepared for the delay, many ladies and children being provided for at the hotels at the expense of the strikers.[54]

The railroad strike in East St. Louis was spreading to other businesses; all the packing houses shut down, and southern Illinois miners declared their support for the strikers. The miners even promised to send a thousand men to East St. Louis to aid the strike.[55] J. H. Wilson had informed Secretary Schurz that East St. Louis had been shut down and requested that two thousand federal troops be sent to the city. In the meantime, local authorities were not interfering with the strikers. The *Globe-Democrat* reported that on Tuesday "no official of the company interfered in the least. A policeman was asked if he could not make any arrests. He laughed, and said as long as the railroad companies did not interfere with the men running the trains for them, it was none of their business."[56]

The WPUSA had taken control of events in St. Louis and established what would become known as the St. Louis Commune. It sought to operate the city in the interests of the working-class while leading the strike against the railroad corporations. Subsequently the party would direct and coordinate all labor actions in St. Louis and, for a time, rule the city itself. Again the elite laid the blame for the disturbances not on the railroad monopolies but on foreigners, the First International, and the Paris Commune. The *Missouri Republican* raised the warning that the events in Paris were about to be repeated in St. Louis: "The Internationalists have taken control of the strike, same as the communists who took control of Paris in 1870."[57] At the same time, other workers than those on the railroads contacted the party for support and advice.

The coopers went on strike and paraded through the St. Louis streets calling out to other workers to join them. Newsboys struck, along with employees of the St. Louis Gas Works. Boatmen on the levee, most of whom were Black, struck and received wage increases almost immediately. A *Missouri Republican* reporter who had infiltrated the strikers' ranks dressed as a tramp, described the strikers, as the *Republican* was wont to do, not as struggling workers attempting to survive but as vicious animals: "The cluster were simply communists, who, when they talked, showed their teeth like wolves."[58] The newspaper sought to dehumanize the strikers and thereby turn the public against them.

Rich and prominent St. Louis leaders feared mob actions and violence. Everyone was familiar with what had occurred in Paris only six years previously, and recently in Baltimore and Pittsburgh. It was clear to them that the unrest had taken on the characteristics of a working-class or proletarian revolt against the railroads and corporate interests generally. There was no doubt in the minds of the "good people" that the European revolutions and the foreign ideology of communism had crossed the Atlantic and taken root and sprouted in the United States. St. Louis, they feared, was on the verge of imitating Paris, where the working class armed itself in preparation for battling the capitalists. The WPUSA, they claimed, was identical to the First International, which they believed was also responsible for the Paris Commune: "Behind the discontent of the poor-paid workingmen, appeared the horrid front of the Commune. It was the 'Workingmen's Party of the United States,' known in Europe as the 'Workingmen's International Association,' that had assumed the reins and were endeavoring to drive the car of civilization over the precipice of destruction."[59] Many of the St. Louis rich prepared themselves for a battle between the social classes; they slept in their clothes, sent their families outside of the city for safety, and hoarded food and water in case of a complete breakdown of society, when necessities would become impossible to obtain.[60]

St. Louis leaders were marked by conflicts of interest with regard to labor and the railroad strike. A group of businessmen met with the mayor on Tuesday and encouraged him to raise up to a thousand volunteers to confront the strikers. Among those meeting with the mayor were Gen. John S. Carender and Erastus Wells, both of whom had significant railroad holdings, and J. H. Wilson, the federal receiver for the St. Louis and Southeastern. Wells was also a director of the Ohio and Mississippi Railroad. No representative of the workers was present at the meeting. Employers agreed to order their employees to join the new militias being organized. The greed of the railroads was highlighted by the fact that employees of one railroad office who joined the militia at the order of their employer were docked pay while they involuntarily served in the employers' militia.[61]

Unlike the mayor of East St. Louis, who supported the strikers, at the secret meeting of what were described as the "good people" of St. Louis, that city's mayor warned of what he described as a conspiracy of thirty thousand socialists who sought to overthrow the municipal government. There was no organized opposition, he said, with which to stop them. It was necessary to organize the good, law-abiding citizens of the city. Like superheroes, those at the meeting and their cohorts were described by the *Globe-Democrat* as superior to common men in intellect and physical prowess, almost god-like, certainly people destined by nature to lead the forces of good: "Those who were thus sworn in appeared to be the pick of the best educated classes of society; men whose light fitting and fashionably cut clothes but partly conceal brawny muscles and magnificent physical powers."[62] A member of the Board of Police Commissioners asked the mayor to call a public meeting for the purpose of organizing the conservative forces in the city.

Since St. Louis was at the time unprepared for a general strike, the Catholic Church's Bishop Patrick John Ryan suggested orchestrating a trick to buy time, during which the authorities and corporate interests would be able to consolidate and prepare their forces. The local managers of the railroad companies, Ryan explained, should agree to the demands of the workers in order to end the strike, then send the resulting agreement to the companies' boards of directors. The boards could meet and reject the previously agreed upon settlement, thereby allowing the city and businesses time in which to organize their forces. Local Catholic organizations were directed to give no aid to strikers and to ally themselves on the side of law and order. The Internationalists, it was argued, were arrayed against the Church and its followers. There was, of course, some truth to the allegation that the socialist leadership opposed the Church. Some of the socialists were atheists or free thinkers. Others resented the Church's historical support for conservative causes and forces both in Europe and in the United States.

Albert Warren Kelsey, a leading member of the militia whose memoir and autobiographical notes described the fear of the city's propertied classes during the general strike, was one of the "good people" of St. Louis who was invited to the mayor's meeting. Other attendees were bank presidents, the police commissioner, and the city's leading businessmen. In his memoir, Kelsey described the meeting's plan for a citizen militia made up of "respectable members of the body politic, who had responded to a call from their employers to come forward and enroll themselves as being willing to assist the State and City authorities in the preservation of law and order."[63] Kelsey ordered that all bottles in his home be filled with water and that all members of the household sleep with their clothes on, ready to rise up from bed and fight or flee at any moment. It was a time of peril, he said, and no one knew whether or when he or she would be able to obtain necessities or be called to action. The entire city was in danger, it seemed, of collapsing: "It appeared as if society was about to be resolved into its original elements."[64]

Although somewhat exaggerating the danger to St. Louis, at the meeting the mayor described the situation as desperate. It was a revolution, he said, which sought to overthrow by force and violence the legitimate authority and government of the city. Kelsey wrote, "Mayor Overstolz went on to say that his information was to the effect that no less than 'thirty thousand socialists' were fully armed and equipped, and had long been arranging for the overturn of the regularly organized forces of the city."[65] The mayor presented a picture of wild-eyed revolutionaries intent on destroying civilized society in St. Louis. In this battle to the death, the mayor stated, the city did not have the forces to guard prisoners and therefore he ordered that no prisoners be taken. Reminiscent of Thiers's order to Versailles troops attacking the Paris Commune, the mayor commanded, "Shoot them on the spot; do you understand me? Kill them; do not bring in any prisoners."[66] That command stands out in light of the fact that the strikers had not engaged in any real violence or destruction of property. The First Amendment's guarantees of speech and assembly were suspended in St. Louis de facto if not de jure. The mayor had effectively ordered death sentences for the striking workers.

Some militia members were ordered to dress as workers, attend the mass meetings called by the WPUSA, and note down the names of the most radical speakers so that they could be arrested at a later date. A major in the citizens' militia, who commanded a battalion of Compton Hill forces, Kelsey maintained that his best company consisted of Germans who had experience fighting in the American Civil War and/or the Franco-Prussian War. Those who led the militia were themselves generally wealthy and thus opposed to the socialists.[67] However, more and more businesses were being shut down, St. Louis businessmen wanted to end the strike by force, and many had lost confidence in the mayor's ability or desire to do so. The mayor talked about the need to end the strike, often in very strong words. He did not, however, take what the businessmen believed to be the necessary steps to suppress the uprising. In their opinion, he was not acting with enough speed or power. It appeared to them that nothing was being done to end the strike. In order to return law and order to the city, they would have to act themselves. That afternoon thousands of St. Louisans gathered at the Union Depot, where the strike committee was directing activities.

It was decided in Washington not to send federal troops unless a governor announced that an insurrection against the state was occurring that the state was unable to control and specifically requested federal troops. That decision was not entirely based in law. Following the Civil War and the end of Reconstruction, the army had been drastically reduced in number, and most of the remaining troops were occupied on the western frontier fighting Indians. Following the Civil War, the army had been drastically reduced in number in an attempt by Congress to pay off the massive debt that was incurred during the war. By 1874 there were only twenty-five thousand troops in the U.S. Army, and that number would decrease even more. A third of the troops were stationed in the South during Reconstruction, leaving a relatively small number to patrol the massive western frontier.[68] Of those, most were illiterate and incompetent, pay was exceedingly low, and desertion rates were staggering. For example, of 1,288 recruits received by the First Cavalry during a three-year period, 928 deserted.[69] The *Missouri Republican* explained, "It is evident that the federal government cannot respond fully to all their demands. The army is small, and has its hands full in fighting the Indians and protecting the government property."[70] Some soldiers could be sent, however, if strikers interfered with trains that were in receivership and under federal control. Still, troops were removed from the South and the West and relocated in an effort to suppress labor unrest.

Whatever the basis eventually decided upon, six companies of federal troops did arrive at the Union Depot in St. Louis on Tuesday, purportedly to protect federal property, a reason that would be given for federal intervention continuing even to today, whether or not such property was endangered. Many of the troops were African American, and the racism that characterized some of the strikers was evident when one East St. Louis striker complained about the "n———" troops that had arrived in St. Louis. The same thing had occurred in other cities, where the government attempted to divide the poor according to race by using Black troops to break up strikes. The troops that were sent to St. Louis were, however, primarily white and well-armed with Gatling guns and established themselves in the federal arsenal.

Also on Tuesday a Committee of Public Safety was organized by St. Louis businessmen, and two generals, A. J. Smith and John S. Marmaduke, were empowered to raise a citizens' militia. Smith had been a Union officer during the Civil War, and Marmaduke a Confederate. The class nature of the confrontation was clear. Adversaries in the war between North and South had come together to rescue capitalists from their workers. Soldiers who had only recently waged war against the United States were now apparently forgiven and placed in charge of suppressing workers seeking a fair wage, many of whom had fought to defend the Union from the former traitors. The Committee of Public Safety included Gen. John W. Noble, Gen. John S. Cavender, and Judge Thomas T. Gantt. In an effort to pit workers against workers, the Committee called on all employees of St. Louis businesses to join the new militia, promising to care for their families in the event they were killed or injured. The *Missouri Republican* attacked what it described as the communist threat to property and called for war veterans to mobilize under the command of Generals Smith and Marmaduke. That day three hundred men of the Twenty-Third Infantry arrived in St. Louis, purportedly to protect federal property.[71]

Among the Committee of Public Safety leadership and rank and file, the overwhelming majority were not of the working class. David Roediger has provided a detailed study of the Committee's demographics. Only 1.3 percent of its leadership and 5.5 percent of its membership were working class. Its leadership was 23.4 percent merchants, 5.2 percent financiers, 23.4 percent manufacturers and builders, 23.4 percent professionals, 5.2 percent government officials, 10.4 percent small business owners, and 6.5 percent railroad managers. Bookkeepers and clerks made up 51.2 percent of the Committee's followers; most of them were employed by the Committee's leaders and forced to join.[72] Thus most of the Committee's leadership and supporters were capitalists and white-collar workers, most of whom were employed by the business owners. Half of the Committee leaders were born in the United States, while there was an overrepresentation of Irish and German elites. Merchants and "their white-collar employees acted decisively against the general strike in St. Louis."[73]

At the time the Committee of Public Safety was organized, there was little need for federal or state troops or the creation of an armed militia of private citizens numbered in the thousands. There had been some intimidation of workers by those encouraging a general strike, but little, if any, violence. The real purpose of the Committee, organized by the businessmen and capitalists of St. Louis, was to crush the working-class action. That was the reason that many of St. Louis's leading capitalists would later call for action against the workers first, and to determine a legal basis for such action later. Using racism and scare tactics, St. Louis's leaders railed against the participation of African Americans in the strike and the threat of foreign communism to real American values.

In the meantime, the WPUSA in St. Louis, which boasted German, French, English, and Bohemian sections and approximately a thousand members, had its headquarters at Turner Hall, a former meeting place for Germans. On Tuesday night the party leaders met with delegates appointed by various unions and formally established an Executive Committee to lead the strike in St. Louis. That night a parade and a mass meeting were held at Lucas Market with upwards of ten thousand people in attendance. The meeting marked the beginning of the general strike. J. P. Kadell, a WPUSA member and cooper, announced that the strikers had seven thousand arms available to them and compared the situation in St. Louis and throughout the country to the French Revolution. Whether he was including in his count arms stored in arsenals or gun shops or was attempting to excite the strikers by exaggerating their power, in fact the workers had virtually no arms available to them. At the Lucas Market meeting, Currlin spoke to the crowd in German, and James McCarthy asked the group to form companies and patrol the streets in order to protect property, but also to meet force with force, if necessary. Attorney J. J. McBride, who was a supporter of the Fenians, called for an eight-hour workday. H. F. Allen called for a general strike in the name of the Executive Committee of the WPUSA and demanded both an eight-hour workday and the end of child labor. There were speeches in a number of different languages, including English, German, Bohemian, and French.

However, the WPUSA, while nominally in control of the strike, had no real strategy or plan of action. The strike took it by surprise, and so no preparations had been made. It did not attempt to bring all of the unions into the movement or to arm the workers, and, like the leadership of the Paris Commune, it made no effort to take control of the banks. There was no real cooperation with strikers in other cities, and control of its own city had virtually fallen into its lap. The WPUSA had not conquered the city by force, but, like the Paris communards, assumed control when city authorities seemingly withdrew their leadership. At the same time, there existed tensions between Black and white and German and Irish workers. The unions that were most active in the strike were the German cabinet makers, the iron molders, and shoe workers.

Tuesday night the Committee of Public Safety wired the secretary of war to request ten thousand rifles, two thousand revolvers, artillery, and ammunition for its private army. General Pope at Fort Leavenworth sent additional troops, and Gen. Jefferson C. Davis, who had marched with Sherman through Georgia, arrived with six hundred troops and two Gatling guns. By Tuesday the strike had spread all over the country and included all trades. In St. Louis thousands paraded through the streets of Carondelet, and Martindale & Eddy's Zinc establishment, Carondelet Zinc Works, and Missouri Zinc Works were all closed down. Two more companies of troops arrived from Fort Leavenworth, leaving only a small number of men on duty there, even though there was little or no violence in St. Louis. There were, instead, a good deal of meetings and speeches, but very little of what could be considered illegal conduct. The need for federal troops, local vigilantes, and thousands of arms was entirely nonexistent. Even the *Globe-Democrat* recognized that the strikers were reasonably well-behaved and reported, "Here in St. Louis the most violent doctrines of Communism are proclaimed, but no harm seems to be done by them."[74] It was clear that the intention was to intimidate the strikers and suppress the strike.

At the Lucas Market meeting that Tuesday night, speakers demanded that the government spend $100 million on public works in order to create jobs and called for a general strike for an eight-hour workday and for the end of child labor. One worker described the hardships suffered by striking workers, asked for support, and invoked the French Revolution:

We have been made the slaves of capital, the serfs of the bondholders. We have been informed year after year that the times would be better, but there has been no improvement. The time has now arrived when we must gather the harvest that has been growing for the last seven years. We ask you all, workingmen of Missouri, to join with us in this righteous and honest cause to protect our wives and children from the rude hand of starvation. This is the beginning of the same kind of revolution that cost a King of France his head, and we must take warning by it. . . . There was a time in the history of France when the poor found themselves oppressed to such an extent that forbearance ceased to be a virtue, and the heads of some hundreds were tumbled into the basket. That turn may have arrived with us, and we will sweep them out of existence. [Loud and deafening applause and wild cheering.][75]

Another speaker also called for radical change, urging the crowd not to be satisfied with a reinstatement of the 10 percent pay cut, but to demand the reorganization of the railroad industry and to place the railroads "in the hands of those who would make them yield their benefits to the people and not to the capitalists only."[76] After the meeting a thousand men marched through surrounding streets behind a flag and a band.

On Wednesday, July 25, strikes continued to spread across the United States, increasing pressure on the cities. Trains did not leave St. Louis or Chicago. The Baltimore and Ohio advised the U.S. Treasury Department that no freight was moving north or west.[77] Businesses were not able to obtain the products they needed in order to survive. New York City was not receiving grain from the West, and even some Canadian railroads joined the strike. Railroad workers struck in Kansas City, Chicago, Indianapolis, Terre Haute, Columbus, Cincinnati, Louisville, Pittsburgh, and Baltimore. Some of the railroads were completely taken over by strikers, who operated the passenger trains and collected fares that they then turned over to the railroad companies. While such conduct did reflect good faith on the part of the strikers, it also proved to be a boon for the railroads, which were able to run their passenger trains without paying their workers. A mass meeting in New York's Tomkins Square was organized by socialists, and the strike was growing in Chicago, where a crowd of forty thousand clashed with police. The headline in the *St. Louis Post-Dispatch* that day exclaimed, "The Strike Spreading Like Wildfire."[78] While it had no effect on the strike generally, the president of the St. Louis, Alton & Terre Haute Railroad agreed to the strikers' demand to reinstate the pay rate which was in effect on July 1, before the latest pay cut took effect.

The St. Louis Committee of Public Safety, having lost confidence in the mayor's ability to control the strike, acted independently of city officials, organizing citizens' militias, supervising their military training, and attempting to obtain arms in order to suppress the strike by force. It became, in effect, a vigilante group that sought to impose its idea of order on the city. All saloons were closed, and municipal governance was all but ignored. Although it had no legal standing, the Committee of Public Safety, having taken over the Four Courts Building, directed the sheriff to raise a *posse comitatus* of five thousand men. Six hundred had joined by Wednesday night, and an order by the sheriff appeared in Friday's *Post-Dispatch* threatening those citizens who had not responded to the sheriff's call: "All citizens who have been served as a *posse comitatus* by Sheriff Finn's deputies and have not reported this a.m., will report at the Court-house between the hours of 4 and 6 p.m. It is proper to state that any failure to report as above stated will subject the person to the full penalty of the law, which in this case will be rigidly enforced. By order of SHERIFF FINN."[79] All citizens of the city were being threatened with arrest and perhaps jail unless they joined the sheriff's posse against the strikers. Even though there had been hardly any violence by the strikers, Missouri's governor ordered the state arsenal to send rifles, ammunition, and artillery to St. Louis.

However, virtually all freight traffic in St. Louis and East St. Louis had been stopped, and only mail and passenger trains were allowed to pass through the cities.[80] The effectiveness of the strike was reflected in a bulletin that was published at the railroad depot in order to alert the public to the status of railroad transportation: "St. Louis and Southeastern—No. 4, abandoned. Wabash—No. 4, on time; mail car only. Vandalia—No. 4, abandoned. Vandalia—No. 6, on time; mail car only. Ohio and Mississippi—No. 5, abandoned. Ohio and Mississippi—No. 1, on time; mail only. Chicago, Burlington and Quincy reported on time, but has not yet arrived."[81] In St. Louis workers also related the Paris Commune to the situation in St. Louis. Carondelet strikers marched through the railroad depot accompanied by a band and waving flags, shouting "Hooray for the Commune."[82] The governor of Illinois announced that the railroads were controlled by strikers in Chicago, Peoria, Galesburg, Decatur, and East St. Louis, and that coal miners had taken over the mines in Braidwood and LaSalle.

On Wednesday morning the executive committee of the WPUSA sent a group of men to the St. Louis levee to stop a steamboat leaving for New Orleans, an act that reflected the party's support for Black workers. A diverse group of several hundred strikers and supporters, Black and white together, demanded that the wages of the Black boatmen be increased by 50 percent. A crowd of over three thousand congregated at the Union Depot in St. Louis that day, while strikers, including two hundred Black boatmen, met at Lucas Market.

However, the racial contradiction that existed within the working class appeared again when Currlin attempted to stop white workers from uniting with Blacks. Currlin purportedly announced that he was shocked by the participation of "n——s."[83] Racial control at the time was achieved by labeling Blacks as inferior and problematic and enlisting working-class whites to enforce the racial order.[84] While Currlin exhibited strong support for the common man, such comradery apparently did not include African Americans. That contradiction was noted by the *Globe-Democrat*, which was itself no friend of the African American community in St. Louis: "The colored element took a hand in the strike yesterday. Several hundred citizens of African descent joined the mob. It will be remembered that there was great indignation among the strikers a day or two ago, when it was falsely reported that the troops to arrive here under General Davis were negroes. The negro, it seems, is good enough for a plunderer, but he is to be abhorred as a soldier."[85]

The WPUSA prepared a list of all businesses still operating in St. Louis that were to be shut down and appointed marshals to maintain control of a parade that was intended to encourage workers to strike. Strikers were sent out ahead of the march to notify those at work that they were coming and to call out those still working to join the strikers. Roustabouts from the levee, carrying sticks and clubs, joined the workers. The parade of strikers was described by a *Globe-Democrat* reporter in completely different terms from its prior description of the members of the Committee of Public Safety and also acknowledged the class nature of the demonstration. It clearly did not consider the strikers as among the attractive "good people" of the city: "The majority of them were negroes, the remainder 'poor white trash!' All were from the dregs of humanity. All were inhabitants of the slums."[86] Strikers marching four abreast and three blocks long paraded through St. Louis's streets, led by a band and English, German, and Irish contingents. Over five thousand marched to the Four Courts Building, and along the way they shut down the Phoenix Planing Mills, the St. Louis Bagging Company, the Machine and Iron Works Company, Shickle, Harrison & Company, and the Wainwright & Brothers malt house. Armed with clubs, Black and white workers also shut down Southern Mills, Saxony Mills, Atlantic Mills, St. Louis Chemical and Zinc Works, and the Wehl Bakery.

Representing the East St. Louis railroad workers, Harry Eastman urged the men to go home and organize their wards and unions in order to support the labor action. The band played the "Marseillaise," and a loaf of bread was inserted at the top of a flagpole, representing the reason for and constituting a symbol of the strike. As the parade passed, Black and white workers walked out of stores, shops, factories, mills, and other businesses and joined the strikers. Beef cannery workers struck, and virtually every building used for business was closed down. When Richardson & Company needed ice to preserve its meats, it requested permission to temporarily operate not from city officials but from the Executive Committee of the WPUSA, which granted its request. "Mr. Richardson, who was present, proposed three cheers for the strikers upon the announcement of their decision."[87] That appreciation was not reflected in the pages of the *Globe-Democrat*, which instead complained, "Citizens of St. Louis must get a permit from a committee of rioters before they can be allowed to proceed with their business."[88]

In St. Louis the strike was no longer limited to railroad workers but had become a general strike of workers of all vocations, a fact recognized by the *Post-Dispatch*: "The mania for striking seems to have become general, and while the excitement is up we need not be surprised if the vendors of peanuts and pies join in the general cry for reform."[89] The businesses closed down on Wednesday included the Levering Bagging Mills, the Gasworks, Douglas Bagging Factory, Park Foundry, O'Fallon Mills, Bain's Atlantic Mills, Phoenix Planning Mills, St. Louis Refrigerator, Wooden Cutting Company, St. Louis Truck Factory, Southern Mills, and Saxony Mills.[90] Even the elevator boy at the Insurance Building went out on strike.[91] The Missouri Pacific abandoned any effort to move freight and published a public notice to that effect: "Notice to Shippers—No freight will be received by the Missouri Pacific Railway until further notice. J. A. Hill, General Freight Agent."[92] Fifty union members were fired at the Excelsior Stove Works, and the remaining employees were forced to man rifles and cannon.[93] Striking workers marched through Carondelet carrying the red flag of revolution.

The WPUSA was unable to entirely control every member of the marching crowd. During the parade there was a limited amount of looting, with some marchers stealing sausages and bread along the way, although in most cases they were stopped by the marshals. Other minor incidents occurred, not committed by workers but by some unemployed, especially in the poorer sections of the city. By the end of Wednesday, virtually all businesses in the city had been shut down. Coal trains no longer delivered to St. Louis, and concern grew with regard to the consequences to the homes and businesses that relied on coal.

As the strike became general, St. Louis gas employees struck and won the reinstatement of a July 1 pay cut. In the St. Louis neighborhood of Cheltenham, which was once the location of a utopian community, a refining company and several brick plants were shut down. Six hundred strikers from Carondelet, led by a band playing music and carrying U.S. and red flags, crossed the Mississippi into Illinois in order to support the East St. Louis strikers. At a strike meeting in Carondelet, Harry Eastman gave a blistering speech attacking capitalists, who, he said, lived a rich life of leisure while working-class people starved. A crowd took control of a zinc works plant in Carondelet as well as the Bessemer Steel Works. The St. Louis Gun Club joined with the Committee on Public Safety, and two companies of the 16th U.S. Infantry from Fort Riley, Kansas, arrived.[94]

Carondelet businessmen called a meeting on Wednesday night for the purpose of creating a militia to confront strikers. The idea backfired, however, when the meeting hall filled with striking workers. WPUSA member Martin Becker was elected chair of the meeting, and an executive committee was chosen, which included Charles P. Chouteau, a descendent of one of the founders of St. Louis and an official of the Vulcan Iron Works. The Committee agreed to ask the mayor to close all saloons in Carondelet and to appoint a special police force chosen by the Committee, which was controlled by strikers. The Executive Committee of the WPUSA attempted a similar action in St. Louis, but after being thanked for its offer to have its members serve the city as special police, it was ignored by the mayor.

Red flags flew over gatherings and marches throughout the metropolitan area. Both men and women and Blacks and whites participated in the events. On Wednesday night over ten thousand attended a rally at Lucas Market, where speakers called on working men to elect to office people of their own class and not lawyers or the rich. Currlin gave a speech in German, and

Thomas Curtis argued that the present labor action was not so much a strike against particular employers as it was a social revolution. Workers' demands should therefore be directed not to the presidents of railroad companies but to the president of the United States.

Since the railroad companies were crying poverty as the reason for the pay cuts, the WPUSA responded that it appeared evident that they were incapable of operating the railroads at a profit, and therefore the government should take over the industry and run the railroads for the benefit of the public and not for the profits of the already rich. At one mass meeting, a worker suggested that a kind of profit-sharing plan would be fair: "The railroad companies say they can't make running expenses. . . . Now I propose that the workingmen take charge of the railroad business of the country, operate them and pay the companies half of the profits."[95] The meeting then passed the following resolution: "In view of the fact that the entire labor element of the United States is in a condition of revolution, and that at the same time the managers of all the railroad companies have confessed their inability to make expenses, we, the working people of the United States, demand that the government proceed at once to take possession of all the railroads and run them for the general welfare of the people, and take immediate measures for paying the present owners by the issue of a national currency."[96] Three other demands were put forth at the meeting: (1) to recall the charters of all national banks; (2) to institute public works projects in order to create jobs; and (3) to adopt a law limiting the workday to eight hours.

By Wednesday night the WPUSA, constituted as the St. Louis Commune, ruled the city of St. Louis. No work was performed without the permission of its Executive Committee. Those businesses that sought to conduct limited operations came to the Committee for its permission rather than to city officials. The WPUSA did permit those businesses with commodities that would spoil to operate on a limited basis, along with those that performed functions needed by the public, such as the baking of bread by bakeries. Other city services were organized by the Executive Committee, such as the patrolling of city streets to prevent crime and to protect property. However, like the Paris Commune, the WPUSA was concerned about public support and acceptance and made no move to affect private property, take control of the banks, or other revolutionary actions. Because of the spontaneity and fast spread of the strike, the Executive Committee had no time to develop a long-term strategy or plan. It instead reacted to events and acted on a case-by-case basis with regard to the power it suddenly found in its hands.

Yet it appeared to the rich residents of the city that socialists were attempting a revolution against the legitimate government, not only in St. Louis but throughout the country. The entire government and social structure of the United States, they feared, was at risk of collapsing. According to David Burbank, "On the evening of Wednesday, July 25, 1877, public officials throughout the United States felt more genuine alarm at the possibility of imminent social revolution than on any occasion before or since."[97] The municipal government was no longer capable of guaranteeing law and order. As a result, the mayor of St. Louis issued a proclamation calling for citizen patrols in the city: "I deem it necessary to invite to the aid of the government the volunteer services of all citizens in favor of law and order within their respective wards for such police duty as may hereafter be assigned to them."[98]

Wednesday appeared to be the height of the strike activities in both St. Louis and throughout the United States. It was at that time that serious reaction to the various labor actions began to take shape. On Wednesday night over twenty thousand attended the socialist rally in New York's Tomkins Square, waving red flags and listening to socialist speakers. Over 1,400 police and national guard troops broke up that rally. Tuesday night strikers in Buffalo burned several railroad cars and engaged in fights with the militia. Gen. Joseph Carr of the New York State Militia decided to end the strike there immediately. Strikers had not been challenged in Indianapolis, where authorities had trouble raising a militia in light of the public support for the workers and the people's distrust of authorities. The Pennsylvania Railroad's Tom Scott did not stop pressuring the federal government to suppress the strikes. He insisted that workers were not only fighting the railroad companies but were actually making war against the United States itself. The governor in Pennsylvania advised the president that his state was in the throes of an insurrection. Strikers in Louisville, Kentucky, marched through the city closing businesses along the way. Louis Brandeis, who would later serve on the U.S. Supreme Court, patrolled the streets as a member of the local militia.

The mayor of Chicago called for federal troops with Gatling guns as police and strikers engaged in firefights. Although the WPUSA was headquartered in Chicago, it did not control the action there.

In St. Louis, however, although there was little violence, there did exist a general strike controlled by a socialist organization. That situation may have caused more concern to the city's leaders than the violence in other cities. On Wednesday, St. Louis businesses, wholesale as well as retail, were closed. Striking barbers marched in a parade behind fifes and drums. There was no business as usual in the city. Farmers arriving at Lucas Market seeking to sell their products turned around and went home. Three thousand men and women protested in front of the Four Courts Building, and levee workers won a 50 percent pay increase.

Mayor Overstolz wired General Pope at Fort Leavenworth claiming that there was imminent danger of mob violence and requested weapons and ammunition. Pope ordered federal troops to St. Louis with the admonition that they not interfere with events except to protect private property. Railroad trustee James Wilson offered to transport the military men and ammunition to St. Louis without charge. One hundred armed men protected the building in which the *Missouri Republican* was published. At the same time, the WPUSA was attempting to preserve order in the city. At another mass meeting at Lucas Market, the Executive Committee, which authorities accused of encouraging an insurrection, passed a resolution denouncing all acts of violence and promised, "We will do all that lies in our power to aid the authorities in keeping order and preventing acts of violence, and will do our utmost to detect and bring to punishment all guilty parties."[99]

On Thursday, July 26, the national strike began to run out of steam, and the railroads and government became more organized in their attempts to end the strikes. New York, Baltimore, and Philadelphia were basically quiet; U.S. troops had taken control of Reading, Pennsylvania; and the strike was almost over in Albany and Buffalo. However, rail traffic was still stopped in Pittsburgh, Cincinnati, and Cleveland, and crowds still controlled the streets in Chicago, where 12 were killed and 150 wounded by gun and cannon fire. Governor Shelby Moore Cullom of Illinois requested six Gatling guns from Washington, and J. H. Wilson telegraphed Secretary Schurz on July 24 and

July 26 requesting that two thousand troops be sent to St. Louis in order to crush the strike, even if such action would be illegal: "Time has come when president should stamp out mob now rampant. A few resolute men can do it here. The law can be found for it after order is restored. Good citizens enrolling by thousands. Mob now threatening *Westliche Post*. Strikers in absolute control at East St. Louis."[100] The suggestion of illegal action made it evident that the law and order demanded by the railroad companies was the kind that enforced the horrible working conditions that compelled workers to take to the streets. That day a Sergeant Finn telegraphed Washington DC from St. Louis, advising that business was "almost entirely suspended" and that no trains, except those carrying mail, could leave East St. Louis.[101] Missouri's governor arrived in St. Louis and discussed the imposition of martial law with the mayor and several prominent citizens. Needless to say, none of those the governor met with were railroad or other workers.

Like the leaders of the Paris Commune, the WPUSA hesitated and allowed opposing forces to organize themselves. In St. Louis the WPUSA Executive Committee realized that the Committee of Public Safety had grown stronger and so attempted to unite all of the unions in the city into an organization that would be able to negotiate a settlement with the railroads and the municipal government. But the unions were faced with divisions within their own ranks. Many of the skilled workers did not want to risk their favorable positions, and there existed the same conflict between Black and white and German and Irish workers. A few union members had even joined the militia. The Four Courts Building was the headquarters for all of the reactionary forces; the mayor had moved his offices there from City Hall, and the police, Committee of Public Safety, Generals Smith and Marmaduke, and militia members all occupied the site. By noon the *Post-Dispatch* estimated that ten thousand men had arrived at the Four Courts Building to join the militia, and each was given approximately sixty rounds of ammunition.[102] Sensing a change in the air or fearful of damage to their property, the owners of Turner Hall evicted the WPUSA. The railroads still refused to discuss any compromise with their workers, and food and fuel were in short supply in the city.

Recognizing that its situation was rapidly deteriorating, the leaders of the WPUSA attempted to salvage what they could before they faced an attack by the opposing forces. The Executive Committee wrote to the mayor describing the scene of starving families and requested that he help in distributing necessities to the poor. The poor were starving, the letter stated, and aid was necessary "to avoid plunder, arson, or violence by persons made desperate by destitution."[103] They asked the mayor to call a meeting of merchants to deal with the destitute and offered to pay for the food distributed: "Each member of all labor organizations will hold himself individually and collectively responsible to pay for all food procured by his order."[104] The Executive Committee also promised not to sponsor any parades or mass meetings until it could guarantee law and order in the city: "Further, in order to avoid riot we have determined to have no large procession until our organization is so complete as to positively assure the citizens of St. Louis of a perfect maintenance of order, and full protection to life and property."[105]

The promise not to hold mass meetings or parades was a major mistake. Meetings and parades were the only way the Executive Committee was able to retain interest and excitement in the strike and to communicate with the workers. There was no way to communicate with such a large group except by continuously scheduled mass meetings. Once that chain was broken, many supporters were permanently lost. For them, participation in the movement would be over. If there were no mass meetings, excitement would die down, and the WPUSA's control of the strike would be lost. That decision would prove to be fatal to the strike.

St. Louis's municipal authority and the Committee of Public Safety had set up their headquarters in the Four Courts Building, where an artillery company was stationed, and the offices at City Hall were vacant or inhabited by strikers. Both the mayor and the governor issued proclamations ordering citizens not to congregate in the streets nor to interfere with operating businesses. When the governor sought weapons for the militia, many St. Louis gun stores transferred their arms to the authorities, and 1,500 weapons were sent to the state armory in St. Louis. The governor ordered that arsonists be shot and, echoing the prior order of the mayor, and the Versailles government during the days of the Paris Commune, also ordered that no prisoners should be taken. This in spite of the fact that there had been only minor incidents of violence and that the WPUSA had offered to preserve peace and order. The only logical reason for such an action was the same as that which motivated Thiers in Paris: to destroy working-class radicalism and to ensure that similar labor uprisings never occurred again.

A former Missouri governor asked President Hayes to declare martial law in St. Louis, and arms and ammunition arriving in the city were immediately taken to the Four Courts Building. The benches in the Four Courts Building had been made into bunks for the soldiers and militia; two thousand Springfield rifles had arrived from the state capital, Jefferson City, and each of the several thousand militiamen received a rifle and ammunition. Several thousand more arms were expected to arrive, sufficient to equip a force of seven thousand.[106] The city braced for an expected attack on the striking workers and the Commune's leaders.

While the city's business interests were preparing for their attack on the WPUSA, St. Louis was still closed down. Nothing passed through the city by rail except the mail. Armaments and troops did arrive, however, and were hastened to the Four Courts Building. That Thursday the WPUSA Executive Committee announced that there would be no parade that day. Still, in the absence of any formal calling of a mass meeting, approximately two thousand workers, Black and white, did meet at Lucas Market, the usual gathering place, and listened to speeches. Some called for seizing the Four Courts Building. While the authorities prepared for battle, the WPUSA still controlled the city, and workers continued to visit the few shops that were still operating in attempts to close them down. On Thursday afternoon the owners of Belcher Sugar Refinery, which had been closed, approached the WPUSA Executive Committee and requested that they be authorized to operate for a period of forty-eight hours so that their sugar supply would not spoil. The Committee approved the request and sent two hundred workers to protect the plant during its temporary operation. Another forty businesses were closed on Thursday, and virtually no business was operating in the city. Strikers were also in control in Carondelet, where a thousand Vulcan Iron Works employees met to discuss wage demands. WPUSA member Martin Becker was in control of Carondelet and its force of eighteen workers who were serving as special police.

On Thursday night, East St. Louis strikers paraded with signs declaring "Liberty, Equality, and Fraternity," reminiscent of the French Revolution.

In St. Louis a mass meeting of local businessmen at Armory Hall agreed to coordinate efforts with the Committee of Public Safety and to raise $10,000 for what they denominated defense, in order to purchase Sharp, Peabody, Winchester, and Springfield rifles and Colt revolvers and to organize an armed force of a thousand men from among their employees. Within six hours they had raised $12,000 among themselves and purchased all the arms within eight hours of the meeting.[107] Suggestive of the Civil War just a few years earlier, the Committee of Public Safety, without any legal basis, requisitioned property from civilian citizens and handed out vouchers to merchants, who were promised later reimbursement by the Committee, which had no legal existence.

At another mass meeting of workers at Lucas Market, no Executive Committee member or WPUSA representative spoke on behalf of the organization, although Currlin made a speech in German, advocating that people enlist their neighbors, collect arms, and report to the Committee the next day. Currlin also warned against rioting and arson, which would force the authorities to react quickly; he was hoping to buy a few days' time, when the city's provisions would be gone, thereby strengthening the strikers' bargaining power. Other speakers demanded that the government create jobs so that all who wished to work could do so, and again called for an eight-hour workday and the prohibition of child labor. There was also discussion about forcefully taking city buildings and the arsenal, but such talk was not sanctioned by the WPUSA, which had no arms and had not engaged in serious violence. The city authorities also were aware that supplies in the city were low and that action needed to be taken before they were forced into a position of weakness. In what some would later describe as hypocrisy, the Catholic Church in St. Louis condemned the strike while the Irish Catholic Society in St. Louis held a picnic for the purpose of raising money to buy arms for Irish revolutionaries. M. W. Hogan, the city's prosecuting attorney, supported the fundraiser for Irish arms but later prosecuted the strikers.

St. Louis had not experienced the death and destruction that had characterized events in Baltimore, Chicago, and Pittsburgh. Yet it was the only city that was under the control of socialists and communists. The massive force being marshaled by the local, state, and federal governments was not indicated by the situation at the time. As would be evidenced later, there was no need to arm and provision thousands of militia members and soldiers to fight against the strikers. The railroad workers had struck, and they had convinced other workers to join them, usually as a sign of solidarity but sometimes by the threat of force. But virtually no real violence had occurred in the city. Seeking public legitimacy and support, as did the Paris Commune, a proclamation by the Executive Committee of the WPUSA directed to the citizens of St. Louis stated, "We give you our positive assurance of a determined effort on our part to suppress all riotous proceedings."[108] The situation hardly called for thousands of armed men, artillery, and Gatling guns. Yet that was the response being prepared by railroad officials, businessmen, and authorities, who were willing to ignore the rights of strikers and the law in order to suppress the strike and overthrow the Commune. Thursday night mounted police patrolled the streets and quietly began to arrest strike leaders who were not violating any laws. In an obvious exaggeration, but one that would excuse the use of overwhelming force against strikers, the St. Louis newspapers again compared the local situation to the Paris Commune.

On Friday, July 27, two more companies of federal troops arrived in St. Louis, together with another 1,200 rifles from the state arsenal. The police were in control of the Union Depot, and workers watched the University Club citizen militia drill there. Authorities reported to Washington that three thousand St. Louis citizens were now under arms. The Committee of Public Safety appeared in the streets on Friday morning, and plainclothes police identified the leaders of the strike and began to arrest them when they found them alone. The WPUSA Executive Committee, realizing that they could be attacked at any time, tried to organize their own militia companies, which included Black and white workers. But the workers had only a few weapons. They had not made any attempt to take the armory, although the *Missouri Republican* had accused them of plotting a coup d'état with a plan to seize the arms at the Jefferson Barracks army base.[109] The shift in momentum was not lost on the newspaper: "There is but one thing for the strikers to do, and that is to go to work for such wages as the railroads offer to pay or to quit work."[110] Without any evidence that the workers had attempted to bring down the government, the paper went on to call for the strike leaders to be hunted down and charged with sedition. The *Republican* thereby equated a strike against railroad monopolies with a conspiracy to overthrow the U.S. government, as if they were one and the same.

The WPUSA Executive Committee issued a circular on Friday once more denouncing mob violence, calling for an eight-hour day, and promising to aid the city in suppressing violence in the event it occurred. It also announced that there would be no march on Friday, although large crowds did gather at its headquarters, now at Schuyler Hall, attempting to determine what was planned for the day and criticizing the Committee for its inaction. The Committee, however, was unsure of what action to take and so hesitated to take any action whatsoever. The workers looked to it for leadership, but none was to be found. A *Missouri Republican* reporter observed, "Another party was roaring around to the effect that if the d—n fool executive committee had taken the arsenal on Tuesday, as they ought to have done, and as fifty good men could have done as easy as wink, there would be no suffering for food in the city today."[111]

The Executive Committee did call for a meeting to take place on Friday afternoon consisting of delegates from the various workers' organizations. The Committee was desperate to negotiate an end to the strike without having to confront the military forces now arrayed against them. A reporter observed the desire for settlement on the part of the workers and the refusal of the railroads to enter into any negotiations: "From what a reporter gleaned in an interview with several leading men among the discontents, it is safe to say they would willingly surrender if the railroad company would meet them half way."[112] A letter to the editor by a striking engineer summed up the desire for a compromise between striking workers and the railroad companies and an end to the strike: "In justice to ourselves, I will let you know how things are. We do not want to prevent passenger trains or mail from going out, but the superintendents will not run these trains, so as to get the public on their sides. Run all passenger and mail trains and we will see that they are not molested. Give us our old pay and cut down the officers of the road, and all will be as ever. The sooner this is done the sooner business will revive."[113]

Some workers demanded guns from the Executive Committee, but it had none to give and had no intention of fighting what appeared to be the overwhelming armed forces of state, federal, municipal, and private troops. The morale of the strikers was sinking, and there was a strong feeling that the end was near. However, railroad workers still controlled the city of East St. Louis and Carondelet, where most of the residents were of the working class. The Committee of Public Safety had no presence whatsoever in Carondelet.

Mayor Overstolz had finally decided that the strike had to end and that the communists had to be crushed. According to the *Globe-Democrat*, "The Mayor had come to the conclusion at last that the Communists were bad men; that they were responsible for the outrages of the week, of the cessation of all industries; that they had incited riots and inaugurated mob law; that they were even then plotting a coup d'etat that would place the city in the control of the lawless; that their existence was a threat against the safety of the city, and that they should be at once arrested."[114]

The Committee of Public Safety decided to attack the WPUSA headquarters before the planned meeting of union members could occur and thereby organize the working-class organizations. Generals Smith and Marmaduke were against the move at that time, and Gen. John D. Stevenson was given command of the police and militia forces. There was no legal basis for federal intervention, and federal troops were not involved in the action. On Friday afternoon, led by cavalry, foot police, an artillery company, and two cannon, seven hundred militia troops left the Four Courts Building and marched through crowded streets of onlookers to Schuyler Hall, where the executive committee was meeting but was entirely unprepared for the assault. Police cavalry filled the width of the street, followed by police on foot, armed with bayonets, swords, rifles, and cannon. There were thousands of spectators and innocent and curious people in the streets, who were attacked by the police. One man was crushed by a horse, while Colonel Armstrong, a leader of the city's forces, shouted, "Ride 'em down! Ride 'em down! They have no business here."[115] According to the *Post-Dispatch*, "Men, women and children thronged the pavements, and the police were obliged to actually ride down, and, in some instance, horsewhip the crowd back."[116]

As the militia approached the hall, an alarm was raised, and men jumped out of windows and raced across the roofs of neighboring buildings to escape. Police arrested everyone in the building and those they could catch, apparently for being in the building, since they had observed no illegal conduct of any kind. The police were ordered to shoot anyone who resisted arrest, although the vast majority of the people arrested were turned loose once it was determined that they had not committed any unlawful act but simply were in the wrong place at the wrong time. The militia was unnecessary, as police made the arrests with little or no resistance and without one shot being fired. Seventy-five men were arrested, and only a few guns were found in the building. Of those arrested, only forty-nine were kept in custody, and none of those were members of the WPUSA's Executive Committee nor leaders of the strike.

After the raid Currlin met with fifty men in a nearby saloon and discussed forming a secret organization. Then he and William Fischer, both members of the WPUSA Executive Committee, walked over to the mayor's office in a last attempt to negotiate an end to the strike, but they were immediately arrested. Even the *St. Louis Times* admitted that the arrests were unlawful. In violation of the Fourth Amendment to the Constitution, authorities had not obtained arrest warrants and those arrested were doing absolutely nothing illegal at the time of their arrests. When a meeting at Moran's Place, a working-class saloon, was broken up by forty-two policemen, Colonel Armstrong was asked about the legality of arresting men who had not done anything illegal. He replied, "Oh, we'll arrest them and discuss that question afterwards."[117] Under the pretext of preserving law and order, authorities purposely and knowingly violated the First Amendment's right of assembly and the Fourth Amendment's prohibition against warrantless arrests. If there was any unlawful activity in St. Louis that day, it was committed by the authorities. The *Missouri Republican*, however, had no sympathy for those killed or injured, even those who were innocent of any wrongdoing and were merely curious spectators watching the events unfold. Instead the editors insisted, "The guardians of the peace have been given guns for no other purpose but to shoot and they and the mob must both bear in mind that when they do shoot they shoot to kill. There must be no sickly sentimentality about innocent people being hurt, for innocent people have no business to be where they can be hurt."[118] The entire area had apparently been designated by authorities a free-fire zone, meaning that anyone found there was subject to being shot.

Of those arrested at the WPUSA headquarters, 63 percent were German-born.[119] Twenty-seven members of the Carondelet Executive Committee were also arrested on Saturday, including Martin Becker, a WPUSA member and chair of the Committee. That the action consisted of a conflict between classes was made clear when only working-class members of the Carondelet Committee were arrested and none of the businessmen on that Committee were arrested or taken into custody. Paradoxically the St. Louis Executive Committee of the WPUSA had arranged for three meetings later that night in a last-minute attempt to unite the people, which was clearly too little and too late. After the arrests, the working class began to split again along racial and ethnic lines. Whites blamed Blacks for the failure of the strike; the Irish blamed the Germans and Blacks; the Germans blamed the Irish and Blacks; and the American-born workers blamed Blacks and foreigners.[120] One thing all white groups had in common was that all blamed Blacks for the failure of the Commune.

A militia company of 130 men descended on Carondelet at midnight and ended the strike there. For all practical purposes, the strike in St. Louis and the rule of the St. Louis Commune were over. There had been no deaths and virtually no violence, damage to property, or looting. Nevertheless the *Republican* blamed the strike on "those blood-thirsty communists."[121] The *Post-Dispatch*, which had been critical of the strikers during the previous week, was more thoughtful in its analysis once the perceived danger was past. The real problem, it concluded, was not so much due to troublemakers as it was systemic and due to hunger and frustration caused by industrial expansion: "Statistics prove that before this strike nearly 4,000,000 toilers were idle in the United States, caused by improved machinery forcing them out of employment, and those who were in forced idleness, through sheer destitution, were compelled to underbid their fellow-workmen, until the wages paid to those fortunate enough to have work became so low as to make even their case desperate; hence, using a homely phrase, 'the chickens came home to roost.'"[122]

Strike leaders James Cope, Thomas McGraw, W. H. Churchill, and Henry Morgan were arrested, and in obvious reference to the events in Paris six years before, the newspaper linked the St. Louis rebellion to the Paris Commune:

"Cope is the well-known leader of the St. Louis Commune, and has been loudest in his denunciation of the wrongs inflicted upon 'workingmen.'"[123] The *Globe-Democrat* emphasized that the rights of corporations were equal to those of people: "And the protection which is extended to the private and personal rights of the citizen must be extended to the property and rights of the corporation."[124] The paper did not point out that it was the citizens' rights, not those of corporations, which were actually being violated. At the same time the paper made clear that in its opinion, the workers who had struck, and those who had led them, were of the lowest class of humanity, again distinguishing their physical attributes from members of the Committee of Public Safety: "The capture was over before it could be told, and in a twinkling a long line of ill-dressed, evil-looking, hard-featured, beetle-browed, grimy unkempt men, with scowling faces, were in the center of the street, under guard, and the battle was won."[125] Some of those the newspaper thus described were actually *Globe-Democrat* reporters who were arrested in the arbitrary sweep made by St. Louis authorities.

The workers in East St. Louis were running the city and policing its streets until the very end. Finally, Governor Cullom declared martial law in East St. Louis. The police there and the Illinois National Guard were sympathetic to the strikers and could not be trusted to do the bidding of the authorities or railroad companies. The Montgomery Guard, a militia, also refused to move against East St. Louis workers. As a result, the federal government decided to act. East St. Louis was an extremely important rail center, especially for goods shipped east or west. The excuse for the use of federal troops was that federal property, including those trains under receivership, needed to be protected.

On Saturday, July 28, federal troops took control of the Eads Bridge, which connected the cities of St. Louis and East St. Louis. Twelve companies of the Twenty-Third U.S. Infantry, under the command of General Davis, crossed the Mississippi River in the dark, early morning hours for an attack on striking workers in East St. Louis. Eight companies marched toward the railroad depot, while four others floated on barges farther down the river in order to attack the other side of the depot. Two other companies marched toward the railway yards from the Eads Bridge, so that almost a thousand men moved toward the headquarters of the railroad strikers. Reinforcements, which included the Belleville Guards, the Fourth Regiment of the Illinois National Guard, and the Illinois militia commanded by Brig. Gen. E. N. Bates, arrived.[126] U.S. marshals descended on the scene and began arresting workers, meeting with no resistance. Reflecting the massive and arbitrary arrests that had occurred in St. Louis, East St. Louis strikers and even the East St. Louis city marshal John B. Carroll were placed under arrest. Several hundred armed coal miners arrived to support the strikers, but they were immediately disarmed and sent home by U.S. troops.

By Sunday the great railroad strike in St. Louis and the rule of the St. Louis Commune were over. The newspapers in St. Louis had all attacked the strike since its beginning, continually demeaning and dehumanizing the workers and distorting their message. The *Globe-Democrat* happily declared an end to the uprising: "The Communistic uprising had died through decapitation, and the police succeeded in driving the rank and file of the movement to their holes."[127] Instead of portraying strikers as they actually were, hardworking men who were attempting to feed their families in the face of greed on the part of massive corporations, the *Missouri Republican* branded the workers so as to instill fear and hatred against them by the general public. Some of its allegations made no sense and were ridiculous; for instance, one article suggested, "The Communist wishes the government to take possession of all existing industries and of every form of accumulated property, and to administer both in the interest of the lazy and vicious."[128] The strikers, the *Republican* explained, sought to take the food out of the mouths of the rich: "No one can say what the revolutionists had in mind, but it is evident they had a scope far beyond a mere strike for higher wages. They sought to seize the city and distribute food to the poor, so the rich would be unable to buy food."[129] There was no question that the *Missouri Republican* had chosen the side of the rich against the poor.

Although the workers lived only one step away from starvation, the *Republican* portrayed them as reckless spenders, living lives of luxury, who wished to take from those who lived responsible lives. That the situation was exactly the opposite did not appear to concern the *Republican*. "The Communists—for it is they we are dealing with . . . we find it to be a claim that those who squander their wages in comforts and luxuries shall be equal partners with those who have saved theirs, through self-denial and privation."[130] In fact, it was, of course, the workers who actually lived lives of self-denial and privation, and the railroad owners and monopolists who squandered their wealth on comfort and luxury. But the *Republican's* agenda was not to report the news or present opinion objectively; it was to turn St. Louis citizens against the strikers.

There were, however, a few holdouts in other places around the country, which included both railroad and other workers. On July 30 the *Globe-Democrat* described Pittsburgh, Erie, Scranton, Urbana, Mattoon, Vandalia, Terre Haute, Kansas City, and Grafton, West Virginia, as quiet, while Fort Wayne, Columbus, Cleveland, Cincinnati, Evansville, Chicago, Quincy, and Galesburg, Illinois, were still active strike locations.[131] East St. Louis strikers made a final unsuccessful attempt on Sunday to enforce the blockade of freight, but they were arrested, not for any violent or illegal conduct but for continuing to strike. One hundred thousand coal miners in Pennsylvania struck, as did miners in Springfield and Du Quoin, Illinois. However, in St. Louis the old order was restored, and the elite of the city were about to demonstrate their power to the general public, "thus giving 'the committee' and their routed adherents a chance to judge the tone and sentiment of the law-abiding citizens."[132]

In the nineteenth century, street parades were a common method of reinforcing or challenging the public order and were part of the public discourse.[133] They were also a source of excitement and entertainment. In a letter dated September 17, 1953, from William Moskop to David Burbank, Moskop related his childhood memories of such parades: "I remember when I was a young lad the great enjoyment I derived from public meetings, especially political, with flag-waving, music, and torchlight parades."[134]

On the Tuesday following the strike, St. Louis business leaders sponsored a military parade in order to show off their power and victory over striking workers, at which over five thousand armed men marched in a victory parade. The *Globe-Democrat* described the sidewalks as full of people watching the scene and all windows of surrounding buildings black with humanity, even long before the start of the parade. Flags waved, bayonets glittered, and uniform buttons dazzled on the five regiments of marching soldiers.[135] The

Post-Dispatch described those who participated as the cream of St. Louis society: "We cannot take the time to make special notice of companies or individuals where all did so well, and all deserving of so much praise. The ranks of some were filled with young men, the glory of the city and its future note. Others were gray-headed and grizzled bearded men who have long been known in business circles here and identified with many of the leading enterprises of St. Louis."[136]

The parade was organized by the same people who had put together the local militia in order to suppress the strike. Row after row of men in uniform with rifles, artillery, and other weapons marched through the streets of St. Louis, including working-class neighborhoods. That the purpose of the massive parade was to intimidate those who might in the future challenge the city's authority was made clear by the *Missouri Republican*: "The value of yesterday's parade to the city of St. Louis is inestimable. It gave to the late turbulent classes a wholesome lesson that rule not be forgotten during this generation, and it afforded the law-abiding the fullest faith in the supremacy of the upholders of peace and order."[137] The *Globe-Democrat* agreed with its colleagues at the *Republican* that troublemakers were not welcome in St. Louis and would not be tolerated: "The display of military force is a solemn warning to Internationalism, Communism and all other forms of disturbing 'isms' that they are attempting to settle in the wrong locality."[138]

In the same issue the *Globe-Democrat* again linked the events in St. Louis to the Paris Commune. In a review of a new book, *Revue des Deux Mondes* by M. Maxime Du Camp, the reviewer wrote that it was necessary to study the author's findings "especially in view of the fact that within the last few days the doctrines of the Commune have been preached in this city and seem to have found advocates even among men who might be supposed to have some sense."[139] The connection of the St. Louis Commune with the Paris Commune was clear to everyone. The St. Louis Commune and the WPUSA, it was alleged, were not just similar to but were actually a "branch" of the Paris Commune: "In St. Louis, a branch of the Commune, the organization which incessantly conspires for the overthrow of the Governments of the world, existed under the '[harmless] title' of the Workingmen's Party of the United States."[140] Of course that statement was a blatant distortion of the truth, since the Paris Commune had made no effort to overthrow the French government, nor did the St. Louis Commune attempt to overthrow the government of the United States. Both, however, were guilty of trying to improve the lives of the poor and working classes. But the newspapers perceived both incidents from the perspective of the bourgeoisie, the class that had emerged in the United States after the Civil War and was in direct conflict with the working class. The leaders of the WPUSA, according to the *Globe-Democrat*, took advantage of the railroad strike in order to attempt to overthrow the government: "Curlin [*sic*] and his crew saw, in the inflamed and excited condition of the railroad men, and the general sympathy of the workingmen of the country with the strikers, what they deemed the opportunity for the revolution long desired by them."[141] The fact that the WPUSA had demanded only a restoration of the recent pay cuts and the end of child labor and had successfully restrained its more violent supporters seemed to be irrelevant or unimportant to the newspapers.

Prior to and during the strike, the streets had possessed a democratic character. The lowest groups in the social hierarchy were free to use them for commerce, recreation, and political statements. After the strike, control of the streets was exercised by and limited to the elite. One parade by the city's ruling class was not the end of their efforts to showcase their power and control of St. Louis. The rich and powerful citizens of St. Louis were determined to continue to display their power over ordinary residents, so they began a tradition that is still celebrated to this day, although its original purpose has been hidden. Several months following the collapse of the railroad strike, members of the city's business elite met secretly for the purpose of creating a public spectacle that would unquestionably demonstrate that there was a social hierarchy in the city, that they were at the top of that hierarchy, and that they, not the working class, possessed the power in the city. In March 1878 a number of St. Louis businessmen received a letter asking them to attend a secret meeting of "prominent gentlemen."[142]

At the secret meeting, St. Louis's elite citizens formed the Veiled Prophet (VP) organization, purportedly based on a mythical kingdom, Khorassan, where the wealthy ruled over ordinary people. A veiled prophet was to be elected each year from the city's rich citizens to reign over a festival and parade. The founders of the VP were geographically a diverse group. Ten were from St. Louis, five from elsewhere in Missouri, and forty-eight from other states. Nine had fought for the Union in the Civil War, and seven had fought for the Confederacy. Most came from Protestant upper-class families, and all were born into wealthy families. Of the original founders, all were Protestant, except one, Moses Fraley, who was Jewish, and three, Charles Chouteau, Pierre Chouteau, and Alexander Garesche, all of whom were Catholic.[143] The Chouteaus were descendants of one of the original founders of St. Louis. A third of the founding group traded or processed agricultural and industrial products. Nine of the organization's founders served as president of the St. Louis Merchants Exchange between 1872 and 1887. What they all had in common was that they were rich, white males, and each was determined that the working class would never again take control of their businesses or their city.

The St. Louis Commune was to be erased from the city's history and to be replaced by the show of power of the city's wealthiest members. The VP founders were largely the same men who crushed the 1877 strike in St. Louis. They included the city's police commissioner, John G. Priest; George Bain and John A. Scudder, who had served as recruiters for the militia; and Leigh O. Knapp, who was an adjutant-general in the city's militia and commanded the troops during the raid on Schuyler Hall. Through the VP organization, they would make important business contacts with other elite members of St. Louis society and introduce their daughters to the sons of the rich in an annual debutante ball. Women, African Americans, and the working class were excluded from the organization.

The founders of the VP organization proposed to hold a huge parade every year, marked by military might and money, so that there was no question as to who controlled the streets and ruled the city. Membership in the organization was limited to two hundred, and the payment of a $100 membership fee was required, which was approximately three times the monthly pay of a working-class laborer at the time. According to Thomas Spencer, the VP celebration was "a symbolic attempt to assert business-class control over the streets of St. Louis."[144] The parade was modeled after the Mystick Krewe of Comus, one of the New Orleans Carnival societies. One of the original founders,

Charles Slaybock, had moved to St. Louis from New Orleans, where he had been a member of the New Orleans Carnival Society; he purchased floats for the parade from friends in New Orleans. Each year a new Veiled Prophet is chosen whose identity is secret, but it is always a successful businessman.

The theme of that first parade was "Festival of Ceres," and it presented Greek and Roman gods advocating capitalist values. Floats portrayed the St. Louis ruling class as royalty, riding high above the common people and dressed as gods and kings. A newspaper description of the first Veiled Prophet reflected his royalty and power; in order to demonstrate his dominion and authority, the dress of the Veiled Prophet resembled the costume of a certain Southern terrorist organization, which was especially active at the time: "A newspaper sketch pictured him in white robes, mask, and pointed hat, carting a pistol and a shotgun, with a second shotgun well within reach."[145] Just in case the message was not clear enough, the Veiled Prophet was joined on his float by an executioner and a butcher's block. So the Veiled Prophet was a masked and unknown person, dressed in a white costume that hid his identity, and he was surrounded with weapons, a picture undoubtedly meant to transmit a clear warning to the ordinary working people of the city. Although the identity of the Veiled Prophet is supposed to remain a secret, the first was John G. Priest, the St. Louis police commissioner, who had helped suppress the strike.

The parade was intended to announce that these were the richest and most powerful men in St. Louis, some descended from the city's founding families, and they, not socialists or workers, controlled the city. Over one hundred thousand people watched the first parade and its thousand torches, hundreds of Japanese lanterns, and fireworks lighting up the night sky. The spectacle was intended to awe the masses with the obvious power of the rich and to serve as its response to the workers' parades during the strike. According to Spencer, "By having a parade every year that showed a make-believe Middle Eastern king and his court, the St. Louis elite asserted the value of social hierarchy both in the mythical kingdom of Khorassan and in the real world of St. Louis."[146] Through the years the VP parade evolved into somewhat of a community celebration in St. Louis, its original purpose almost, but not entirely, forgotten. In 1952, as part of a protest against the

Smith Act, a 1940 statute that made it a crime to advocate the overthrow of the U.S. government, the St. Louis Emergency Defense Committee published a circular titled "The Veiled Prophet, How It Began":

> Big business and the press have conspired to hide the true origins of the VP parade. . . .
>
> The [St. Louis general] strike was broken. To celebrate, St. Louis business leaders held a victory march of 3000 armed troops and a battery of cannon to intimidate St. Louis working people and prevent the organization of unions.[147]

Ultimately the prosecution of those involved in the railroad strike and the St. Louis Commune reflects the fact that the legal actions were primarily directed toward ending the strike and not for any serious, illegal misconduct on the part of the strikers. Threats of long sentences as a result of violating conspiracy laws or treasonous conduct did not come to fruition. Generally those who were not leaders but who had only participated in closing factories were fined up to $300. Those who were financially unable to pay the fine were sentenced to six months in the city's workhouse. Since the strikes were largely peaceful and the strikers had attempted to curtail any violence and the destruction of property, charges of "riot" failed due to a lack of evidence. Many of the charges against the workers were for peace disturbance, a broad charge used to remove people from the streets rather than to punish them for serious misconduct. An attempt was made to treat leaders of the strike, who were members of the WPUSA Executive Committee, more harshly. Albert Currlin, Louis Fischer, Peter Lofgreen, John Glenn, Henry Allen, Thomas Curtis, and James Cope were eventually charged with associating "together for the unlawful purpose of preventing men from plying their lawful avocations, and did prevent, according to their purpose, by means of terrorism, intimidating, etc."[148] Bail for each of them was set at $3,000. The law was used, however, primarily to break the strike and to neutralize its leadership.

The prosecution of the East St. Louis and other Illinois strikers was held in Springfield. It was led by Bluford Wilson, the brother of James Wilson, the railroad receiver who had advocated the use of federal force against legal strikers. Several cases were dismissed outright, including that against John

Carroll, the East St. Louis city marshal. Twenty-six strikers on the Indianapolis, Bloomington and Western Railroad were sentenced in federal court to ninety days in jail for contempt of court, most likely for interfering with trains under federal receivership. Some Peoria strikers received sentences of four months.[149] Others were released on $500 recognizance bonds on the condition that they not interfere with federal property for a period of one year.

Authorities in St. Louis were clearly more concerned with removing strikers from the streets than with seriously punishing them. First and foremost, they desired the return of order to the city, the kind of order that was in effect when they controlled the city's businesses and government. The authorities believed that the arrest of the leaders would result in the collapse of the strike and the end of the rule of the Commune. While the authorities did attempt to bring serious felony charges against a few leaders, most of those arrested were charged with lesser crimes.

Currlin, Lofgreen, Fischer, and other leaders of the general strike and the St. Louis Commune were originally taken into custody and held in jail without being charged with any crime. They finally filed for a Writ of Habeas Corpus, alleging that they were being illegally imprisoned by the government and held against their will without being charged and brought before a magistrate, a right that had existed as a part of Western civilization since the time of the *Magna Carta* in 1215.

Some workers who were convicted as a result of their conduct during the strike received only fines, others were sentenced to six months in the city workhouse, while still other cases were dismissed. Daniel Price, a worker who had assisted in closing shops, was fined $100; Barney Coyle was convicted of peace disturbance and fined $50; and Patricia Curtin was fined $25 for peace disturbance. On August 10 the strike leaders Currlin, Lofgreen, Cope, Glenn, Curtis, Fischer, and Allen, having finally been charged, appeared in court. Currlin had participated in forming the WPUSA in Philadelphia in 1876, served as an editor of the *Arbeiter-Zeitung*, and was later a speaker at the funeral of the Haymarket martyrs in Chicago.[150] Cope was one of the founders of the First International in England in 1864. Glenn was a secret official in the Knights of Labor. The leaders were the only ones who were charged with serious felonies, such as rioting. However, the authorities had no real evidence against any of them; they had not directed illegal acts publicly and there were no witnesses against them, so the charges against all were ultimately dismissed.[151] E. A. Owens, a member of the International, was charged with "language calculated to provoke a breach of the peace." That charge was clearly in violation of the U.S. Constitution, violating the First Amendment's guarantee of free speech and being so overbroad in its definition of an alleged crime that it was unclear what language was allowed and what was prohibited. The charge was, in fact, later determined to be defective and was dismissed.[152]

In Carondelet, Joseph Morge and August Musser were each charged with disturbing the peace by riotous and tumultuous conduct and interfering with an officer. Both, together with George Strothold, who was accused of disturbing the peace, were acquitted. It was probably the only time in American history when cavalry, artillery, and cannon were used to effect the arrest of persons charged with misdemeanors, such as peace disturbance, which raised the question of the real reason for the show of state and federal force against striking workers.

The St. Louis general strike consisted of railroad workers, workers in other industries and businesses, and the unemployed, those whom Pinkerton referred to as "vagrants." The strikers were supported by artisans, skilled and unskilled workers, small business owners, and a large portion of the general public. With some exceptions, Black and white workers united in their opposition to capital and authority. Many strikers were veterans of the 1848 revolutions and the Paris Commune. The strike was largely led in St. Louis by German workers, who were members of the First International and the WPUSA. Most were socialists and, at least to some extent, followers of Karl Marx. Together they created the St. Louis Commune, the only time in the history of the United States that communists controlled a major American city.

When the strike was over, thoughtful commentators on what had occurred suggested that reforms in the relationship between labor and capital were necessary. A failure to confront and resolve the problems associated with industrial capitalism had the potential to result in violent revolution. Twenty-seven prominent St. Louis residents, including Thomas T. Gantt and John W. Noble, both leaders of the Committee of Public Safety, signed an open letter to the St. Louis community stating that the workers had legitimate grievances against the railroad companies, that some had survived only day to day, that others had not been paid for several months, that still others were paid only in company scrip, and that it was time for the railroad companies to face up to and deal with those grievances in a reasonable manner.[153] Even J. A. Dacus, who had no sympathy for socialism, recognized the problem, writing, "Even in America, the proletariat is becoming great in numbers and dangerous in disposition. A policy that increases the number of poor, that depresses the condition of the working people is unwise, and must inevitably end in the destruction of social order and the ruin of the country."[154]

There were many lessons to be learned from the events that occurred around the country and in St. Louis during the summer of 1877. Unfortunately the only lesson learned from the strike and the Commune by the St. Louis mayor was that there was a proven need for a larger police force. In his message to the city's legislative body following the strike and fall of the Commune, Mayor Overstolz explained what, in his opinion, was needed: "Every large city that has suffered during the recent strike and riots has acquired a new experience as to defects in its municipal system that should be remedied. In St. Louis the lesson most strongly enforced is the necessity of increasing the police force."[155] The *Missouri Republican* agreed, adding that since the militias could not be counted on to oppose the people, a large standing army would be necessary in the future.[156] What was necessary, added the *Republican*, was "a large increase of the forces for the maintenance of order—the federal army, the state militia, and the municipal police."[157] Military force was required, not to protect the American people from foreign enemies but to protect capital and property from the working class. Philip Foner suggests that capitalists generally recognized the need for the establishment of armories throughout the United States, a better trained national guard, and a larger standing army.[158] In the future, it appeared that the government would have to fight not only Indians and foreign nation-states but also the country's own working class, and those military forces would be necessary to wage that battle.

Epilogue

The fall of the St. Louis Commune marked the end of socialist rule in St. Louis. But it did not represent the end of the socialist movement in the city or in the United States. Fully one-fourth of the WPUSA's national membership was in St. Louis. Most of the members were German, but they also included French, Bohemian, Irish, English, and native-born Americans. The WPUSA continued to work for electoral progress in St. Louis after the strike. Between 1876 and 1881 St. Louis socialists, led by the German community, achieved success in a number of elections. The four wards in St. Louis that were strongly socialist were also 75 percent ethnically German.[1] In September 1877 thousands attended a mass meeting at Lucas Market called by the WPUSA, and in October the party elected its candidates for school directors in five of St. Louis's twenty-eight wards. The WPUSA became the Socialist Labor Party in 1878, and that year two of its members were elected to the St. Louis municipal House of Delegates. Joseph Weydemeyer would serve as the St. Louis County auditor.

The divisions that had haunted socialist organizations for many years did not disappear after the end of the railroad strike and the fall of the St. Louis Commune. The conflict between Marxists and Lassalleans was still alive and arose again in the WPUSA; there was still disagreement as to whether socialists should immediately participate in electoral matters or whether such participation should wait until labor organizations were stronger and more powerful. J. P. McDonnell, the Marxist editor of the *Labor Standard*, called for the organization of unions as the primary goal of the party. Support for the major political parties without an already strong union organization and a developed working-class consciousness, he argued, could only result in the exploitation of labor by the bourgeois parties. "You have neglected your unions," explained McDonnell, "and allowed yourself to be led by the nose by every swindling politician. . . . You are sheep without a shepherd. Union is your shepherd."[2] Union growth, in other words, was a prerequisite to success in electoral politics.

In September 1877 the New Haven, Connecticut, section of the WPUSA sought to participate in a local election but was opposed by Marxists. Unless a workers' party was strong enough to stand on its own, Marx had argued, there was a danger that labor's efforts would be appropriated by the liberal bourgeoisie for its own benefit and purposes, much like what had occurred in the European revolutions in 1830 and 1848. During those years the working class had fought together with the emerging middle classes in attempts to overthrow kings, aristocrats, and other remnants of feudalism, only to be betrayed by their purported allies.

The Lassalleans were somewhat successful in their political efforts, especially in places with large German populations. Socialist candidates received large numbers of votes in elections held in New Haven, Chicago, and Cincinnati, and six socialists were successfully elected to public office in Milwaukee. In Louisville, Kentucky, the WPUSA won five of the seven seats it contested in an election for the state legislature and received 8,850 of the 13,578 votes cast. In Pittsburgh the socialists and the Greenback Party ran a joint ticket, while Peter Clark ran for state superintendent of schools in Cincinnati on the WPUSA ticket. An attempt to bring together the factions in New York failed when a proposed compromise between Marxists and Lassalleans was rejected by the latter. Thus the division between the followers of Marx and those of Lassalle that began in Europe continued in the United States.

Social instability characterized the United States after 1877. Depressions and labor strife were rife during the last years of the nineteenth and the beginning of the twentieth centuries. In 1892 strikes again occurred across the country.

There was a general strike in New Orleans and miners' strikes in Tennessee and Coeur d'Alene, Idaho, which were marked by firefights between workers and authorities. Ten thousand workers and supporters fought private militias in the Homestead strike in Pittsburgh that year. In 1894 the Pullman strike that started in Chicago spread across the nation. Two years before the Triangle Shirtwaist fire in New York City, thousands of garment workers struck over the issues of long hours and poor working conditions, and many joined the International Ladies Garment Workers Union. Following the Triangle fire, which took 146 lives in 1911, over 100,000 union members and supporters marched down Broadway.[3] Thousands of members of the Industrial Workers of the World (IWW) marched in Spokane, Washington, in 1909, and hundreds were arrested. In July 1903 Mother Jones organized a Children's March to Washington to protest child labor. In 1914 a strike by Colorado miners resulted in the Ludlow Massacre, when twenty-six miners were killed by Gatling-gun fire. Sixty thousand workers struck in Seattle in 1919, and that same year martial law was declared in Gary, Indiana, in order to defeat striking steel workers.

Nevertheless the socialist philosophy continued to spread following the end of the St. Louis Commune, although not necessarily in its revolutionary form. Many of the reforms demanded by the WPUSA in St. Louis, such as the eight-hour workday and the end of child labor, became part of the platforms of the Socialist Labor Party and later the Socialist Party and ultimately part of American labor law.

Socialist ideas spread throughout the United States following the fall of the Commune. The German nucleus of the socialist movement in the United States eventually gave way to other immigrant groups, such as the Jewish socialists in New York and Abraham Cahan's *Forward*, a Yiddish-language daily, which was especially popular in New York's Lower East Side and in its needle trades.[4] German socialist thought also spread from urban centers and was adopted or fused into an American brand of socialism. While German immigrants continued to play a role in the spread of a socialist philosophy, it began to take on an American personality.

The Midwest became a center of socialist activity. Oklahoma boasted over twelve thousand members of the Socialist Party, and over one hundred socialists held local offices in the state. Kansas became a focal point for both populist and socialist politics. The People's Party was formed in 1890, demanding radical reforms, especially in rural areas. The new party adopted many of the demands of the socialists, and it was successful in winning numerous elective offices, its members ultimately dispersing among the Democratic and Socialist parties. The populists and socialists agreed on the need for many of the same reforms, but the populists appeared to focus more on what the socialists viewed as the symptoms rather than the causes of the inequalities in American society.

By the end of the nineteenth and the beginning of the twentieth centuries, several different perspectives of socialism had emerged. Utopian socialism appeared again, for example, in Christian Hoffman's creation of the Sinaloa community, which offered "free land, free money, and free education."[5] Many German immigrants in Chicago were anarchists; some were active in the founding of the IWW, and a number of them were involved in the Haymarket incident in 1886. The IWW was especially strong in the West; its members did not believe in participating in electoral politics and met corporate and state violence with violence of their own. Other socialists would eventually follow what today would be called democratic socialism, which would ultimately be led by Eugene Debs, who was a candidate for president five times on the Socialist Party ticket and received almost 1 million votes in 1920 when he campaigned for the office from his Atlanta prison cell. According to his biographer, Nick Salvatore, the root of Debs's socialism was Jefferson and Lincoln rather than European thinkers.[6]

Kate Richards O'Hare was introduced to socialism by Mother Jones, the famous organizer of coal miners in Pennsylvania and southern Illinois. O'Hare moved to St. Louis in 1911 to edit a socialist weekly with her husband, Frank O'Hare. She worked for women's rights, served as a delegate to the 1917 socialist antiwar convention in St. Louis, and served time in a Missouri prison along with Emma Goldman for violation of the Espionage Act.[7] Socialism had almost become mainstream in the United States when in 1911 over 1,200 local officials, including seventy-three mayors, were elected on socialist tickets in the United States.[8]

In 1895 Julius Wayland edited the *Appeal to Reason*, a socialist periodical published in Girard, Kansas, which at one time boasted a readership of up to

4 million, the largest circulation of any left-wing paper in American history. Its roots in American culture were reflected in its name, which was drawn from Thomas Paine's *Common Sense*.[9] The paper published Upton Sinclair's *The Jungle* in 1904 and was Girard's largest employer. The city of Girard later elected a socialist mayor, and Crawford County, Kansas, was the first U.S. county to be controlled by socialists.

Divisions within the left weakened American socialists. Followers were divided on issues such as whether efforts and money should be spent on organizing unions or on participating in electoral politics, the effectiveness of a general strike or the use of violence, and the correct strategy for moving from a capitalist to a socialist society. The Socialist Labor Party, led by the Marxist Daniel DeLeon, ultimately split over tactics following the Russian Revolution, from which the Socialist Party of America and the American Communist Party ultimately emerged.

There is no question that current events are strongly affected by history, and what came before has a direct effect on later events. The awareness of the effect of history on present events has made its way into literary culture, such as Shakespeare's comment, "What's past is prologue," and William Faulkner's observation, "The past is not dead. It isn't even past." Marx made a similar observation in *The Eighteenth Brumaire of Louis Napoleon*, which was originally published as a series of weekly articles in Weydemeyer's *Die Revolution*: "Men make their own history, but they do not make it just as they please; they do not make it under circumstances chosen by themselves, but under circumstances directly encountered, given and transmitted from the past. The tradition of all the dead generations weighs like a nightmare on the brain of the living."[10] Depending on the situation, history may drive or restrain current events.

The 1877 railroad strike and the St. Louis Commune did not emerge without historical roots. They were born as a result of and shaped by both European and American history. The European revolutions of 1848 were rebellions by the working and middle classes against the remnants of feudal society. The emerging bourgeoisie and proletariat challenged the power of kings, aristocrats, and the Church, which had ruled Europe for over a thousand years. They sought to share in a more equitable division of wealth and power as they matured and grew more numerous and powerful. Their challenge called for a fairer and more meritorious kind of world, with greater freedoms for all members of society. Many were republicans who called for a sharing of power by the existing classes. Others were nationalists who sought to unite their countries into more powerful and successful entities, as occurred in the German and Italian states. Still others, especially those from the working and lower classes, called for socialism, whereby political power and wealth would be in the hands of the people. Ultimately, however, the middle classes were more concerned with what they considered the threat of the working classes and made their peace with royalty and cooperated in the suppression of workers, especially socialists.

Following the revolutions in 1848 there occurred the Franco-Prussian War. Crushed by the Prussians, the French acceded to Prussian demands at the same time that a movement for a republic swept over France. The people of Paris refused to accept the French surrender, declared a republic in Paris, and established the Paris Commune, a working-class experiment in self-government. During its three-month existence, the Paris Commune passed legislation favorable to the working class, prompting Marx to describe it as the dictatorship of the proletariat, when the working class would begin to remake society without economic classes and class conflict.

As a result of the failure of the 1848 Revolution in Germany and the fall of the Paris Commune, many working-class leaders were forced to flee Europe and settled in the United States, bringing with them their revolutionary fervor and philosophies. Most settled in New York and in the midwestern cities of St. Louis, Milwaukee, and Cincinnati. St. Louis possessed a culture friendly to both the French and German immigrants. It was an old French city that had attracted many Germans during the 1830s and early 1840s. So it was a friendly environment for those who arrived in the 1850s.

Those later immigrants came to America at an especially opportune time. The nation was about to explode in a civil war over the issue of slavery and attracted the participation of those already steeped in republican values. German immigrants joined the Union army and fought valiantly against slavery and for freedom and republicanism. Many of them were socialists who had previously fought on the barricades during the 1848 Revolution and the Paris Commune. The emergence of large monopolies and corporations after the Civil War, together with the exploitation of workers by unbridled and unregulated capitalism, provided a new enemy for them to confront. German radicals became leaders in the American labor movement, the 1877 railroad strike, and the St. Louis Commune. Their revolutionary fervor crossed the Atlantic with them and brought a new element to the conflict between American labor and capital. Thus one might say that the perfect storm arose, fueled by the revolutionaries of 1848, the Paris Commune, the First International, the Panic of 1873, and the instability and greed that characterized American society in the 1860s and 1870s.

There was no feudal class in the United States in the 1860s and 1870s, except perhaps the great plantation class in the South. The North was marked by industrial growth, public works, and the extension of railroads, while the South was mired in agriculture and slave labor. The conflict between North and South was not only a moral one involving slavery but also a result of the economic differences between the two sections. In many ways it was, as Marx described, a battle between feudalism and capitalism, which ended in the victory of the new corporate entities that had emerged in the North. As in Europe, the conflict then primarily became one between the new capitalism and those who served it by selling their labor. Similar to what had occurred in Europe, steam power brought about the increased use of machinery in factories, the use of unskilled workers to operate the machines, the disappearance of artisans who were no longer needed, and the exploitation of the working class by the new capitalists.

The Panic of 1873 affected both capitalists and workers. The speculative expansion of railroads, loans by banks to support that expansion, corruption in government, and fare wars between the railroads brought about and fueled the Panic. The rich, however, were in a much better position to survive the depression than was the working class. When the railroad owners instituted a number of pay cuts in 1877, laid off workers, increased the work load of remaining workers, and refused to reduce their own salaries or the shareholder dividends paid by their companies, it was a formula for disaster. Once the 1877 railroad strike began, it spread thousands of miles within only a few days. Repressed frustration and hatred exploded throughout the United States, as railroad workers were joined by other workers in their battle against the new corporatization of the country. Those who wished to usher in a new socialist society, more democratic and more equal with regard to political power and the distribution of wealth, combined with those who desired only a living wage to create a massive working-class movement that shook the foundations of American society. The cries of the capitalists against revolutionaries and the threat of another Paris Commune were not completely without merit. In many ways the events in the United States were merely a continuation of the nineteenth-century European revolutions. The past, it appeared, was not only prologue. It also was not even past.

The WPUSA and the St. Louis Commune, though both were short-lived, succeeded in affecting American society in several ways. They showed working people that they could accomplish reforms by uniting. At the time of the strike, unions and labor solidarity were young. National unions were only emerging and were weak. The Civil War and the 1873 depression almost destroyed most unions, though some managed to survive. But it became clear to all that working people could accomplish much more when united than they could by acting as individuals. Strong unions were the only weapon available to the working class.

The St. Louis Commune also showed that workers were capable of leading a major American city. During its life, the Commune operated city services, controlled manufacturing and business, and policed the city. At the same time that they battled the massive railroad companies, state militias, and other adversarial groups, they carried on the workings of a large metropolitan area. The Commune proved that the working class was capable of administering the city.

It also revealed clearly that the interests of the rich capitalists and the poor workers were incompatible. The railroads attempted to operate by paying their workers less than a living wage, so that the profits for its officers, owners, and shareholders were maximized. The large corporations had one goal: not to provide a fair wage to their workers but to maximize their profits as much as possible by any means available. In the end, the workers did not even demand wages that would provide their families with comfortable lives but only that which would enable them to survive.

Although racism permeated the nineteenth century in both the North and the South, the struggle between labor and capital showed that people of different ethnic backgrounds could share the same interests and work together toward a common goal. While racism did exist in the WPUSA and the St. Louis Commune, both were composed of people of different ethnic backgrounds and races. Although there were conflicts between the different groups, in St. Louis Germans, Irish, Bohemians, French, Swedes, and African Americans were conscious of their shared interests, and they united against what they saw as a common enemy. They identified as workers first, and only secondarily ethnically. For a time during the life of the St. Louis Commune, workers, Black and white and of several ethnicities, came together in their struggle for better lives.

The WPUSA revealed the necessity of conducting battles on two fronts, economically and politically. It was not sufficient to seek only economic goals; it was also important to seek political power. The WPUSA and the St. Louis Commune significantly influenced the American labor movement by attempting to educate workers about the effects of capitalism on the working classes and the class nature of American society.[11]

Finally, both introduced the American working class to the philosophy of socialism. European immigrants, especially Germans, brought European ideas with them when they immigrated to the United States, and socialism was at the heart of both the WPUSA and the St. Louis Commune. Those ideas did not die with the WPUSA and the Commune but became a part of the American labor movement. Robert Bruce suggests that Debs was so impressed with St. Louis Commune leader Peter Lofgreen's book, *The Cooperative Commonwealth*, that he became a socialist as a result.[12]

The birth of the WPUSA and the St. Louis Commune made it appear as if the 1848 revolutions in Europe were continuing in the United States, influenced by the First International and the Paris Commune. Many of their members had fought in the European revolutions and on the barricades in Paris. Their effect on the events in St. Louis is clearly evident and cannot be denied. Members of the St. Louis Commune were veteran Forty-Eighters and Paris communards, and many belonged to the First International. Even the newspapers at the time continuously compared the strikes to the Paris

Commune and blamed members of the International for the unrest. Allan Pinkerton, who was responsible for destroying many unions and crushing many more strikes, called the 1877 strikes the greatest peril ever to hit the United States. It was like the Paris Commune, he said, the result of vile men with no human attributes. The strikes in the United States, he argued, were a direct result of the Paris Commune and the First International. Unions themselves, in Pinkerton's opinion, were secret, communist organizations of the most vile members of society.[13] There is also no doubt that the 1877 strikes were a working-class struggle against monopoly and industrial capitalism. In Pittsburgh almost all those arrested were working-class citizens; in Buffalo, 60 percent of those arrested were of the working class; in Baltimore they were 80 percent and in St. Louis 94 percent.[14] The uprisings throughout the country clearly had a working-class character.

There also was a strong socialist flavor to the strikes, the WPUSA, and the St. Louis Commune. The railroads were a symbol of industrial capitalism and all of the problems that went along with it. They fed at the public trough, invaded cities, bought legislators, and were responsible for a good deal of the corruption in the nation. The Pennsylvania Railroad was the largest corporation in the world at the time. Although the railroad strike began over the issue of wages, it quickly grew to criticize industrialism generally, capitalism and the rich in American society, which it saw as parasites and exploiters of working people.

This change was in no small way attributable to the German revolutionaries who settled in the United States following the 1848 revolution, the French participants in and supporters of the Paris Commune, and both French and German members of the First International. While participants in the German Revolution also included those whose primary interests were nationalism, republicanism, or the unification of the German states, there was a strong socialist element that supported and, in many cases, led the revolution. The Paris Commune, although born in patriotism and a rejection of France's humiliating surrender to Prussia, supported a republic and legislated a number of socialist reforms in the city. The First International, organized by Marx, focused on uniting working people of all countries in order to overthrow capitalism and replace it with socialism. Many of the German immigrants to the United States, and to St. Louis in particular, brought socialist thought with them, which they attempted to apply to American labor struggles. The constitution, propaganda, and philosophy of the WPUSA all emphasized socialism as the solution to labor's problems. The leaders of the St. Louis Commune were socialists who attacked capitalism and monopoly as the scourge of the working man. At least in St. Louis, the strike movement had a strong socialist bent.

There were certainly revolutionaries active in the railroad strike, the WPUSA, and the St. Louis Commune. Once again, many of the German immigrants had participated in the German Revolution and carried their beliefs with them when they immigrated to the United States. A good number of them were Marxists who advocated revolution in all industrial nations and the ascendency of the working classes to power. Weydemeyer was one such advocate in St. Louis. The writings and speeches of the leaders of the St. Louis Commune were certainly of a revolutionary nature. Time after time they called for the overthrow of capitalism, either peacefully or in a violent manner. Yet the Commune's immediate goals were more economic than political. The historian Harvey Goldberg's description of the French socialist Jean Jaurès could equally apply to the WPUSA and the leaders of the St. Louis Commune: "More than most of his socialist colleagues, he grasped the central paradox of unionism, that however revolutionary its rhetoric and goals, its *raison d'être* was amelioration of existing social conditions."[15]

Witnesses to the railroad strike believed that a working-class revolution was possible in the United States at that time. The state militias were badly trained, unorganized, and, in many instances, sympathetic to the strikers. The U.S. Army had only approximately fifteen thousand men, most of whom were stationed on the frontier fighting Indians. The strike had become general, and workers of all trades participated. Had the railroad employees desired to overthrow the government in 1877, Dacus believes they could have succeeded: "With a purpose of revolution, with organization and leadership, it was within the grasp of the railroad employees and other classes of laborers to have taken absolute possession of every commercial center in the nation; aye! Even to have overturned the Government itself!"[16]

But, Dacus adds, there was no evidence that the First International had attempted to overthrow the American government.[17] Like the Paris Commune's failure to march on Versailles or to capture the Bank of France, American workers hesitated to take the steps that may have resulted in their complete victory. Leaders of the St. Louis Commune, although they controlled the city for all practical purposes, did not attempt to take the city's armories or banks. They appeared satisfied to organize mass meetings and parades and to condemn the use of violence.

While authorities warned of a proletarian revolution, even Marx, who followed events in the United States closely, recognized that the workers in the United States were not in a position to carry out a successful revolution. Recognizing that the U.S. government was strong enough to crush the strikers, Marx wrote to Engels that the 1877 strike was a movement that would ultimately fail, but he hoped that it would be the beginning of the creation of a labor party supported by the working class in the United States: "What do you think of the workers of the United States? This first explosion against the associated oligarchy of capital which has occurred since the Civil War will naturally again be suppressed, but can very well form the point of origin of an earnest worker's party."[18]

But the 1877 railroad strike did not cause the working class to make an attempt to overthrow the government, as had occurred in Europe. Workers in the United States were faced with certain obstacles to organization that did not exist in Europe. The American labor movement was not a homogeneous group but was divided over gender, race, social mobility, and ethnicity. Although women were active in the 1877 strikes, the railroad industry's workers were overwhelmingly male and white. There were conflicts between African Americans and whites, Irish and German, and Irish and Black workers. European countries were much more homogeneous and were not compelled to resolve those differences. A united working class had to overcome those conflicts in order to be successful.

In addition, because the United States, unlike European countries, already was a republic, most American-born workers were willing to work through accepted political channels rather than engage in revolutionary action. European workers did not have those seemingly open channels through which to achieve reform. American individualism, the Protestant ethic, and the acceptance of republican values were part of American culture. Class warfare, which was endemic in Europe, was challenged in the United States by ideas of justice and democracy. Even Engels concluded that America's German revolutionaries attempted to impose a system that was foreign to the American experience.[19]

What was fatal to the St. Louis Commune, however, was a lack of revolutionary leadership. The railroad strike that resulted in the establishment of the Commune was not organized on a national basis and did not have any national leadership or coordination. Those national unions that did exist were young and weak. Workers struck independently in various locales. While the First International did have a national organization, it did not possess the numbers to realize revolutionary change.

The takeover of St. Louis by striking workers was the result of a combination of the expansion of the railroad strike into a general strike in the city and the failure of the municipal government to react to events in a timely way. The WPUSA leadership in St. Louis was successful in exciting the working class and presenting inspiring parades and speeches, but it failed to take the steps necessary to achieve radical change. It did not arm the workers, even for their own defense, and did not attempt to take the armories, not even to prevent the militia and Committee of Public Safety from obtaining those arms. Commune leaders halted mass meetings and parades, resulting in little or no communication with the striking workers. Leaders of the St. Louis Commune, having taken leadership of the strike in St. Louis and control of the city, then hesitated and appeared to be unsure of what actions to take with their newly discovered power. As occurred to their predecessors in Paris, their hesitation allowed the reactionary forces time to regroup, organize, and arm themselves, resulting in the Commune's defeat. Still, the St. Louis Commune represented the product of a hundred years of historical actions and philosophies that covered two continents thousands of miles apart, beginning with the French Revolution and ending, at least for a time, on the streets of St. Louis. Ron Chernow summarized the socialist legacy of the St. Louis Commune this way: "In St. Louis, the intellectual and political heirs of Sigel and Weydemeyer mounted a final battle. The St. Louis General Strike of 1877 provided the nation with the era's most compelling example of interracial radicalism."[20]

NOTES

INTRODUCTION

1. P. S. Foner, *History of the Labor Movement*, 170–73.
2. P. S. Foner, *History of the Labor Movement*, 183.

1. REVOLUTION COMES TO ST. LOUIS

1. "The Internationals," *Missouri Republican*, July 27, 1877, 4.
2. "The Big Strike," *Westliche Post*, July 24, 1877, 3.
3. "Situation at St. Louis," *Globe-Democrat*, July 22 1877, 2.
4. "The Little Rolling Mill," *Globe-Democrat*, July 24, 1877, 4.
5. Roediger, "Not Only the Ruling Classes," 213–39, 221.
6. "The Public Meeting," *Globe-Democrat*, July 23, 1877, 3.
7. "International," *Westliche Post*, July 25, 1877, 3.
8. "Meeting at Lucas Market," *Missouri Republican*, July 24, 1877, 5.
9. "Terre Haute," *Missouri Republican*, July 25, 1877, 2.
10. "Meeting at Lucas Market," *Missouri Republican*, July 25, 1877, 5.

2. REVOLUTION IN EUROPE

1. Hobsbawm, *Age of Revolution*, 109.
2. Sperber, *Rhineland Radicals*, 6.
3. Hobsbawm, *Age of Revolution*, 111.
4. Hobsbawm, *Age of Revolution*, 112.
5. Rapport, *1848*, 18.
6. Hobsbawm, *Age of Revolution*, 112.
7. Hobsbawm, *Age of Revolution*, 170.
8. Stadelman, *Social and Political History*, 64.
9. Rapport, *1848*, 2.
10. Hobsbawm, *Age of Revolution*, 172.
11. Rapport, *1848*, 47.
12. Rapport, *1848*, 58–59.
13. Rapport, *1848*, 60–63. Kossuth later became governor of the Kingdom of Hungary, and Metternich became chancellor of the Austrian Empire.
14. Stadelman, *Social and Political History*, 22.

15. Stadelman, *Social and Political History*, 4.
16. Siemann, *German Revolution*, 15.
17. Sperber, *Rhineland Radicals*, 155.
18. Sperber, *Rhineland Radicals*, 149.
19. Rapport, *1848*, 73.
20. Rapport, *1848*, 73–78.
21. Rapport, *1848*, 2.
22. Hammen, *Red '48ers*, 122.
23. Marx, "Germany at the Outbreak of the Revolution," 5.
24. Marx and Engels, *Communist Manifesto*, 13–15.
25. Roberts, *Napoleon*, 406.
26. Sperber, *Rhineland Radicals*, 21.
27. Sperber, *Rhineland Radicals*, 24.
28. Sperber, *Rhineland Radicals*, 162.
29. Sperber, *Rhineland Radicals*, 161.
30. Hammen, *Red '48ers*, 335–36.
31. Siemann, *German Revolution*, 64–66.
32. Sperber, *Rhineland Radicals*, 219.
33. Stadelman, *Social and Political History*, 15.
34. Stadelman, *Social and Political History*, 101.
35. Hammen, *Red '48ers*, 336.
36. Hammen, *Red '48ers*, 337.
37. Stadelman, *Social and Political History*, 181.
38. Hammen, *Red '48ers*, 392.
39. Sperber, *Rhineland Radicals*, 366–68.
40. Stadelman, *Social and Political History*, 184.
41. Stadelman, *Social and Political History*, 111.
42. Sperber, *Rhineland Radicals*, 477.
43. Siemann, *German Revolution*, 187.
44. Stadelman, *Social and Political History*, 196–97.

3. AFTER THE CIVIL WAR

1. E. Foner, *Short History of Reconstruction*, 9.
2. Cozzens, *The Earth Is Weeping*, 207.
3. Cozzens, *The Earth Is Weeping*, 197.
4. Chernow, *Grant*, 153.
5. Chernow, *Grant*, 143, 149.
6. Chernow, *Grant*, 694, 715.
7. Chernow, *Grant*, 147.
8. Axelrod, *Gilded Age*, 406.

9. Turner, *Frontier in American History*.

10. Brands, *American Colossus*, 316–19.

11. Riis, *How the Other Half Lives*, 85, 2, 229.

12. Brands, *American Colossus*, 413–18.

13. Trachtenberg, *Incorporation of America*, 39.

14. Trachtenberg, *Incorporation of America*, 12.

15. Chernow, *Grant*, 729.

16. E. Foner, *Short History of Reconstruction*, 202.

17. Twain, *Gilded Age*, 236.

18. Brands, *American Colossus*, 6.

19. Chernow, *Grant*, 819.

20. Chernow, *Grant*, 710.

21. Chernow, *Grant*, 752.

22. Chernow, *Grant*, 729.

23. Corbett and Miller, *Saint Louis in the Gilded Age*, 4–6.

24. Hodes, *Divided City*, 17.

25. Nini Harris, presentation, St. Louis Oasis, June 18, 2019.

26. A. F. Holland, "African Americans," 51–78.

27. Harry Purdy, "An Historical Analysis of the Economic Growth of St. Louis 1840–1945," I.C.C. Finance Document No. 15365, p. 51, St. Louis Public Library Archives.

28. Johnson, *Broken Heart of America*, 175.

29. Heinrichs, "Carondelet," 160–82, 167, 170.

30. Van Ravenswary, "Years of Turmoil."

31. Hagen, *This Is Our*, 294.

32. Hodes, *Divided City*, 657–58.

33. Chernow, *Grant*, 173.

34. Hodes, *Divided City*, 38.

35. Primm, "Economy of Nineteenth Century St. Louis," 103–35.

36. Hodes, *Divided City*, 115.

37. Primm, *Lion of the Valley*, 272.

38. Primm, "Economy of Nineteenth Century St. Louis," 117.

39. Chernow, *Grant*, 118.

40. Chernow, *Grant*, 172.

41. Johnson, *Broken Heart of America*, 41.

42. Gates, "Railroads of Missouri," 126–41.

43. Hodes, *Divided City*, 178–79.

44. Twain, *Gilded Age*, 97.

45. Guese, "St. Louis and the Great Whiskey Ring."

46. Johns, "Joseph Pulitzer."

47. Chernow, *Grant*, 748.

4. THE PARIS COMMUNE

1. Lissagaray, *History of the Paris Commune*, 8.
2. Edwards, *Paris Commune*, 3.
3. Marx, *Civil War in France*, 13.
4. Lissagaray, *History of the Paris Commune*, 32–33.
5. Hobsbawm, *Uncommon People*, 55.
6. Gluckstein, *Paris Commune*, 86.
7. Merriman, *Massacre*, 21.
8. Edwards, *Paris Commune*, 54.
9. Gluckstein, *Paris Commune*, 3.
10. Edwards, *Communards of Paris*, 56.
11. Lissagaray, *History of the Paris Commune*, 72.
12. Edwards, *Communards of Paris*, 16.
13. Gluckstein, *Paris Commune*, 122.
14. Hobsbawm, *Revolutionaries*, 95.
15. Merriman, *Massacre*, 37.
16. Gluckstein, *Paris Commune*, 127.
17. Marx, *Civil War in France*, 16.
18. Edwards, *Paris Commune*, 34.
19. Gluckstein, *Paris Commune*, 22.
20. Michel, "Memories of the Commune," 14.
21. Gluckstein, *Paris Commune*, 10.
22. Merriman, *Massacre*, 65–66.
23. Gluckstein, *Paris Commune*, 23.
24. Edwards, *Communards of Paris*, 106.
25. Edwards, *Communards of Paris*, 128.
26. Merriman, *Massacre*, 161.
27. Lissagaray, *History of the Paris Commune*, 2.
28. Merriman, *Massacre*, 206.
29. Merriman, *Massacre*, 240.
30. Horne, *Fall of Paris*, 422.
31. Lissagaray, *History of the Paris Commune*, 344.
32. Gluckstein, *Paris Commune*, 158.
33. Edwards, *Paris Commune*, 351.
34. Horne, *Fall of Paris*, 424.
35. Horne, *Fall of Paris*, 429.
36. Marx, *Civil War in France*, 60.
37. Bakunin, "Paris Commune and the Idea of the State," 42.
38. Bernstein, "American Labor," 154.

39. Hobsbawm, *Revolutionaries*, 92.

40. Morris et al., "Short Account," 21.

41. Katz, *From Appomattox to Montmartre*, 32, 37.

42. Katz, *From Appomattox to Montmartre*, 57.

43. Katz, *From Appomattox to Montmartre*, 53.

44. Katz, *From Appomattox to Montmartre*, 63.

45. Katz, *From Appomattox to Montmartre*, 173.

46. Katz, *From Appomattox to Montmartre*, 171.

47. Katz, *From Appomattox to Montmartre*, 112–13.

48. Katz, *From Appomattox to Montmartre*, 112.

49. Katz, *From Appomattox to Montmartre*, 131, 135.

50. Katz, *From Appomattox to Montmartre*, 157, 158.

51. Katz, *From Appomattox to Montmartre*, 157–59.

52. Mark Rudd, email dated July 24, 2020; Katz, *From Appomattox to Montmartre*, 2.

53. Katz, *From Appomattox to Montmartre*, 173.

5. THE FIRST INTERNATIONAL

1. Fernbach, *The First International and After*.

2. Sperber, *Karl Marx*, 59.

3. Marx and Engels, *German Ideology*, 64.

4. Mehring, *Karl Marx*, 72.

5. Mehring, *Karl Marx*, 105.

6. Wheen, *Karl Marx*, 275–76.

7. Marx, "Inaugural Address," 77–80.

8. Carolyn J. Mattern, ed., "Papers of the International Workingmen's Association," 1972, p. 316, Wisconsin Historical Society.

9. Mattern, "Papers of the International Workingmen's Association," 316.

10. Marx, "Inaugural Address," 87–91.

11. Sperber, *Karl Marx*, 183.

12. Mehring, *Karl Marx*, 354–55.

13. Bernstein, *First International in America*, 31.

14. Wheen, *Karl Marx*, 324.

15. Bernstein, *First International in America*, 48.

16. Marx, "Report to the Basle Conference," 99.

17. Marx and Engels, "Resolution of the London Conference," 270.

18. Bell, *Marxian Socialism*, 18.

19. Marx, "Report to the Hague Congress," 321.

20. Marx, "Report to the Hague Congress," 322.

21. International Working Men's Association, "Programme of the Internationals," broadside, Newberry Library.

22. Gerth, *First International Minutes*, 171.

23. Gray, *Socialist Tradition*, 352.

24. Mehring, *Karl Marx*, 405.

25. Gray, *Socialist Tradition*, 359–60.

26. Gerth, *First International Minutes*, 297–98.

27. Wheen, *Karl Marx*, 326.

28. Bell, *Marxian Socialism*, 22.

29. Bernstein, *First International in America*, 9.

30. Fried, *Socialism in America*, 180–81.

31. Bernstein, *First International in America*, 18.

32. Bernstein, *First International in America*, 39.

33. Bernstein, *First International in America*, 93.

34. Gray, *Socialist Tradition*, 341.

35. Bernstein, *First International in America*, 102–4.

36. Mattern, "Papers of the International Working Men's Association."

37. Sperber, *Karl Marx*, 514.

38. Bernstein, *New Papers*, 455.

39. F. A. Sorge et al., letters to St. Louis sections, August 19, 1874, October 6, 1874, February 17, 1875, and June 17, 1876, Collection of Documents of the First International, Wisconsin Historical Society.

40. Burbank, "First International," 163–72.

41. Burbank, "First International."

42. Sperber, *Karl Marx*, 372.

6. CONDITION OF THE AMERICAN WORKING CLASS

1. Currarino, *Labor Question in America*, 14.

2. Gutman, *Work, Culture and Society*, 28.

3. Ware, *Industrial Worker*, 15.

4. Ware, *Industrial Worker*, 14–15.

5. E. Foner, *Free Soil, Free Labor*, 27–28.

6. P. S. Foner, *History of the Labor Movement*, 199.

7. Ware, *Industrial Worker*, 127.

8. Ware, *Industrial Worker*, 75.

9. Ware, *Industrial Worker*, 75.

10. Ware, *Industrial Worker*, 76.

11. P. S. Foner, *History of the Labor Movement*, 225.

12. Swacker, *New York City History*, 576.

13. "The New York Communists," *Globe-Democrat*, July 26, 1877, 2.

14. *Who Was G.*, 54.

15. Gutman, *Work, Culture and Society*, 121.

16. Gutman, *Work, Culture and Society*, 264–67.
17. Gutman, *Work, Culture and Society*, 327–30.
18. P. S. Foner, *History of the Labor Movement*, 461.
19. Gutman, *Work, Culture and Society*, 295–96.
20. Gutman, *Work, Culture and Society*, 298–300.
21. Gutman, *Work, Culture and Society*, 300–301.
22. Gutman, *Work, Culture and Society*, 320.
23. P. S. Foner, *History of the Labor Movement*, 344–45.
24. P. S. Foner, *History of the Labor Movement*, 381.
25. P. S. Foner, *History of the Labor Movement*, 339–40.
26. Laboring Man, "Conditions of the Laborers of St. Louis," *Missouri Republican*, July 13, 1877, 4.
27. Zinn, *People's History*.
28. Ware, *Industrial Worker*, 193–94.
29. Ware, *Industrial Worker*, 195.
30. Ware, *Industrial Worker*, 196.
31. Leikin, *Practical Utopians*, 1.
32. Leikin, *Practical Utopians*, 5.
33. Leikin, *Practical Utopians*, 12–13.
34. Leikin, *Practical Utopians*, 93–94.
35. Leikin, *Practical Utopians*, 104.
36. Leikin, *Practical Utopians*, vii.

7. GERMAN IMMIGRATION

1. Daniels, *Coming to America*, 70.
2. Wittke, *Refugees of Revolution*, 6.
3. Daniels, *Coming to America*, 150.
4. Daniels, *Coming to America*, 156.
5. Rowan, *Germans for a Free Missouri*, 35.
6. Elisha Burch, letter to Abram Clement, September 12, 1831, Immigration to Missouri Collection, Missouri Historical Society.
7. Kargan, "Missouri's German Immigration," 23.
8. Eugenia Busch Kircher, "Excerpts from Friedrich Muench's Last Words," Immigration to Missouri Collection, Missouri Historical Society.
9. Wittke, *Refugees of Revolution*, 116–20.
10. Kargan, "Missouri's German Immigration," 24.
11. Julius Muench, "The German Contribution to Missouri," speech, January 1947, Immigration to Missouri Collection, Missouri Historical Society.
12. Wittke, *Refugees of Revolution*, 49.
13. Wittke, *Refugees of Revolution*, 56.

14. Olson, "The Nature of an Immigrant Community," 343.
15. Emil Mallinckrodt, letter, July 4, 1847, Emil Mallinckrodt Papers, Missouri Historical Society.
16. Churchill, *The Crisis*, 117.
17. Emil Mallinckrodt, letter, July 4, 1847, Emil Mallinckrodt Papers, Missouri Historical Society.
18. Emil Mallinckrodt, letter, April 29, 1841, Emil Mallinckrodt Papers, Missouri Historical Society.
19. Emil Mallinckrodt, letter, November 20, 1849, Emil Mallinckrodt Papers, Missouri Historical Society.
20. Boernstein, *Memoirs of a Nobody*, 81.
21. Blatter, "Emigration from Germany," 77.
22. Freitag, *Friedrich Hecker*, 27–28.
23. Freitag, *Friedrich Hecker*, 169.
24. Kargau and Tolzmann, *German Element in St. Louis*, 212.
25. Wittke, *Refugees of Revolution*, 134.
26. Daniels, *Coming to America*, 162.
27. Boernstein, *Memoirs of a Nobody*, 79.
28. Joseph Elder, letter to James Broadhead, June 18, 1861, James O. Broadhead Papers, Missouri Historical Society.
29. Wittke, *Refugees of Revolution*, 334.
30. Wittke, *Refugees of Revolution*, 338.
31. Kargau, and Tolzmann, *German Element in St. Louis*, 151.
32. Gerteis, *Civil War in St. Louis*, 92.
33. Wittke, *Refugees of Revolution*, 149–50.
34. Kargau and Tolzmann, *German Element in St. Louis*, 216–17.
35. Benson and Kennedy, *Lincoln's Marxists*, 59–60.
36. Obermann, *Joseph Weydemeyer*, 60.
37. E. Foner, *Free Soil, Free Labor*, 226.
38. Wittke, *Refugees of Revolution*, 185.
39. Gerteis, *Civil War in St. Louis*, 43.
40. E. Foner, *Free Soil, Free Labor*, 257
41. Olson, "The Nature of an Immigrant Community," 347.
42. Krause, "German Americans," 301.
43. Hodes, *Divided City*, 203.
44. Griffin, "Strange Story," 405.
45. Sandweiss, *St. Louis*, 87–89.
46. "Germans Arouse!," broadside, October 25, 1864, Civil War Collection, Missouri Historical Society.
47. Chernow, *Grant*, 134.

48. Hamilton, "Enrolled Missouri Militia," 421.

49. Gerteis, *Civil War in St. Louis*, 103.

50. McCoskrie and Warren, *Civil War Missouri Compendium*, 33.

51. Chernow, *Grant*, 397.

52. Sperber, *Rhineland Radicals*, 492.

53. Brands, *American Colossus*, 266.

54. Chernow, *Grant*, 134.

55. Marx and Engels, *Civil War in the United States*, 224.

56. Marx and Engels, *Civil War in the United States*, 167.

57. Rowan, *Germans for a Free Missouri*, 31.

58. Gerteis, *Civil War in St. Louis*, 255.

8. THE RAILROAD STRIKE

1. L. Marx, *Machine in the Garden*, 191.

2. Adams, *Education of Henry Adams*, 361.

3. Smith, "Chicago Railway Review," 3.

4. Bruce, *1877*, 15.

5. Smith, "Chicago Railway Review."

6. Adamic, *Dynamite*, 23–26.

7. Zinn, *People's History*, 238–39.

8. Zinn, *People's History*, 238.

9. Commission of Railroads and Telegraphs of Ohio, "Eleventh Annual Report," 165, 174, 175, 475, 474.

10. Gutman, *Work, Culture and Society*, 51.

11. P. S. Foner, *Great Labor Uprising*, 32.

12. Gutman, *Work, Culture and Society*, 320.

13. "The Outlook for Washington," *New York Tribune*, July 25, 1877, 1.

14. Stowell, *Streets, Railroads*, 1.

15. Stowell, *Streets, Railroads*, 15, 26.

16. Gutman, *Work, Culture and Society*, 309.

17. Walker, "Railroad Strike," 21.

18. Brecher, *Strike*, 29.

19. "The German Bank," *Missouri Republican*, July 11, 1877, 4.

20. "Another Collapse," *Missouri Republican*, July 12, 1877, 8.

21. "The Banks: Two of Them Closed Suddenly on Yesterday," *Missouri Republican*, July 17, 1877, 8.

22. "Monetary," *Missouri Republican*, July 18, 1877, 4.

23. P. S. Foner, *Great Labor Uprising*, 44.

24. "Railroad Matters," *Missouri Republican*, July 3, 1877, 2.

25. Walker, "Railroad Strike," 19.

26. Brecher, *Strike*, 14.

27. Dacus, *Annals of the Great Strikes*, 18.

28. Dacus, *Annals of the Great Strikes*, 13.

29. Dacus, *Annals of the Great Strikes*, 47.

30. C. Holland, *Blood on the Tracks*.

31. P. S. Foner, *Great Labor Uprising*.

32. Brecher, *Strike*, 23.

33. Dacus, *Annals of the Great Strikes*, 49.

34. "The Martinsburg Strike," *Missouri Republican*, July 19, 1877, 4.

35. Editorial, *Missouri Republican*, July 21, 1877, 2.

36. Barry, *The 1877 Railroad Strike in Baltimore*, 27.

37. P. S. Foner, *Workingmen's Party*, 171.

38. "Glutted with Gore," *Globe-Democrat*, July 22, 1877, 1.

39. Dacus, *Annals of the Great Strikes*, 78.

40. "Glutted with Gore," *Globe-Democrat*, July 22, 1877, 1.

41. Bruce, *1877*, 131.

42. Bruce, *1877*, 176–80.

43. "The Nation's Woe," *Globe-Democrat*, July 23, 1877, 1.

44. Boyer and Morais, *Labor's Untold Story*, 58.

45. "Erie Railroad Matters," *Missouri Republican*, July 1, 1877, 3.

46. Dacus, *Annals of the Great Strikes*, 83.

47. Jones, *Goddess of Anarchy*, 40–48.

48. "Chicago's Commune," *Globe-Democrat*, July 26, 1877, 1.

49. Boyer and Morais, *Labor's Untold Story*, 59.

50. "At the National Capitol," *Globe-Democrat*, July 26, 1877, 2.

51. Jones, *Goddess of Anarchy*, 66.

52. "The New York Central," *Globe-Democrat*, July 24, 1877, 1.

53. J. H. Wilson, letter to Carl Schurz, July 22, 1877, David Burbank Collection, State Historical Society of Missouri.

54. *Who Was G.*, 43.

55. "The Newsboys Strike," *Globe-Democrat*, July 21, 1877, 5.

56. "The Feeling at Cincinnati," *Globe-Democrat*, July 23, 1877, 5.

57. Mandel, "The 'Great Uprising' of 1877."

58. Bell, *Marxian Socialism*, 24.

59. P. S. Foner, *Great Labor Uprising*, 8.

60. "A Splendid Pageant," *Globe-Democrat*, August 1, 1877.

61. Bruce, *1877*, 135.

62. Dacus, *Annals of the Great Strikes*, 6.

63. P. S. Foner, *History of the Labor Movement*, 471.

9. THE ST. LOUIS COMMUNE

1. Wittke, *Refugees of Revolution*, 4.
2. Wittke, *Refugees of Revolution*, 20.
3. Wittke, *Refugees of Revolution*, 25.
4. Reznek, "Distress, Relief," 495–97.
5. Reznek, "Distress, Relief," 497n11.
6. Reznek, "Distress, Relief," 502.
7. Reznek, "Distress, Relief," 506.
8. P. S. Foner, *Workingmen's Party*, 16.
9. P. S. Foner, *Workingmen's Party*, 21.
10. Graff, "Race, Citizenship," 50.
11. Nolan, "Labor Movement in St. Louis Prior to the Civil War," 18–19.
12. Graff, "Race, Citizenship," 56.
13. Nolan, "Labor Movement in St. Louis Prior to the Civil War," 19.
14. Deborah Henry, "Politics, Economics and the Shaping of Worker Ideology in Antebellum St. Louis," unpublished paper in author's possession, 1996; Houf, "Fifty Years of Missouri Labor," 43.
15. Nolan, "Labor Movement in St. Louis Prior to the Civil War," 25.
16. Nolan, "Labor Movement in St. Louis from 1860 to 1890," 158.
17. Nolan, "Labor Movement in St. Louis from 1860 to 1890," 158.
18. P. S. Foner, *Workingmen's Party*, 25.
19. P. S. Foner, *Workingmen's Party*, 33.
20. P. S. Foner, *Workingmen's Party*, 34.
21. P. S. Foner, *Workingmen's Party*, 34–35.
22. Workingmen's Party of the United States, *Papers for the People, No. 1*, Workingmen's Party of the United States Collection, Newberry Library.
23. A. Douai, *Better Times*, 4, International Workingmen's Association Collection, Newberry Library.
24. Douai, *Better Times*, 24.
25. Douai, *Better Times*, 27.
26. Douai, *Better Times*, 31.
27. Constitution of the Workingmen's Party of the United States, Article I, Workingmen's Party of the United States Collection, Newberry Library.
28. Constitution of the Workingmen's Party of the United States, Article IV.
29. Constitution of the Workingmen's Party of the United States, Article I.
30. Constitution of the Workingmen's Party of the United States, "Women's Rights."
31. Letter regarding interview with Peter Clark, unknown parties, June 18, 1919, Peter Clark Collection, Missouri Historical Society.
32. P. S. Foner, *Workingmen's Party*, 51.

33. P. S. Foner, *Workingmen's Party*, 68.

34. Robert Harris, letter, August 6, 1877, Chicago, Burlington & Quincy Correspondence Collection, Newberry Library.

35. Burbank, *Reign of the Rabble*, 6.

36. "The Big Strike," *Westliche Post*, July 24, 1877, 3.

37. "The Public Meeting," *Globe-Democrat*, July 23, 1877, 3.

38. "International," *Westliche Post*, July 25, 1877, 3.

39. Johnson, *Broken Heart of America*, 219.

40. "The Strike," *Post-Dispatch*, July 24, 1877, 1.

41. J. H. Wilson, telegram to Carl Schurz, July 22, 1877, David Burbank Collection, State Historical Society of Missouri.

42. J. H. Wilson, letter to Carl Schurz, July 22, 1877, David Burbank Collection, State Historical Society of Missouri.

43. "The Internationals," *Globe-Democrat*, July 24, 1877, 5.

44. "The Internationals," *Globe-Democrat*, July 24, 1877, 5.

45. "In Conversation," *Missouri Republican*, July 23, 1877, 5.

46. "In Conversation," *Missouri Republican*, July 23, 1877, 5.

47. "In Conversation," *Missouri Republican*, July 23, 1877, 5.

48. J. F. Hartranft, telegram to President Hayes, July 23, 1877, David Burbank Collection, State Historical Society of Missouri.

49. John Welsh, letter to President Hayes, July 24, 1877, David Burbank Collection, State Historical Society of Missouri.

50. W. K. Ackerman, *President's Daily Reports*, Chicago Office, April 7–December 4, 1877, Illinois Central Railroad Company Collection, Newberry Library.

51. "The Strike at Home," *Globe-Democrat*, July 24, 1877, 4.

52. "The Internationals," *Globe-Democrat*, July 24, 1877, 5.

53. "Very Latest," *Post-Dispatch*, July 24, 1877, 1.

54. "Letters," *Missouri Republican*, July 26, 1877.

55. "East St. Louis," *Post-Dispatch*, July 24, 1877, 1.

56. "On the Ragged Edge," *Globe-Democrat*, July 25, 1877, 4.

57. "The Internationals," *Missouri Republican*, July 24, 1877, 4.

58. "The Great Strike," *Missouri Republican*, July 24, 1877, 1.

59. Dacus, *Annals of the Great Strikes*, 197.

60. David Burbank Collection, State Historical Society of Missouri.

61. "Ways of Iron," *Missouri Republican*, August 2, 1877, 3.

62. "On the Ragged Edge," *Globe-Democrat*, July 25, 1877, 4.

63. Kelsey, *Autobiographical Notes and Memoranda*, 93.

64. Kelsey, *Autobiographical Notes and Memoranda*, 95.

65. Kelsey, *Autobiographical Notes and Memoranda*, 95–96.

66. Kelsey, *Autobiographical Notes and Memoranda*, 110.

67. Kelsey, *Autobiographical Notes and Memoranda*, 106.

68. Cozzens, *The Earth Is Weeping*, 54.

69. Cozzens, *The Earth Is Weeping*, 59.

70. "The Real Demand," *Missouri Republican*, July 24, 1877, 4.

71. Primm, *Lion of the Valley*, 310.

72. Roediger, "Not Only the Ruling Classes," 216.

73. Roediger, "Not Only the Ruling Classes," 218.

74. "The Strike Yesterday," *Globe-Democrat*, July 25, 1877, 4.

75. "At Turner Hall," *Globe-Democrat*, July 25, 1871, 4.

76. "Internationalists," *Missouri Republican*, July 25, 1877, 3.

77. "The Outlook from Washington," *New York Tribune*, July 25, 1877, 1.

78. "The Strike Spreading Like Wildfire," *Post-Dispatch*, July 25, 1877, 1.

79. "Attention, Citizen Soldiers," *Post-Dispatch*, July 27, 1877, 1.

80. "The Outlook from Washington," *New York Tribune*, July 25, 1877, 1.

81. "The Union Depot," *Globe-Democrat*, July 26, 1877, 4.

82. "The Union Depot," *Globe-Democrat*, July 26, 1877, 4.

83. P. S. Foner, *Workingmen's Party*, 87.

84. Spencer, *Other Missouri History*, 54.

85. "Discussing the Situation," *Globe-Democrat*, July 26, 1877, 3.

86. "The International Procession," *Globe-Democrat*, July 26, 1877, 4.

87. "Ice for Preserving Meats," *Globe-Democrat*, July 26, 1877, 5.

88. "Discussing the Situation," *Globe-Democrat*, July 26, 1877, 3.

89. "Pacific Railroad," *Post-Dispatch*, July 25, 1877, 1.

90. "Manifesto," *Post-Dispatch*, July 26, 1877, 1.

91. "Steamboat Strikers," *Post-Dispatch*, July 26, 1877, 1.

92. "A Frightful Affair," *Globe-Democrat*, July 24, 1871, 1.

93. Primm, *Lion of the Valley*, 312.

94. Nolan, "The Labor Movement in St. Louis from 1860 to 1890," 167.

95. "Bloody Week," *Post-Dispatch*, July 26, 1877, 1.

96. "Manifesto," *Post-Dispatch*, July 26, 1877, 1.

97. Burbank, *Reign of the Rabble*, 87.

98. "Mayor's Proclamation," *Post-Dispatch*, July 25, 1877, 1.

99. "Bloody Week," *Post-Dispatch*, July 26, 1877, 1.

100. J. H. Wilson, telegrams to Carl Schurz, July 24, 1877, and July 26, 1877, David Burbank Collection, State Historical Society of Missouri.

101. Sergeant Finn, telegram, July 26, 1877, David Burbank Collection, State Historical Society of Missouri.

102. "The Sheriff's Posse," *Post-Dispatch*, July 27, 1877, 1.

103. Scharf, *History of St. Louis City and County*, 1847.

104. "Workingmen to the Mayor," *Globe-Democrat*, July 27, 1877, 5.

105. "Workingmen to the Mayor," *Globe-Democrat*, July 27, 1877, 5.

106. "The Strike," *Post-Dispatch*, July 27, 1877, 1.

107. "The Meeting at Armory Hall," *Globe-Democrat*, July 27, 1877, 5.

108. "Law and Order," *Post-Dispatch*, July 27, 1877, 1.

109. "The *Coup D'Etat*," *Missouri Republican*, July 28, 1877, 4.

110. "The Task That Remains," *Missouri Republican*, July 28, 1877, 1.

111. "The Capture," *Missouri Republican*, July 28, 1877, 5.

112. "Getting Hungry," *Post-Dispatch*, July 27, 1877, 1.

113. "Striker's Views," *Post-Dispatch*, July 27, 1877, 1.

114. "Scattering the Mob," *Globe-Democrat*, July 28, 1877, 4.

115. "Scattering the Mob," *Globe-Democrat*, July 28, 1877, 4.

116. "Captured," *Post-Dispatch*, July 27, 1877, 1.

117. "The Four Courts at Night," *Globe-Democrat*, July 28, 1877, 3.

118. "Railroad Matters," *Republican*, July 28, 1877, 4.

119. Roediger, "Not Only the Ruling Classes," 230.

120. Burbank, *Reign of the Rabble*, 148.

121. "Railroad Matters," *Missouri Republican*, July 28, 1877, 4.

122. "Law and Order," *Post-Dispatch*, July 27, 1877, 1.

123. "Come to Grief," *Post-Dispatch*, July 28, 1877, 1.

124. "Executive Committee," *Globe-Democrat*, July 28, 1877, 4.

125. "Scattering the Mob," *Globe-Democrat*, July 28, 1877, 4.

126. Scharf, *History of St. Louis City and County*, 1847.

127. "At East St. Louis," *Globe-Democrat*, July 29, 1877, 4.

128. "Not That, but This," *Missouri Republican*, August 1, 1877, 3.

129. "General Notes and Incidents of Yesterday," *Missouri Republican*, July 28, 1877, 4.

130. "The Kernel of Communism," *Missouri Republican*, August 2, 1877, 4.

131. "After the Storm," *Globe-Democrat*, July 30, 1877, 1.

132. "Suspension of Manufacturing Industries That Were Running before the Strike," *Post-Dispatch*, July 28, 1877, 2.

133. Spencer, *St. Louis Veiled Prophet Celebration*, 1.

134. William Moskop, letter to David Burbank, September 17, 1953, David Burbank Collection, State Historical Society of Missouri.

135. "A Splendid Pageant," *Globe-Democrat*, August 1, 1877, 4.

136. "The Parade," *Post-Dispatch*, August 1, 1877, 1.

137. "Yesterday's Parade," *Republican*, August 1, 1877, 4.

138. "A Splendid Pageant," *Globe-Democrat*, August 1, 1877, 4.

139. "Mob Rule," *Globe-Democrat*, August 1, 1877, 2.

140. "A Splendid Pageant," *Globe-Democrat*, August 1, 1877, 4.

141. "A Splendid Pageant," *Globe-Democrat*, August 1, 1877, 4.

142. Spencer, *St. Louis Veiled Prophet Celebration*, 8.

143. Spencer, *St. Louis Veiled Prophet Celebration*, 176n57.

144. Spencer, *St. Louis Veiled Prophet Celebration*, 3.

145. Spencer, *St. Louis Veiled Prophet Celebration*, 7.

146. Spencer, *St. Louis Veiled Prophet Celebration*, 18.

147. St. Louis Emergency Defense Committee, "The Veiled Prophet, How It Began," circular, October 10, 1952, Veiled Prophet Papers, Missouri Historical Society.

148. "The Habeas Corpus Cases," *Missouri Republican*, August 2, 1877, 8.

149. "The Labor Agitation," *Missouri Republican*, August 1, 1877, 1.

150. David Burbank, letter to Ursula Holtermann, May 24, 1950, David Burbank Collection, State Historical Society of Missouri.

151. William C. Breckenridge Papers, State Historical Society of Missouri.

152. "Cases of Rioters," *Missouri Republican*, August 3, 1877, 8.

153. Burbank, *Reign of the Rabble*, 179.

154. Dacus, *Annals of the Great Strikes*, 269.

155. "Mayor's Message, August 10, 1877," *Journal of House of Delegates*, April 1877–April 1878, 252–53.

156. "A History of Strikes," *Missouri Republican*, August 2, 1877, 3.

157. "Standing Forces," *Missouri Republican*, August 3, 1877, 3.

158. P. S. Foner, *History of the Labor Movement*, 473.

EPILOGUE

1. Kanter, "Class, Ethnicity," 49.

2. P. S. Foner, *Workingmen's Party*, 93.

3. Zinn, *People's History*, 319.

4. Buhle, *Marxism in the United States*, 46.

5. Lee and Cox, *When Sunflowers Bloomed Red*, 10–15.

6. Salvatore, *Eugene V. Debs*, 153.

7. Lee and Cox, *When Sunflowers Bloomed Red*, 87–96.

8. Zinn, *People's History*, 346.

9. Lee and Cox, *When Sunflowers Bloomed Red*, 38.

10. Marx, *Eighteenth Brumaire*, 15.

11. P. S. Foner, *Workingmen's Party*, 104.

12. Bruce, *1877*, 320.

13. Pinkerton, *Strikers, Tramps and Detectives*.

14. Stowell, *Streets, Railroads*, 118–20.

15. Goldberg, *The Life of Jean Jaures*, 271.

16. Dacus, *Annals of the Great Strikes*, 63.

17. Dacus, *Annals of the Great Strikes*, 80.

18. Bruce, *1877*, 276.

19. Messer-Kruse, *Yankee International*.

20. Chernow, *Grant*, 155.

BIBLIOGRAPHY

ARCHIVES AND MANUSCRIPT MATERIALS

Missouri Historical Society, St. Louis.
    Civil War Collection.
    Emil Mallinckrodt Papers.
    Immigration to Missouri Collection.
    James O. Broadhead Papers.
    Peter Clark Collection.
    Veiled Prophet Papers.
Newberry Library, Chicago.
    Chicago, Burlington & Quincy Correspondence Collection.
    Illinois Central Railroad Company Collection.
    International Workingmen's Association Collection.
    Workingmen's Party of the United States Collection.
State Historical Society of Missouri, St. Louis.
    David Burbank Collection.
    William C. Breckenridge Papers.
St. Louis Public Library Archives.
Wisconsin Historical Society, Madison.
    Collection of Documents of the First International.

PUBLISHED WORKS

Adamic, Louis. *Dynamite*. New York: Harper & Row, 1958.
Adams, Henry. *The Education of Henry Adams*. New York: Penguin, 1995.
Axelrod, Alan. *The Gilded Age*. New York: Sterling, 2017.
Bakunin, Mikhail. "The Paris Commune and the Idea of the State." In *The Commune: Paris, 1871*, edited by Andrew Zonneveld. Atlanta GA: On Our Own Authority!, 2013.
Barry, Bill. *The 1877 Railroad Strike in Baltimore*. N.p.: Self-published, 2014.
Bell, Daniel. *Marxian Socialism in the United States*. Ithaca NY: Cornell University Press, 1996.

Benson, Al, Jr., and Walter Donald Kennedy. *Lincoln's Marxists*. Gretna LA: Pelican, 2011.

Bernstein, Samuel. "American Labor and the Paris Commune." *Science and Society* 15, no. 2 (Spring 1951): 144–62.

———. *The First International in America*. New York: August M. Kelley, 1962.

———, ed. *New Papers of the General Council of the International Workingmen's Association: New York 1872–1876*. New York: New York Public Library, 1961.

Blatter, Mississippi. "Emigration from Germany to America." In *Germans for a Free Missouri*, translated by Steven Rowan. Columbia: University of Missouri Press, 1983.

Boernstein, Henry. *Memoirs of a Nobody: The Missouri Years of an Austrian Radical, 1849–1866*. Translated and edited by Steven Rowan. St. Louis: Missouri Historical Society Press, 1997.

Boyer, Richard O., and Herbert M. Morais. *Labor's Untold Story*. New York: United Electrical, Radio & Machine Workers of America, 1972.

Brands, H. W. *American Colossus*. New York: Anchor, 2011.

Brecher, Jeremy. *Strike*. Cambridge MA: South End Press, 1997.

Bruce, Robert B. *1877: Year of Violence*. Chicago: Ivan R. Dee, 1989.

Buhle, Paul. *Marxism in the United States: A History of the American Left*. London: Verso, 2013.

Burbank, David. "The First International in St. Louis." *Missouri Historical Society Bulletin* 18 (January 1962): 163–72.

———. *Reign of the Rabble*. New York: Augustus M. Kelley, 1966.

Chernow, Ron. *Grant*. New York: Penguin, 2017.

Churchill, Winston. *The Crisis*. New York: Macmillan, 1901.

Commission of Railroads and Telegraphs of Ohio. "Eleventh Annual Report of the Commission of Railroads and Telegraphs of Ohio for the Year Ending June 30, 1877." *Ohio Railroad Report*, 1878.

Corbett, Katherine T., and Howard S. Miller. *Saint Louis in the Gilded Age*. St. Louis: Missouri Historical Society Press, 1993.

Cozzens, Peter. *The Earth Is Weeping: The Epic Story of the Indian Wars for the American West*. New York: Vintage Books, 2017.

Currarino, Rosanne. *The Labor Question in America: Economic Democracy in the Gilded Age*. Urbana: University of Illinois Press, 2011.

Dacus, J. A. *Annals of the Great Strikes in the United States*. Reprint edition. Urbana: University of Illinois Library, 2009.

Daniels, Roger. *Coming to America*. New York: HarperCollins, 2002.

Edwards, Stewart. *The Communards of Paris, 1871*. Ithaca NY: Cornell University Press, 1981.

———. *The Paris Commune 1871*. New York: Quadrangle, 1973.

Fernbach, David, ed. *The First International and After: Karl Marx*. London: Verso, 2010.

Foner, Eric. *Free Soil, Free Labor, Free Men: The Ideology of the Republican Party before the Civil War*. Oxford: Oxford University Press, 1995.

———. *A Short History of Reconstruction*. New York: Harper and Rowe, 1990.

Foner, Philip S. *The Great Labor Uprising of 1877*. New York: Pathfinder, 1977.

———. *History of the Labor Movement in the United States*. New York: International Publishers, 1998.

———. *The Workingmen's Party of the United States: A History of the First Marxist Party in the Americas*. Minneapolis: MEP Publications, Anthropology Department, University of Minnesota, 1984.

Freitag, Sabine. *Friedrich Hecker: Two Lives for Liberty*. Translated by Steven Rowan. St. Louis: University of Missouri, Mercantile Library, 1998.

Fried, Albert, ed. *Socialism in America from the Shakers to the Third International: A Documentary History*. New York: Columbia University Press, 1992.

Gates, Paul W. "The Railroads of Missouri 1850–1870." *Missouri Historical Review* 26 (January 1932): 126–41.

Gerteis, Louis S. *Civil War in St. Louis*. Lawrence: University Press of Kansas, 2001.

Gerth, Hans, ed. *The First International Minutes of the Hague Congress of 1872*. Madison: University of Wisconsin Press, 1958.

Gluckstein, Donny. *The Paris Commune: A Revolution in Democracy*. Chicago: Haymarket Books, 2011.

Goldberg, Harvey. *The Life of Jean Jaures*. Madison: University of Wisconsin Press, 1968.

Graff, Daniel A. "Race, Citizenship, and the Origins of Organized Labor in Antebellum St. Louis." In *The Other Missouri History*, edited by Thomas M. Spencer. Columbia: University of Missouri Press, 2004.

Gray, Alexander. *The Socialist Tradition: Moses to Lenin*. New York: Harper & Row, 1968.

Griffin, Lawrence E. "The Strange Story of Major General Franz Sigel: Leader and Retreater." *Missouri Historical Review* 84 (July 1990): 404–27.

Guese, Lucius E. "St. Louis and the Great Whiskey Ring." *Missouri Historical Review* 36 (January 1942): 160–83.

Gutman, Herbert. *Work, Culture and Society in Industrializing America*. New York: Vintage Books, 1977.

Hagen, Harry M. *This Is Our . . . St. Louis*. St. Louis: Knight, 1970.

Hamilton, James A. "The Enrolled Missouri Militia: Its Creation and Controversial History." *Missouri Historical Review* 69 (July 1975): 413–32.

Hammen, Oscar J. *The Red '48ers: Karl Marx and Friedrich Engels*. New York: Charles Scribner, 1969.

Heinrichs, Gustav. "Carondelet Formerly and Now, Part Two." *Missouri Historical Bulletin* 17 (January 1961): 160–82.

Hobsbawm, Eric. *The Age of Revolution*. New York: Vintage, 1962.

———. *Revolutionaries*. New York: New Press, 1973.

———. *Uncommon People*. New York: New Press, 1998.

Hodes, Frederick A. *A Divided City: A History of St. Louis 1851 to 1876*. St. Louis MO: Bluebird, 2015.

Holland, Antonio F. "African Americans in Henry Shaw's St. Louis." In *St. Louis in the Century of Henry Shaw*, edited by Eric Sandweiss. Columbia: University of Missouri Press, 2003.

Holland, Cecilia. *Blood on the Tracks*. Lexington: n.p., 2008.

Horne, Alistair. *The Fall of Paris*. London: Penguin, 2007.

Houf, Walter R. "Fifty Years of Missouri Labor, 1820–1870." PhD dissertation, University of Missouri, 1958.

Johns, George S. "Joseph Pulitzer: Early Life in St. Louis and His Founding and Conduct of the Post-Dispatch up to 1883." *Missouri Historical Review* 25 (April 1931): 404–20.

Johnson, Walter. *The Broken Heart of America: St. Louis and the Violent History of the United States*. New York: Basic Books, 2020.

Jones, Jacqueline. *Goddess of Anarchy: The Life and Times of Lucy Parsons, American Radical*. New York: Basic Books, 2017.

Kanter, Elliot J. "Class, Ethnicity, and Socialist Politics: St. Louis, 1876–1881." *UCLA Historical Journal* 3 (1982): 36–60.

Kargan, E. D. "Missouri's German Immigration." *Missouri Historical Society Bulletin* 2, no. 1 (January 1900): 23–34.

Kargau, Ernest D., and Don Heinrich Tolzmann, eds. *The German Element in St. Louis*. Translated by William G. Bek. Baltimore MD: Clearfield, 2000.

Katz, Philip. *From Appomattox to Montmartre: Americans and the Paris Commune*. Cambridge MA: Harvard University Press, 1998.

Kelsey, Albert Warren. *Autobiographical Notes and Memoranda*. Baltimore MD: Munder-Thomsen Press, 1911.

Krause, Bonnie J. "German Americans in the St. Louis Region, 1840–1860." *Missouri Historical Review* 83 (April 1989): 295–310.

Lee, R. Alton, and Steven Cox. *When Sunflowers Bloomed Red: Kansas and the Rise of Socialism in America*. Lincoln: University of Nebraska Press, 2020.

Leikin, Steve. *The Practical Utopians: American Workers and the Cooperative Movement in the Gilded Age*. Detroit MI: Wayne State University Press, 2005.

Lissagaray, Prosper Olivier. *History of the Paris Commune of 1871*. Translated by Eleanor Marx. London: Verso, 2012.

Mandel, Bernard. "The 'Great Uprising' of 1877." *Cigar Makers Official Journal* 77, no. 12 (December 1953): 3–5.

Marx, Karl. *The Civil War in France: The Paris Commune*. New York: International Publishers, 1968.

———. *The Eighteenth Brumaire of Louis Napoleon*. New York: International Publishers, 1968.

———. "Germany at the Outbreak of the Revolution." In *Revolution and Counter-Revolution.* New York: Odin, 1851.

———. "Inaugural Address of the International Working Men's Association." In *The First International and After: Karl Marx,* edited by David Fernbach. London: Verso, 2010.

———. "Report to the Basel Conference." In *The First International and After: Karl Marx,* edited by David Fernbach. London: Verso, 2010.

———. "Report to the Hague Congress." In *The First International and After: Karl Marx,* edited by David Fernbach. London: Verso, 2010.

Marx, Karl, and Friedrich Engels. *The Civil War in the United States.* New York: International Publishers, 1969.

———. *The Communist Manifesto.* Chicago: Henry Regnery, 1965.

———. *The German Ideology.* New York: International Publishers, 1996.

———. "Resolution of the London Conference on Working-Class Political Action." In *The First International and After: Karl Marx,* edited by David Fernbach. London: Verso, 2010.

Marx, Leo. *The Machine in the Garden.* Oxford: Oxford University Press, 1967.

McCoskrie, James W., Jr., and Brian Warren. *The Civil War Missouri Compendium.* Charleston SC: History Press, 2017.

Mehring, Franz. *Karl Marx: The Story of His Life.* Translated by Edward Fitzgerald. Ann Arbor: University of Michigan Press, 1969.

Merriman, John. *Massacre: The Life and Death of the Paris Commune.* New York: Basic Books, 2014.

Messer-Kruse, Timothy. *The Yankee International: Marxism and the American Reform Tradition, 1848–1876.* Chapel Hill: University of North Carolina Press, 1998.

Michel, Louise. "Memories of the Commune." In *The Commune: Paris, 1871,* edited by Andrew Zonneveld. Atlanta GA: On Our Own Authority!, 2013.

Morris, William, et al. "A Short Account of the Commune of Paris of 1871." In *The Commune: Paris, 1871,* edited by Andrew Zonneveld. Atlanta GA: On Our Own Authority!, 2013.

Nolan, Russell M. "The Labor Movement in St. Louis from 1860 to 1890." *Missouri Historical Review* 34, no. 2 (1940): 157–81.

———. "The Labor Movement in St. Louis Prior to the Civil War." *Missouri Historical Review* 34, no. 1 (1939): 18–37.

Obermann, Karl. *Joseph Weydemeyer: Pioneer of American Socialism.* New York: International Publishers, 1947.

Olson, Audrey. "The Nature of an Immigrant Community: St. Louis Germans 1850–1920." *Missouri Historical Review* 66 (April 1972): 342–59.

Overstolz, Henry. "Mayor's Message." *Journal of House of Delegates,* April 1878.

Pinkerton, Allen. *Strikers, Tramps and Detectives.* Lexington KY: G. W. Carlton, 2017.

Primm, James Neal. "The Economy of Nineteenth Century St. Louis." In *St. Louis in the Century of Henry Shaw*, edited by Eric Sandweiss. Columbia: University of Missouri Press, 2003.

————. *Lion of the Valley: St. Louis, Missouri, 1764–1980*. St. Louis: Missouri Historical Society Press, 1998.

Rapport, Mike. *1848: Year of Revolution*. New York: Basic Books, 2008.

Reznek, Samuel. "Distress, Relief, and Discontent in the United States during the Depression of 1873–1878." *Journal of Political Economy* 58, no. 6 (December 1950): 494–512.

Riis, Jacob. *How the Other Half Lives*. New York: Dover, 1971.

Roberts, Andrew. *Napoleon: A Life*. New York: Viking Penguin, 2014.

Roediger, David. "Not Only the Ruling Classes to Overcome, but Also the So-Called Mob: Class, Skill and Community in the St. Louis General Strike of 1877." *Journal of Social History* 19, no. 2 (December 1985): 213–39.

Rowan, Steven. *Germans for a Free Missouri: Translations from the St. Louis Radical Press, 1857–1862*. Columbia: University of Missouri Press, 1983.

Salvatore, Nick. *Eugene V. Debs: Citizen and Socialist*. Urbana: University of Illinois Press, 2007.

Sandweiss, Eric. *St. Louis in the Century of Henry Shaw*. Columbia: University of Missouri Press, 2003.

Scharf, J. Thomas. *History of St. Louis City and County*. Philadelphia: Louis H. Everts, 1883.

Siemann, Wolfram. *The German Revolution of 1848–49*. Translated by Christiane Baner. New York: St. Martin's Press, 1998.

Smith, Willard A. "Chicago Railway Review." *Railway Review* 20, no. 1 (January 3, 1880): 3.

Spencer, Thomas M. *The Other Missouri History: Populists, Prostitutes and Regular Folk*. Columbia: University of Missouri Press, 2005.

————. *The St. Louis Veiled Prophet Celebration: Power on Parade 1877–1995*. Columbia: University of Missouri Press, 2000.

Sperber, Jonathan. *Karl Marx: A Nineteenth Century Life*. New York: Liveright, 2013.

————. *Rhineland Radicals*. Princeton NJ: Princeton University Press, 1991.

Stadelman, Rudolph. *Social and Political History of the German 1848 Revolution*. Translated by James G. Chastain. Athens: Ohio University Press, 1975.

Stowell, David O. *Streets, Railroads, and the Great Strike of 1877*. Chicago: University of Chicago Press, 1999.

Swacker, Bob. *New York City History*. New York: McNally Jackson, 2017.

Trachtenberg, Alan. *The Incorporation of America: Culture and Society in the Gilded Age*. New York: Hill and Wang, 1994.

Turner, Frederick Jackson. *The Frontier in American History*. Tucson: University of Arizona Press, 1994.

Twain, Mark. *The Gilded Age.* New York: Quill Pen Classics, 2008.

Van Ravenswary, Charles. "Years of Turmoil, Years of Growth: St. Louis in the 1850s." *Missouri Historical Bulletin* 23 (July 1967): 303–24.

Walker, Samuel C. "Railroad Strike of 1877 in Altoona." *Railway and Locomotive Historical Society Bulletin,* no. 117 (October 1967): 18–25.

Ware, Norman. *The Industrial Worker 1840–1860.* Chicago: Ivan R. Dee, 1990.

Wheen, Francis. *Karl Marx: A Life.* New York: Norton, 2001.

Who Was G.: Being a Truthful Tale of the Seventh Regiment in the Armory, during the Railroad Strikes in July, 1877. London: FB&C, 2015.

Wittke, Frederick. *Refugees of Revolution: The German Forty-Eighters in America.* Philadelphia: University of Pennsylvania Press, 1952.

Zinn, Howard. *A People's History of the United States.* New York: HarperPerennial, 1995.

INDEX

abolitionism, 51, 133, 135, 144, 148, 149, 153, 155

Ackerman, W. K., 205

Adams, Henry, 159

agriculture, 51, 58, 135, 138, 140–41, 191–92

Akerman, Amos, 47

Albany NY, 165, 180, 181–82

Allegheny PA, 178

Allen, Henry F., 10, 11, 200, 214, 240, 241

Allen, Thomas, 56, 59

Alsace-Lorraine region, 49, 65, 94, 95

American Communist Party, 249

American Confederation of the International Workingmen's Association, 107

American Labor Union, 190

American press. *See* newspapers

American Workers' League, 101, 150

Ammons, Robert, 172

anarchists, 7, 14, 99, 191; goals of, 67, 105–6, 112; International and, 101, 104, 105–6, 107–8, 109; IWW and, 248

Andrews, Stephen Pearl, 105

Anthony, Susan B., 122

anticlericalism, 29–30, 72–73, 144

Antiplaft of St. Louis, 143

Anti-Socialist Law, 95

Anzeiger des Westens, 50, 135, 147; anticlericalism of, 143, 144; antislavery views of, 153; attack on, 152; integration opposed by, 39

Apache people, 38, 86

Appeal to Reason, 248–49

Arbeiterbund, 109

arms. *See* weapons

Armstrong, Colonel, 230, 231

artisans, skilled, 11–12, 111; craft unions of, 112, 118, 129, 130, 150, 199; in France, 64, 79; German immigrants as, 49, 134, 135, 199; in Germany, 20, 24, 29, 35; in industrial capitalism, 11–12, 64, 115–16, 132, 178

Astor, James, 53

atheism, 142, 143, 210. *See also* free-thinkers

Atlantic and Pacific Railroad, 54, 59

Austrian Empire: emigrants from, 49; International members in, 93, 96; nationalism in, 22–23, 31; railroads in, 19; revolution in, 19, 21, 22–23, 26, 30, 31, 35; Social Democratic Party in, 96; suppression of liberalism by, 20, 31

Babcock, Orville E., 60

Bain, George, 238

Bakunin, Mikhail, 35, 81, 94, 112; followers of, 105, 108; Marx challenged by, 98–99, 104, 110

Baltimore and Maine Railroad, 162

Baltimore and Ohio, 12; doubleheaders run by, 167; federal government billed by, 170; shareholder profits of, 162; shutdown of, 179, 216; strikes on, 164, 166–73; troops requested by, 169–71, 172; wages cut by, 166, 167

Baltimore MD, 166, 167, 168–69, 254

Buffalo and Jamestown Railroad, 182
Buffalo NY, 180, 182–83, 222, 254
Burbank, David, 200, 222
Busch, Adolphus, 52
bushwhackers, 154

Cabet, Étienne, 90, 102, 109, 198
Cahan, Abraham, 247
Cairo and Fulton Railroad, 57, 59
Cairo Short Line, 206
Cambria Iron Works, 123–24
Camden Yards. *See* Baltimore MD
Campbell, Robert, 54
Camp Spring Garden, 146–47
Canada Southern Railroad, 188
cannery workers, 219
cannibalism, charges of, 84
capitalism: boom and bust cycles of, 29,
    48, 117–18, 132; defeat of, 91; democracy
    threatened by, 44, 204, 206; injustice
    of, 195; vs. labor, 177, 181; Mark Twain
    on, 59; railroads as symbols of, 164, 254;
    regulation of, 242–43; Republicans as
    party of, 46; violence of, 203–4. *See also*
    industrial capitalism
capitalists: asserting control of St. Louis,
    237–40; cooperation with, 101, 106;
    divisions between workers exploited by,
    96, 192; fear of, over strike, 184, 208–9,
    210; foreigners blamed by, 207–8; greed
    of, 44, 61, 117, 162, 209, 234, 235, 252; as
    parasites, 254; profiting from unemploy-
    ment, 13–14, 119, 160, 166; revolution
    feared by, 13, 184, 208–9, 210, 222; state-
    run railroads bought by, 59; as tyrants,
    172; workers' grievances conceded by,
    242–43; workers mistreated by, 13–14,
    43–44
Carender, John S., 209
Carnegie, Andrew, 43, 55
Carnegie Steel, 42, 43
Carondelet Executive Committee, 232

Carondelet neighborhood, 136; arrests in,
    232; charges against workers in, 242;
    Committee of Public Safety and, 230;
    economy of, 52, 56, 140; kindergarten
    started in, 145; strike gatherings in, 10,
    201, 203, 215, 217, 219, 220, 226
Carr, Joseph, 222
Carroll, John, 168, 234, 240
Catholic Church: in France, 72–73, 80, 84,
    87; free-thinkers opposed to, 143, 144;
    and French Catholic families, 50; Inter-
    national denounced by, 87, 103, 210; Irish
    revolutionaries supported by, 227; Irish
    workers and, 126; Know Nothings and,
    143, 152; in the Rhineland, 29–30, 32–33,
    34; silence of, on slavery, 153; strike of
    1877 and, 209–10, 227; and women's
    rights, 74
cattle and cattle trains, 9, 169
Cavender, John S., 212
Central Committee of the International, 106
Central Organization of Cigarmakers, 183
Central Pacific Railway Company, 42, 45, 46
Central Railroad of New Jersey, 163
Chenango County NY, 178
Chernow, Ron, 47, 48, 257
Chesapeake and Ohio Canal, 170
Chicago, Burlington & Quincy, 198, 206
Chicago and Alton Railroad, 57
Chicago and Northwestern, 180
Chicago and St. Louis, 206
Chicago IL: depression in, 178–79; Great
    Fire of, 86, 97; railroad strike (1877)
    in, 179–80, 205, 216, 223, 235; socialist
    politicians in, 246; St. Louis competing
    with, 8, 54, 57, 58
children, 29, 73, 75, 164, 247; killing of,
    76–77, 78, 174; laboring in textile mills,
    119; labor of, European reforms of, 24;
    labor of, restricting, 92, 194, 215, 247; in
    tenements, 29, 43, 145, 160; wages of, 61,
    100, 111. *See also* education

Frémont, John C., 39, 58, 59, 110

French Revolution, 4, 5, 63, 67, 257; the Church and, 72; Paris Commune inspired by, 99; revolutions of 1848 inspired by, 17, 18, 31, 33, 35, 137; strikers invoking, 9, 179, 200, 214, 215, 219, 226

fur trade, 53

Galliffet, Gaston, 77

Gantt, Thomas T., 212, 242

Garesche, Alexander, 238

Garfield, James, 47

Garibaldi, Giuseppe, 89, 91

garment workers, 247

Garrett, John, 12, 168

Garrison, Daniel R., 55

gas and gasworks, 29, 220

General Orders, 9, 200, 206

general strike of 1877, 157, 200, 203, 213–22, 223, 241–42, 255, 257; Black workers in, 204–5, 208, 213, 214, 217–18, 219, 220, 224, 226, 242; capitalists' fear over, 184, 208–9, 210; Catholic Church and, 209–10; First International and, 88, 108, 110, 210, 242; French Revolution invoked during, 9, 179, 200, 214, 215, 219, 226; historic nature of, 3, 6, 242, 249, 257; marches during, 215, 216, 218–19; Paris Commune compared to, 82; peacefulness of, 203, 211, 215, 223; race and, 218–19, 220; railroad strike leading to, 3, 167, 183, 203; as revolution, 221, 255–56; union involvement in, 192, 199, 214, 219, 224; women in, 220, 256. *See also* Committee of Public Safety; Executive Committee of St. Louis Commune; militias in strike of 1877; St. Louis Commune

Geneva Convention of 1864, 72

George, Henry, 44

"The German Contribution to Missouri" (J. Muench), 138

The German Ideology (Marx), 27, 90

German Triangle, 134

Germany, 19–20, 26–29, 31–36, 96, 194; consolidation of, 28, 64, 250; constitutional government in, 19, 34, 35; extended suffrage in, 104; Frankfurt National Assembly of, 32–33; French Revolution ideals in, 18, 28, 30; hunger in, 24, 26, 28, 33, 134, 137; immigrant ties to, 141; industrialization of, 24, 28–29, 137; International members in, 93, 96–97; poverty in, 24–25, 29, 137; repression in, 135, 148; revolution in, 5, 6, 10, 17, 22, 23–26, 30–36, 137, 201; rural, 25, 26, 28–29; socialism in, 26, 31–32, 95

Gerneau, Joseph, 52

Geyer, Henry, 51

"Gilded Age" (term), 46, 59

Gindele, John, 146

Girard KS, 248–49

Glenn, John, 240

Glenn, Joseph, 11, 203

Globe-Democrat, 85, 184, 207, 209, 218, 233, 235, 236–37; reporting by, on violence, 174, 175, 176, 179–80, 215; on strikers, 218, 219, 230, 233, 234, 235

Godkin, E. L., 86

Goebel, David, 138

Goldberg, Harvey, 255

Goldman, Emma, 248

gold market, 43

Gompers, Samuel, 183

Gotha Congress, 184, 194

Gould, Jay, 42–43, 44, 56, 160, 162

Gowen, Frank, 124

Grafton WV, 170, 171

Granger movement, 42, 130, 193

Grant, Orville, 47

Grant, Ulysses, 42–43, 46–47, 60, 157

Greece, 19

greed, 44–46, 61, 117, 131, 162, 209, 234, 235, 252; poor conditions resulting from, 43–44, 48, 61–62, 117, 173; reactions to, 173, 251

Greeley, Horace, 4

Pennsylvania Railroad, 12, 162, 164, 165, 167, 222, 254; losses of, 175, 176; Pittsburgh strike against, 173–75; wages cut by, 163, 166, 173

People's Party, 42, 248

Phelps, John S., 10, 217, 224, 225–26

Philadelphia PA, 103, 105, 110, 174, 199

Phillips, Wendell, 62, 82, 99, 100, 200

Pinkerton, Allan, 85, 242, 254

Pinkerton Agency, 43, 124, 174

Pitcairn, Robert, 173

Pittsburgh PA, 12, 173–77, 201, 223, 246, 254

Pixley, Frank M., 85

police, 168, 209, 230–31, 243; private, 127, 174, 230; special force of, 220, 226; violence, 120–21, 171, 179–80, 230–31. *See also* militias in strike of 1877; national guard

politics, 96, 104, 112, 121, 122–23, 127, 162, 192–93, 253; vs. labor organizing, 104, 112, 129, 184, 190, 193–94, 245–46, 249, 256; labor parties in, 126, 128, 145, 148, 184, 194, 245, 247–49, 256; Lassalleans vs. Marxists on, 104–5, 112, 126, 184, 190, 193–94, 196, 245–46; Marx on, 104–5, 112, 121, 184, 193–94, 256; unions and, 112, 126–27, 128, 129, 184, 190, 193–94, 245–46. *See also* corruption

the pope, 97

Pope, John, 12, 214–15, 223

posse comitatus, 216–17

potato blight, 21, 25, 28, 49, 137, 151

Pottier, Eugène, 102

poverty, 104, 189–90, 225; boom and bust cycle causing, 29, 48, 117–18, 132; in Germany, 24–25, 29, 137. *See also* hunger

Praetorius, Emil, 144

Price, Daniel, 241

Priest, John G., 238, 239

printers, 20, 32, 120, 193

prison labor, 194

private property, 3, 87, 100, 214, 221, 233; abolishing, 4, 14, 20; troops protecting, 201, 212, 213, 223, 243

profit-sharing, 221

"Program of the Internationals," 97–98

Proletarian League, 150

proletariat, 27, 28, 172; and bourgeoisie, conflict between, 5, 27–28, 78, 90, 95–96, 172–73, 184; dictatorship of, 98, 99, 104

property. *See* private property

Proudhon, Pierre-Joseph, 67, 69, 74, 81, 92, 99, 104, 112

Prussia, 24, 25–26, 31, 32–34. *See also* Franco-Prussian War; Germany

Pulitzer, Joseph, 61, 135

Pullman strike, 247

Putnam, Mary, 84

Quakers, 134

race: of federal troops, 212; labor organizing and, 123, 126, 192, 196–97, 204–5, 217, 253, 256; and racism in the St. Louis Commune, 212, 218, 232, 253; workers divided by, 121, 123, 192, 213; WPUSA on, 196–97, 217–18, 253. *See also* Black workers; ethnicity

railroad corporations, 2, 37–38, 41–42, 44–47, 59, 159, 165, 189, 216, 221; agreeing to strikers' demands, 180, 216; corruption by, 45–47, 48, 61, 166, 198, 201, 223–24, 254; dangers of working for, 2, 9, 160, 161; grievances against, capitalists conceding, 242–43; investors of, failing, 38, 56, 59, 187–89, 251; land given to, 162; Panic of 1873 affecting, 44, 124, 163–65, 166, 198, 251–52; post–Civil War boom of, 37, 158, 160, 187; public relations attempts by, 206–7; refusing to meet with strikers, 177, 181, 201, 229; wage reductions by, 2–3, 12, 128, 160, 162–63, 198, 200, 202, 205–6, 251; and worker housing, 128, 162–63; work schedules of, 205–6. *See also* Baltimore and Ohio; Erie Railroad; Pennsylvania Railroad

railroads: agricultural goods moved by,
42, 45, 52, 162, 216; bridges for, 55, 57;
European expansion of, 19; government
ownership of, 42; investment in, 41–42,
55–59; nationalization of, demanded,
179, 216; public unhappiness with, 44,
159, 164–65, 168–69, 198, 254; regulation
of, 185; St. Louis as hub of, 8, 55, 56–57;
as symbols of capitalism, 164, 254; transcontinental, 37, 42, 45, 55–56
railroad strike (1873–74), 124–25, 160, 163–
64, 165; troops called out for, 124, 162,
165, 167, 169–70
railroad strike (1877), 2, 8, 159–85, 202–3,
251–52; arming of workers during, 175,
180, 182, 214; beginning of, 2, 163, 166–67,
198–99, 200; as coup attempt, 209, 210,
228–29, 230, 236–37, 239–40, 255–56;
demands of, met by bosses, 180, 216;
general strike arising from, 3, 167, 183,
203; as "insurrection," 12, 169, 174; International blamed for, 97; looting during,
175, 219–20; Paris Commune blamed for,
85, 252, 253–54; and property damage, 9,
12, 175, 176, 178, 180–81, 182; prosecution
of members of, 240–42; spontaneity of,
2–3, 12, 97, 167, 184, 201, 222; spread of,
167–68; support for, 167, 172–73, 178, 184,
199, 201, 207, 233; WPUSA unprepared
for, 198–99, 214, 222. See also general
strike of 1877; militias in strike of 1877;
St. Louis Commune; violence
rape, 76
Raymond, Emmeline, 84
Reading PA, 171, 177, 205, 223
real estate boom, 54
realism, 41
Reavis, L. U., 48–49
Reconstruction, 37, 39, 46, 86, 212
reformers, 104, 105–6, 119
regulation: of banking, 32, 104; of industry,
75, 107, 185; lack of, causing panics, 187

Reign of the Rabble (Burbank), 200
religion, 17, 25, 87, 153; anticlericalism and,
29–30, 72–73, 144; conservatism of, 74,
80; and education, 30, 73, 90, 143, 145;
in France, 72–73, 80, 84, 87; freedom of,
18, 23, 90, 136; free-thinkers and, 126, 133,
142–43; of German immigrants, 50, 133,
134, 136, 142–43, 145, 153; in Germany, 25,
29–30, 33; immigrants divided by, 50, 126,
142–43; monarchies supported by, 23, 25,
29, 33, 72, 80. See also atheism; Catholic
Church; Lutherans
rent collection, 191
Report of a Journey to the Western States of
North America (Duden), 136
Republican Party, 37, 61, 152–53, 154, 197;
corruption in, 46–47, 60–61; German
members of, 141, 144–45, 153; labor
support sought by, 121
revolution, 14, 27, 98–99, 156, 249; in
Austrian Empire, 19, 21, 22–23, 26, 30, 31,
35; capitalist fears of, 13, 184, 208–9, 210,
222; general strike as, 221, 255–56. See also
French Revolution
revolutions of 1848, 5, 15, 17, 21–36, 133, 137,
201, 249–51; American support of, 141–
42; Civil War and, 157; ethnic tensions
and, 22–23, 31; French Revolution
inspiring, 17, 31, 33, 35, 137; German
immigration and, 11, 36, 62, 101, 109–10,
120, 125, 142–46, 157, 250–51; repression
following, 5, 23, 93, 137–38; socialism
and, 21, 26, 31–36, 90, 101, 120, 133–34,
137, 249–51, 254; troops called out for,
30–31, 35
Rheinische Zeitung, 21, 27
Rhineland, 18, 26, 28–30, 134. See also
Germany
ribbon weavers, 123
Rigault, Raoul, 72, 76
Riis, Jacob, 43–44
river transport, 37, 54, 55, 57

urbanization, 41, 111–12, 164

utopian communism, 3–4, 90, 151

Valentin, Louis, 76

Vanderbilt, Cornelius, 42

Vanderbilt, Cornelius, II, 40

Vanderbilt, George Washington, II, 40–41

Vanderbilt, William, 40, 180–81, 182

Van Patten, Philip, 8, 10

Veiled Prophet (VP), 237–40

Venice, 23

Vesinier, Pierre, 78

Vienna Congress, 18, 137

Vigilance Committees, 66

Villard, Henry, 146

violence, 167, 168, 171, 178, 249; A. Douai on, 196; against immigrants, 152; against spectators, 9, 174, 176, 230, 231; against the Paris Commune, 72, 76–78, 79; against workers, 203–4; WPUSA denouncing, 223. See also militias in strike of 1877

Voltaire (François-Marie Arouet), 18

voting rights. See suffrage, extended

Vulcan Iron Works, 52, 203, 220, 226

wages, Panic affecting, 122–24, 128–29, 160, 162–64, 165–67, 173, 198–200, 202, 205–6

Walther, C. F. W., 142

Ware, Norman, 116

Warmoth, Henry Clay, 45

War of Spanish Succession, 134

Warren, Josiah, 105

Washburne, Elihu, 84

Wayland, Julius, 248–49

wealth, 38, 40–41, 43–44, 48, 51, 61–62, 63, 195. See also greed

weapons: common people bearing, 25, 31, 32, 33–34, 67, 92; in shows of force, 236, 239; stores donating, 225; strikers lacking, 227, 257; strikers rumored to have, 214, 228; workers bearing, 182, 228

Weigel, Philipp, 145

Weitling, Wilhelm, 109, 151

Wells, Erastus, 209

Welsh, John, 205

the West, 117, 121; Manifest Destiny and, 39–40, 55; transcontinental railroad opening, 37, 42, 45, 187; troops stationed in, 170, 211–12, 255

Westliche Post, 61, 141, 144, 156, 224

Weydemeyer, Joseph, 27, 101, 109–10, 149–50, 255; American Labor Union led by, 190; as county auditor, 245; Marx and, 27, 101, 109–10, 149–50

Weydemeyer, Otto, 102

Whig Party, 49, 154

Whiskey Ring, 47–48, 60–61

Wilkes, George, 84–85

Willard, Mrs. F. J., 83–84

Wilson, Bluford, 240

Wilson, J. H., 181, 203, 206, 207, 209, 223–24, 240

winemaking, 52

Wisconsin Synod Lutherans, 153

Wittke, Carl Frederick, 138, 143

women, 36, 50, 122; garment workers, 247; in the general strike, 220, 256; in the Paris Commune, 73–74; rights of, 86, 87, 104, 194–95, 196, 248; rights of, vs. workers' rights, 107, 122; status of, in Marxism, 74; suffrage of, 122; in unions, 74, 118, 122; WPUSA on, 194, 196, 197

Woodhull, Victoria, 106–7

Woodward, Jesse, 60

workday: contracts stipulating, 118–19, 127, 199; eight-hour, 92, 99, 112, 127–28, 191, 199, 215, 221, 247; ten-hour, 118, 119, 192–93

workers, 13, 31–32, 91, 92, 116, 121, 160, 166; African American, 101–2, 123, 183, 196, 208, 217–18, 253, 256; capitalists exploiting division between, 96, 192; Chinese, racism against, 183; Civil War generals fighting, 127, 158, 212; company housing of, 127, 128, 162–63; divisions among, 96, 119, 214, 224, 232, 249, 253, 256; ethnic diversity and divisions among, 41, 102–3, 111, 150, 217–18, 224, 253, 256; European, 19–20, 24–25, 28–29, 31–32; facing death, 13–14, 160; government fighting, 158, 243; impoverishment of, 117–18, 188; injury of, 2, 160, 161–62, 164–65, 194; international unity of, 89–93, 112–13, 125; in militias, 169; in the Paris Commune, 74–75, 76; political party as necessity for, 96, 112; poor conditions of, 43–44, 48, 61–62, 100, 115–32, 157–58, 160, 195, 198, 232; rights of, vs. women's rights, 107, 122; solidarity among, 20, 91, 92, 120, 127, 172, 183, 197, 228; victory of, Marx on, 95–96; wage reductions of, 122–24, 128–29, 160, 162–64, 165–67, 173, 198–200, 202, 205–6. *See also* artisans, skilled; class consciousness; cooperatives; unemployment

Workingmen's Party (Illinois), 179, 193, 194

Workingmen's Party (New York), 96

Workingmen's Party of the United States (WPUSA), 3, 194–96, 252–55; arrests at, 230–32; Black workers and, 196–97, 217, 228; Chicago meeting of, 179; Committee of Public Safety attacking, 230–31; divisions within, 198; in East St. Louis, 10, 11, 200–201; eight-hour workday and, 10, 199, 214, 221, 229, 247; in electoral politics, 246; ethnic groups represented in, 11, 253; First International and, 6, 15, 108, 194; formation of, 110, 126, 178–79, 184, 194, 241; headquarters of, 126; legacy of, 252; mayor appealed to by, 224–25; militias organized by, 228; on nationalization, 10, 179, 196, 199, 221; order preserved by, 223, 225, 228; peacefulness of, 196, 227–28, 229; police attacking, 199; profit-sharing proposed by, 221; promising not to hold meetings, 225, 257; prosecution of members of, 240, 241–42; publications of, 195–96, 197; on race, 196–97, 217–18, 253; railroad strike supported by, 172–73, 184, 199, 201; in St. Louis, 6, 12–13, 110, 184, 197–98, 203–8, 213–14, 221, 245, 257; strikers urged to join, 179; unpreparedness of, for strike, 198–99, 214, 222; violence condemned by, 223; and workers' cooperatives, 194, 196

Workingmen's Union of Trenton, New Jersey, 121

World's Fair of 1876, 41

WPUSA. *See* Workingmen's Party of the United States (WPUSA)

zinc works, 215, 220

Lightning Source UK Ltd.
Milton Keynes UK
UKHW041421030822
406770UK00009B/344